Metamorphosis

Metamorphosis

Who We Become after Facial Paralysis

FAYE LINDA WACHS

RUTGERS UNIVERSITY PRESS

NEW BRUNSWICK, CAMDEN, AND NEWARK, NEW JERSEY

LONDON AND OXFORD

Rutgers University Press is a department of Rutgers, The State University of New Jersey, one of the leading public research universities in the nation. By publishing worldwide, it furthers the University's mission of dedication to excellence in teaching, scholarship, research, and clinical care.

LIBRARY OF CONGRESS CATALOGING-IN-PUBLICATION DATA

Names: Wachs, Faye Linda, author.
Title: Metamorphosis : who we become after facial paralysis / Faye Linda Wachs.
Description: New Brunswick : Rutgers University Press, [2023] | Includes bibliographical references and index.
Identifiers: LCCN 2022056494 | ISBN 9781978805316 (paperback) | ISBN 9781978805323 (hardcover) | ISBN 9781978805330 (epub) | ISBN 9781978805354 (pdf)
Subjects: LCSH: Paralytics—Social conditions. | Facial paralysis—Social aspects. | Facial expression—Social aspects. | Self-perception. | Social perception.
Classification: LCC HV3011 .W23 2023 | DDC 362.4/041—dc23/eng/20221201
LC record available at https://lccn.loc.gov/2022056494

A British Cataloging-in-Publication record for this book is available from the British Library.

Copyright © 2023 by Faye Linda Wachs

All rights reserved

No part of this book may be reproduced or utilized in any form or by any means, electronic or mechanical, or by any information storage and retrieval system, without written permission from the publisher. Please contact Rutgers University Press, 106 Somerset Street, New Brunswick, NJ 08901. The only exception to this prohibition is "fair use" as defined by U.S. copyright law.

References to internet websites (URLs) were accurate at the time of writing. Neither the author nor Rutgers University Press is responsible for URLs that may have expired or changed since the manuscript was prepared.

♾ The paper used in this publication meets the requirements of the American National Standard for Information Sciences—Permanence of Paper for Printed Library Materials, ANSI Z39.48-1992.

rutgersuniversitypress.org

For Ziya—who always reminds us difference is a gift.

CONTENTS

1   When Life Gives You Lemons . . . Interview Lots of
Other People Also with Lemons   1

2   Theorizing Change: Culture, Identity, and the Face   23

3   Microaggressions, Internalizations, and Contested
Ideological Terrain   39

4   It's My Face–Why That Matters   76

5   Disrupted Selves   101

6   Someone I Would Rather Be   131

7   Walking Away: The Challenge of Change   158

Appendix A:
Summarizing Facial
Difference   171
Appendix B:
Overview of Methods   173
Appendix C:
Summary of Participants
with Facial Differences   176
Acknowledgments   187
Notes   191
References   193
Index   207

Metamorphosis

1

When Life Gives You Lemons . . . Interview Lots of Other People Also with Lemons

NOVEMBER 2009

It was a stressful time. Furloughed by the state of California, I was receiving 10 percent less pay after years of missed contractually obligated increases. Recently divorced, I was in the process of moving to a small apartment I wasn't sure I could now afford. A pain in my ear led me to take a decongestant before bed, so when I woke up feeling strange I checked the interaction effects. Numbness was listed. No big deal. I went for a run with my dogs. But something was off, so I called a friend. "My face feels weird. I feel weird." "Hope it's not Bell's palsy!" she joked. "What's that?" I remember asking. "Oh, it's rare, it's probably not that." I was working from home anyway, so I stopped obsessing and got to work.

But something wasn't right! Passing by the window, I caught my reflection. My face looked weird. I went to the bathroom mirror. I was having trouble blinking. So I googled the symptoms. Bold red flashing letters across my screen: YOU ARE HAVING A STROKE. GO DIRECTLY TO THE EMERGENCY ROOM. Panic is creeping around the edge of my consciousness.

Wait a second. I am not having a stroke. My mother is a gerontologist. I know the signs, and I am completely clear headed. I stand up: on one foot, then the other. No balance issues. Still, just to be sure I run to my bookcase and grab the two most difficult books I see, Foucault's *Discipline and Punish*, and my advanced stats textbook. I read a few pages of Foucault first. Yes, I understand it. That took me years to achieve, so that's good. And then I open up the stats book and read a few pages at random. Yes, I can also understand discussions about regression equations.

OK, so probably not having a stroke. But something is really wrong. I text my childhood friend, a family practice doctor at my local Kaiser. She asks for a picture, and tells me it is likely Bell's palsy and to go immediately to the emergency room [ER]—to get a ride, don't drive.

It is flu season. The ER is packed. There's a woman being sick in the bathroom. And after looking at me, they take me in first. Now I am really, really scared. I look worse than all these other people—worse than the woman who can't stop vomiting or the man lying on the floor. But, fortunately, it is indeed, Bell's palsy. They don't have much else to say. Just give me antivirals and steroids, a promise that it will go away, and a suggestion to follow up.

Though I followed the doctor's advice, I am in the 15 to 20 percent that don't fully heal, and I have synkinesis.

Bell's palsy is damage to the seventh cranial nerve, cause unknown. Some studies link it to being exposed to a virus, such as herpes simplex, herpes zoster, infectious mononucleosis (Epstein-Barr), or some other infection. Pregnancy is also a risk factor. Most of those I've spoken to who have Bell's palsy don't really know what elevated their risk, with the exception of those who were pregnant. The majority heal and would have regardless of any intervention, although intervention does hasten the healing (Slatery and Azzizadeh 2014). Unfortunately for me, I am among the approximately 20 percent in whom synkinesis occurs (Bylund et al. 2017).

Bell's palsy is a neurological problem—paralysis because of nerve damage—but synkinesis is a movement disorder. Synkinesis may look like the paralysis did not resolve or the nerve did not heal, but in fact it is a different challenge. With synkinesis, when the nerves heal and regrow they do so too much and in too many places: paralysis occurs because too many things try to move at once, so nothing moves at all. Parts of the face and neck are perpetually "tight"; one may find individual parts, such as the corner of the mouth, pulled back. Unwanted movement also can occur. A common example is the affected eye involuntarily closing when one purses one's lips. There can be other sorts of cross wiring: for instance, the eyes may tear up while one eats, but one may not salivate, which can lead to ongoing dental problems. There can be vision problems as well.

Synkinesis can be painful, and the pain is very different for different people. Those affected have described it as constant awareness, tightness, heaviness, bruising, old bruises, knots, discomfort, or pain. During onset, many—myself included—have described the sensations as resembling having been in a recent fight, leaving one bruised or sore. I have complained about it less over time, but it's more that I simply started to get used to it, adapting to the ongoing pain and discomfort.

One of my early interviewees was a midcareer, graduate-school-educated software engineer, Maggie V. She had a casual appearance, identified as cisgendered

WHEN LIFE GIVES YOU LEMONS 3

and queer, and had been suffering from synkinesis for eight years. She described it as life changing.

> There's a constant pulling in my cheek; it's really, really tight. Even with the Botox, I still notice it. My eye waters a lot when I eat, like I'm crying. That's kind of a pain, too; just every time you eat, it's always tearing up and stuff. Then my nose, it's pulling so much to the side. . . . And the pulling, it's moving my teeth. My teeth are actually moving; I'm getting spaces between my teeth. My nose is getting pulled over so much so that one side of my nose—there's this huge, big canal. The other side is almost closed off. So on the side it's really opened, [and] my nose runs all the time, like all the time. I'm like always blowing my nose every ten minutes, it seems like, and that is just so annoying. I mean, it sounds stupid, but it's really annoying. And then there's my expressions . . . ugh. I can't communicate. I look awful. It feels awful.

Individuals with synkinesis have raised changes to vision, challenges with prescription glasses and contact lenses, a host of dental problems, and muscular skeletal complaints as ongoing challenges. As patient advocacy groups, support groups, and online communities expand, new studies have responded to patient complaints, identifying vision changes, breathing difficulties, dental challenges, vertigo, temporomandibular joint pain, and a host of other consequences. Too often, each problem is treated piecemeal instead of understood as part of an ongoing health challenge.

Synkinesis isn't exclusive to Bell's palsy. Potentially it can result from other causes of facial paralysis or facial nerve damage. Other causes of acquired facial paralysis include Ramsay Hunt syndrome, acoustic neuroma, parotid gland tumors or other tumors and their removal, or trauma; sometimes the cause is unknown. There are other origins of facial paralysis that generally do not include synkinesis, such as genetic causes. Those born with Moebius syndrome, for example, have facial differences but not synkinesis. However, people who are born with single-sided paralysis might develop synkinesis in time.

As an acquired condition, synkinesis generally results after a medical ordeal, and the initial onset can be traumatic. Despite being college educated and working in health care, Loretta H., a white, cisgendered woman in her early thirties, recounted the experience of initial onset as frightening and alienating:

> I was really scared. . . . So I went to the ER, and they basically just gave me the drugs and sent me on my way, and that was it. [She laughs.] And I was like, okay, so my face is gone—all of a sudden. And they were like, great it's Bell's palsy, no big deal. Umm, to you, no big deal.
>
> And this is standard. I mean I even used to work in the ER—this is about a year and a half ago—I was working in the ER and . . . and I see this

4 METAMORPHOSIS

guy—and he didn't speak very good English, and my Spanish isn't much—but with his English and me trying, it was enough for us to communicate. And he is so upset. And I was registering him, and I saw his face, and I was pretty sure it was Bell's palsy. So I was like, "Do you mind me asking what they diagnosed you with?" And he said, "Well, I have this thing called Bell's palsy. I didn't know what it is, but they're just giving me drugs and sending me on my way."

So I just sat with him for a good thirty, thirty-five minutes just talking to him about my experience. We just talked. I just don't feel like they understand how hard this is, and he wasn't getting any answers, and they're acting like this is going to get better, and he wants to know, "How long it will take?" And I was like, "Well, I don't know, like it took me this long to get to where I am now." And he was getting married in a couple of weeks . . . and he was so worried. And I was like, "Oh my gosh."

I can't imagine how he must feel and how he has to explain this to his wife to be. . . . And he's there all alone . . . and he's going into self-blame. . . . He asked me, "Is this 'cause I went drinking?" and I don't know what to say. There is really no answer. I don't really have any answer why this happens, but it does. And so I just felt really bad for the guy and—there's no answer for it . . .

It's scary. It's hard. You can't just give us drugs and send us away.

And yet what Loretta has described has been a common experience for most individuals. Most were told things would resolve or heal. For Bell's palsy, they would be given steroids or antivirals. Those with Ramsay Hunt syndrome might require additional medication, and it was frequently initially misdiagnosed as Bell's palsy. Those with surgical or trauma-based causes were usually told to "wait and see." And, although the initial onset of facial paralysis is challenging, the lack of follow-up care and lack of awareness have meant so many with synkinesis were left undiagnosed, misdiagnosed, or untreated for an extended period of time.

Synkinesis can vary, and it's important to remember that visibility of impaction is not necessarily the same as degree of impaction. People may experience and describe similar challenges but in dissimilar ways. Overall, struggles with verbal and nonverbal communication, pain, tightness, muscle knots in the face and neck, unwanted movement, and lack of, inexplicable overabundance of, or cross-wiring of tears/saliva were largely ubiquitous. People also noted changes to their taste, vision, and balance along with vertigo, increased anxiety, and exhaustion.

Fundamentally synkinesis includes chronic pain. But people with chronic pain who aren't getting help will "learn to live with it." I was one of the "discomfort" people. Convincing oneself it is not chronic pain because it's tolerable is a

WHEN LIFE GIVES YOU LEMONS

wonderful trick of the mind. And many people, myself included, came to describe the perpetually cramping muscles as "tightness" or "discomfort."

In some cases, synkinesis can progress to intolerable levels. Brad A., an entertainer, found his synkinesis spreading down his neck and into his chest, with muscles tightening into perpetual cramps that were becoming intolerable. Brad is a white, cisgendered man with a college education, who had long struggled his weight. I would see Brad regularly at support events; the change in him was noticeable, and his discomfort was increasing. All this took a toll: Brad was open about his struggles with food and depression. Although Brad did the work, prioritizing his mental and physical health, the synkinesis continued to worsen. After several years of arguing with his health insurer, he found the only workable solution to afford surgery was to start a GoFundMe account to collect donations. He messaged me only hours after awaking from the operation, elated at the immediate change he experienced.

Similarly, Rachel B., a late-career, white, cisgendered, college-educated sales representative, found the side effects difficult to endure after tumor removal had left her with severe synkinesis.

> I don't know what it is, the muscles that pull or what, when I try to relax, if I'm like, I'm reading. It happens when I'm watching TV. I'll look, just like this [she tilts her head toward the affected side], or I'm watching TV like this [she adjusts her head straight up], and about an hour later I'm like this [she tilts her head]. And my husband will come by and push my head back up, it's like, "Oh, that feels better." It's my neck. It's so tight it pulls my head if I try to relax. I get Botox in my neck also because the neck muscles and everything are so bad. That's why I used to need pain killers and muscle relaxers, and these hot pads, and—even now, look. [Her head had started to tilt as she became absorbed in the conversation.] I don't even know I'm doing it, but my head is pointing to the side. [She shakes her head in distress.] And they say there's nothing to be done.

Although these were extreme cases, it was fascinating to speak to over 100 people who were experiencing chronic pain yet instead would use words like uncomfortable, distressing, distracting, frustrating, or difficult. But it's *pain*. It's knots in the face, it's constant pulling in wrong directions and having to adjust one's face, it's pulling in the neck that descends into the shoulders, it's possibly dental issues, or it's vision not being right—the list goes on. Almost everyone highlighted how exhausting it was to live with synkinesis. The chronic pain, combined with needing to manage one's face, took a tremendous amount of energy.

The long-term cost of chronic pain should not be underestimated. Chronic pain is associated with a negative impact on quality of life, including depression, lost time, and impaired performance, as well as negative impacts on physical and mental health (Kawai et al. 2017). For myself, even after three surgeries there is a painful tightness in my neck and a strangeness to my left eye socket. I can't explain my chin and the internal pulling. It's a lot to ignore all the time. Sometimes I need to spend considerable time stretching my left check so I can use my mouth effectively—if I focus hard, I can just barely do things most people do innately such as talking and chewing. I know when my Botox is due owing to the distracting discomfort in my left eye. How does one explain a tight eyeball?

Although I spoke with my interviewees at length about their physical challenges, the most compelling discussions centered on a self-transition necessitated by the experience. Being and communicating self had been immediately, irrevocably altered. Along with the difficulties they encountered, people experienced loss, grief, and growth. For instance, Lori M. is an affable, middle-aged, white, cisgendered woman with a college education and a successful career in marketing. She has found synkinesis to be her central challenge. "It blocks the you-ess of you. That's a grief place. I felt betrayed by myself. It blocks your personality, and you can't communicate who you are. You can't be who you are."

It wasn't just the change in their appearance or the change in how their appearance was valued; rather, it was a jarring disruption to their ability to experience and express their self that the participants described. This is the disruption that we live. People with synkinesis tend to describe intense anxiety, distress, and confusion over social interaction, and often it is expressed in how one feels one looks to others. Were I not living with synkinesis myself, I might not have thought to ask my interviewees, "So was there a mirror?" It really isn't about how we appear—most of the time, we don't really know how we appear—but rather we have a *perception* of how we appear. We have an experience of self as an object, which is always mediated through the subjective experience. It isn't really about how we look; it's about the subjective experience of being a communicative object. That means quite a bit more than simply how one feels one is perceived.

By feel, I don't mean believe—I mean, literally, *feel*. Embodiment is experienced, and synkinesis fundamentally disrupts that experience. On top of the challenges of a potentially visible disability and the extra effort that all communication now requires, there is also this series of social cue alarm bells going off in my head, which normally signal a need to adjust or exit the situation. They're going off all the time—but no, that's just my face.

The Project

Confronting the scope of a disability that impacts oneself in interview after interview, at events, online . . . I look/sound/feel too much like the subjects. It was too real. Too raw to be reminded over and over again of something that causes so much grief and anxiety. I didn't want it to be as hard as it is, didn't want to acknowledge, legitimate, a new status, a changed life. Then your fears become true.

People often tell me they would never know. Sure, if you assume I am a person with very little affect. Which I wasn't before. I was very expressive nonverbally. I enjoyed being that person. The double entendre with the wink or evil grin . . . I wish I could grin. A small smile, that's the best I can do. Or I look like a freak. The joker in Batman. When you smile at someone, having them recoil in horror is not the intended response. Is that a disability?

But I don't want to be disabled. Oh, damn, that's ableism reminding me of my moral imperfections. But I don't want to be marked. Abnormal. I don't want to be writing about how people like me cope with our abnormality. I don't want to know I am coping by turning it into a research project I am both uniquely suited to undertake and using to normalize my stigma. But maybe I need to.

I never wanted to "do autoethnography." That was a stated career goal of mine— I think my actual graduate school pledge was "No weird middle-age exploration as research." It was neither a methodology of interest to me as a scholar, nor a style I chose to embrace as a writer. I have nothing against it; I genuinely appreciate the methodology as a reader, I prefer my sociology in stories with supporting data, and I find my students are more likely to engage with well-written personalized texts. But another overeducated Jewish (white privilege) cis woman's self-exploration of the array of "First World" challenges I overcame didn't seem necessary or productive. It seemed like something that one should only do if one has experienced something unique, emblematic, or somehow worthy of note— circumstances that matched one's area of expertise. It's not that. Interesting things hadn't happened to me. I scuba dove through a tsunami in 2004, which was a life-changing event. But any wisdom I could impart from that experience already has been said by others, in more impactful ways.

But then I was handed a life experience—one that at once brought together my academic specialties, my passion for education and advocacy, and an impossibility of understanding without embodied perspectives. The constant and ongoing misunderstandings, frustrations, and unacknowledged griefs pushed me into the abyss. I won't say I am eating my own words—after I made that student pledge, a voice in my head reminded me that by making the statement I was ensuring I would indeed one day be doing just that. And here I am now, looking back at my twenty-something self, and in my mind I hug that person close. I cry, a gentle flow of tears, full of love and understanding, for who I once was and who I am now. I wish I still had that smile. But I have no regrets.

So what is autoethnography, and how did I end up doing it when it was the only method that this mixed methodologist planned to avoid? Autoethnography refers to work produced through the collective process of contextualized storytelling from an experienced standpoint (Denzin 2014). The value of "analytic" autoethnography conducted by a social scientist with a research-oriented goal comes in part from the reflexive dialogue of the researcher as both a person experiencing something and as a trained methodologist or expert (Anderson 2006). Through this process, one captures the dialogic process of performance of the self, revealing the nuanced experience of embodied social relations and their histories through real-world experiences. In my case, I combined personal experience with in-depth qualitative interviews and participant observation. I continue to attend advocacy events, conferences, and maintain an online presence in support groups. Some of the people who facilitate the groups and events became key informants and have provided insights over several years.

When I first began the project, I expected to focus on inequity in access to care and a self being impacted by internalized experiences of discrimination, discounting, and microaggressions. By extension, internalizing these things impacts the self—which I did find and will discuss. As described by the attractive, relatively young, and likely to be viewed as white cisgendered event planner Maggie D., synkinesis creates an ongoing challenge in making a first impression:

> I think we all judge one another even though we shouldn't. We most likely don't like to admit that we do. . . . But first impressions, we all kind go off of first impressions. When you didn't have this for thirty-five years of your life, and then you do have it—I'm thirty-six—you're kind of having to create almost like a new person. You're still that same person, but it's like a new outward appearance of a person, I think. People treat you differently. You can't talk properly, you can't smile. . . . You're just not comfortable with it because you're not functioning properly still in your own mind. I think that's the hardest adjustment.

Maggie expressed frustration at the encumbrance of assumptions regarding physical, mental, and social capacities and the burden of having to prove otherwise in every interaction. As will be discussed, Maggie D. is facing a real, problematic challenge that will at times result in experiencing and perhaps internalizing the systemic devaluing of bodies viewed as "disabled." This experience is part of discussing synkinesis. But throughout my study, while talking to people who share a rare condition, there was a deeper injury to the experience of self.

When she returned to school as an adult after Bell's palsy had left her with synkinesis, BIPOC (black, Indigenous and people of color), cisgendered

WHEN LIFE GIVES YOU LEMONS

Eva B. now faced both racism and ableism. Beyond the experiences of microaggressions shared, something about her synkinesis never allowed her to relax, even in safe spaces. Even when she should be able to relax, she was perpetually haunted: "I wish there was something I could do about the synkinesis. I think it's in my subconscious. It's always there talking at me. It's always there even when I try not to think about it. But I can't. I can always *feel* it, I can't make this *feeling* stop. It's a constant distraction. I have to think around it. I can always feel it, and I would be so much happier otherwise."

I began with a focus on equity and access, and I found so many doing amazing work in those areas. But I also found a disconnect in the understanding of the experience of synkinesis. When I began to explore this piece in depth, what emerged was a narrative about the embodied self, about loss, and growth. This project is effectively about the process of performance of the self, when that process is irrevocably altered, and performance is permanently inhibited. As I will discuss in depth, it's not only a shift in identity status but a challenge in that experience which needs to be acknowledged and addressed. This feeling is not a metaphor or a product of the experience; it's a literal physiological shift. But people also adapted and found new, resilient, reflective selves. The challenge faced by those with synkinesis further provides a valuable metaphor for self-reflexive critically informed growth. And, though this seems like a unique medical situation, I believe this process has larger applicability to understanding selves and narratives in transition.

What I Did

So I'm debating what to do with my sabbatical over dinner with two close friends from grad school. The people you implicitly trust; the people who get you, and it. And [they] will be honest. And I am musing over on what to focus my research. "Maybe I should consider the facial paralysis thing. . . . You know, a sociology of the body, insider/outsider thing?" "Took you long enough to get there" was the response.

There's so much there. The obvious myriad of intersections that make it easier for some to navigate careers, medical care, and the impact on your life. . . . Bodily capital, normativity, stigma—I could just use it to explain the progression of social theory. But there's something else there, hard to wrap words around . . . a way it changes one's fundamental experience of communication, one's essential experience of everything. It's not just what I can and cannot do, but how faces, expression, are wired into thought, into feeling, into being, into self.

But I don't want to . . . because it hurts. To have to confront that loss. Publicly. Over and over. To be that vulnerable in a world I knew to be more cruel than kind. I really didn't want to.

But despite the challenge of ongoing self-confrontation, maybe I could find something . . . I don't know what the word is. It's a smooth rock that feels good in the hand; it's birdsong in summer; it's a breeze on a hot day; it's the ocean's ever-changing depths. Because after this process, I don't use the word "good" anymore. It's a loaded word, full of histories of colonization, hierarchy, and judgment. And that's the journey this helped prepare me to take. I lost my smile, and I will eternally mourn that loss. But I also lost the word "good." And I gained a process.

But more importantly, I've started a journey. I may not yet know where I'm going, but I've started walking. Becoming is painful and discomforting, and one is always feeling wrong-footed. But I like better the person that I try to be when I'm this way.

I wasn't comfortable with pure autoethnography, uninterested in my story as a stand-alone epic, and preferred to find commonalities and divergences across stories, experiences, and views. My options, my resources, my ability to access resources, my level of empowerment, all made me atypical. I spent a sabbatical year and much of the subsequent year interviewing primarily people with synkinesis; I also interviewed people with acquired facial paralysis and congenital facial paralysis. Some who thought they didn't have synkinesis followed up to let me know they do. I interviewed medical professionals, family members, and partners as well. In addition, I talked to people at conferences, advocacy events, support groups, and support conferences. Some I came to know well over time. And I became more involved: volunteering at the annual walk, moderating support groups, and collaborating with the foundation.

In the end, I conducted 113 interviews with people with facial paralysis, six with family or spouses, and eight with medical professionals. Of the 113 people with facial paralysis, eighty-one had a diagnosis of synkinesis, nine most likely had synkinesis but did not have an official diagnosis, and eleven had an unclear condition—they were currently seeking a diagnosis, or were still healing/too soon to diagnose, or had other health issues that compounded diagnosis. Fourteen had facial paralysis but not synkinesis, though since being interviewed, one person shared with me that they do actually have some synkinesis. The average interview lasted about an hour and a quarter, with most interviews ranging between forty minutes and just over two hours. I attended support groups, support events, and online events for several years, and I continue to attend these. In addition, I collaborated on additional projects with Kathleen Bogart and Amanda Hemmesch, and their insights immeasurably improved my thinking and approach.

Though I remained true to the narrative conveyed to me, this type of work falls under what Arthur Bochner and Carolyn Ellis (2016) describe as evocative autoethnography.[1] Through narration, the author strives to create empathetic

WHEN LIFE GIVES YOU LEMONS

understanding (in the tradition of Weber's *verstehen*[2]). I could well imagine how others might view using narratives of experience as data and including not only my own narrative but my internal dialogue with the narrative I was producing out of my experience of collecting participant's narratives. It is meta but also micro. There's no hypotheses. There's no absolute proof. But there was something else there—something beyond elevated scores on depression and isolation indexes, something beyond correlations, that tugged at intersections hard to measure, hard to fathom.

That missing piece I struggled to articulate was something experienced and felt through the process of communicating with others and with oneself. If I hadn't lived it (insert a no longer attainable sardonic grin), could I truly understand it? From the outside, concern with appearance seems central, but from the inside the experience of communication and ability to self-present, the experience of emotion and experience of self, superseded but also somehow blended into feelings about "how I look." But "how I look" complicated it, as microaggressions revealed a new social status. I could not ignore the experiential embodied and visceral aspects of the experience. And it hurt(s). But it also forces growth as it makes me think more deeply about the relationship between my deepest fears and the structure of a system that needs monsters. That our darkest fears are of ourself becoming monster. Werewolves, vampires, and zombies are us, corrupted. Much of our culture embraces the idea that evil is embodied, that venal corruption is displayed on our visage. Struggling against that to find self-acceptance while also acknowledging the reality of a frustrating physiological impairment challenged me into a fruitless yet fruitful struggle with the systemic reified within self. I hope, these challenges have value for the reader.

I also cannot ignore the fact that autoethnography is a position. To use qualitative interviews and to combine personal experience is to embrace a specific line of inquiry and to take a stance, as it were, as a scholar and a methodologist. To be clear, I consider myself a mixed methodologist, and I see tremendous value in big data, quantitative data, and hypothesis testing. But not every project and not every problem lend themselves to quantification. There is no "masterlist" or "sampling frame" for those with rare diseases. Despite the challenges, tremendous work has already been done on identity, relationships, and psychological impact, for which I am eternally grateful. Rather than standing on the shoulders of giants, I imagine myself surfing a wave of revolutionary scholarship that has informed my thinking.

This project is a different piece. It's an attempt to share a visceral and academic journey or process of growth, of understanding, of acceptance. It's a challenge to set aside ideals and beliefs about what should be and instead spend some time with what is. The goal here is to share the journey. This deep disruption to self, coupled with a change in status, is a lived experience—one that

I lived. It challenged and pushed me in unexpected ways. I don't know what the value of sharing this is, only that so many of us emerged wounded but working toward something, which just seemed more meaningful than what had come before.

There was a letting go of the mask I thought I needed to wear, along with anger and shame. I don't know if I could have started to figure so much out without all these other people struggling with me: that's intersectional feminist scholarship. I'm not going to give you any answers, but I will describe a journey, a process, and a development, precipitated by a radical shift in the understanding and experience of self. Finally, I will explore what it is to undergo a radical shift in status and identity.

The journey began with an abrupt foray into visible, socially stigmatized "otherness." It was brutal—and still is. This project arose out of my attempt to think through and wrestle with the complexity of the experience as a scholar, as a person who lives with synkinesis, and as a member of growing advocacy movement.

> The ethical conundrums abound, and not the usual ICF [informed consent form] ones. I got that. The line between research and life blurs with autoethnography. I wasn't a member of a community when I started the project, but now I am. Many of my participants I recruited out of support groups I now socialize with as the increasingly active communities grow.
>
> Even during the pandemic, online support groups allowed relationships to continue. As I met more people with facial difference online, eventually some of us become "friends" through social media. Can I include comments from a participant's parent who, after hearing about my project, shares with me how much discrimination her son faces? Will people read this, recognize themselves, or be disappointed that they don't? . . . How are they going to feel about me, themselves, everyone else after reading this?
>
> And though throughout, the response is overwhelmingly in favor of visibility, I still don't know how I feel about myself and my process. I know some will hate this—a privileged person, who lost a little bit of that, complaining. Others will endow us with virtues overstated, that feel heavy with impositions and assumptions. But all we can do is take what helps, and leave the rest, and try to grow our humanity.

Knowledge and research are inherently tied to political positions and struggles. It was impossible not to see the need for and to participate in patient advocacy. There is so much commonality in what is neglected, what was needed, and our shared vulnerabilities. Attending conferences with recognized experts, I was able to eventually find guidelines and recommendations, and to piece together a solid understanding of what had happened and continued to happen as well as what my options should have been and currently are. But it's unrealistic to expect the average person or even the average family practice specialist or neurologist to put in the time I have had to put in on a single rare disease.

Guidelines, patient advocacy, and working to create standards of care that maximize quality of life seem like a bare minimum of what work like this should be informing, and to which I should be committing my time. But the medical model, of broken and fixed, leaves one feeling overwhelmed. To sit and listen to people describe what's "wrong" with your face, and what's covered and what isn't, is taxing. Moving from having things done to you to participating as an active partner in treatment is an essential first step. Advocating for increased integration of the patient experience reflects a politicized view, one I was excited to see become increasingly common among doctors, health professionals, and advocacy groups. This work, however, isn't about the causes, advocacy, or the cures, but rather about the experience of living with synkinesis, though I do hope it assists with advocacy.

For critical feminist methodologists, the visceral is foregrounded as a legitimate metric, rather than hidden behind the traditional mask of scientific objectivity. We argue that it should be for a very obvious reason: life is lived. Life is experienced by real people, and quality of life is as much a social-emotional metric as any other type of measure. Fear, anxiety, joy, safety, acceptance, and isolation—all the things that improve or devolve quality of life—are experienced. Feminist theory, critical race theory, and cultural studies challenge scholars, activists, and policy makers to consider the lived experience of individuals as central. Feminist disability studies provide amazing examples of work that centers embodied lived experience (Fine and Asch 1988; Begum 1992; Bogart and Matsumoto 2010; Browne, Connors, and Stern 1985; Deegan and Brooks 1985; Hahn 1989; Krnjacki et al. 2018; Richards 2008).

To capture the place where the social and the corporeal meet requires an acknowledgment of the primacy of experience that has often been ignored or devalued in academic work (Ettorre 2017). More recently, black feminist scholars, intersectional feminists, and body scholars have centered understanding privilege, oppression, and inequity as embodied (Collins 1990; Ettorre 2017; Howson 2013; Richards 2008; Schalk 2022; Shakespeare 1999; Wynter 1999).

Sociology of the body wrestles with studying what one is, while being the vantage point from which we study (Howson 2013). Bodies are complicated. They are the physical manifestation of social relations, experience, and physical possibilities/limits, but they are also us. Relations of power materialize in experience(s), through normalizing practices that produce docile and conforming bodies, that write critical essays about bodies. Although each body has a unique place in space and time, with a specific personal and cultural history, commonalities across place and time highlight the ways relations of privilege and oppression compel and define categories. How is the embodied experience reflected in who does and what is scholarship? How does that impact what knowledge is and who is able to produce it?

Self-Reflexive Scholarship

The self-reflexive social scientist considers not only the object of study but also the conditions that produce the "science of society" (Bourdieu and Wacquant 1992). Pierre Bourdieu and Loïc Wacquant (1992) suggest that what one sees as legitimate knowledge may be a source of bias. This isn't to say there aren't facts; but interpretations suggest outcomes that benefit, validate, include, and exclude. How does the social construction of what should be bothering us interfere with our assertions of what is? How does the language we are already using shape what we express and how we express it, and how might that be limiting discourse?

Autoethnography involves accessing this "reflexive" self (Ettorre 2017; Kleinman 2003; Reed-Danahay 1997; Wheatley 2005). One becomes part of the project as a subject, an object, and the tools of analysis. The process is part of the project as the researcher-subject considers the self-subject and the relationship between participants, how one sees oneself, how one sees oneself as seen by others, and how none of it is quite right. The parameters of traditional knowledge exclude research subject position as a critical factor in understanding the production of knowledge.

Feminist and critical race theorists share this idea of "legitimate knowledge" needing to include the visceral. In our bodies we experience privilege and oppression, adequate nourishment, pleasures and indignities, probable achievements, and envied impossibilities. What we are made to feel as objects and the limits of our subjecthood are where social structures produce, normalize, and legitimate our existences. Interlocking axes of oppression mean that the experience of otherness will be different for those at different social locations (Collins 1990; Crenshaw 1989).

Autoethnography provides one valuable way to explore an embodied subject, a social object, and the complicated experience of the relationship between those things. Research on the long-term impact of trauma on addiction (Ettorre 2017) provides one example. The silencing of people with disabilities within medical models and studies has highlighted the disjuncture between our experiences as subjects and objects within a system of meanings and dis(empowerings). Disability theorists and activists note the tragedy in being rendered so irrelevant as to not be included in the understanding of one's daily milieu.

Although doctors and medical professionals are considered experts, they lack the crucial aspect of experience (Richards 2008). One expert revealed to me how his practice improved after he truly listened to his patients' concerns: there is a "disconnect between medical understandings, and patient needs. . . . What looks fine to me may not feel fine to the patient. What bothers me as a doctor may not be what most distresses the patient, and isn't the point to help the patient?" More than one doctor told me Bell's palsy doesn't hurt even as I was describing my painful reality and the start of synkinesis. I said it felt like my head was being jerked around, that it felt like really bad pins and needles, that it felt like tightness, soreness, and being beaten. I could see my descriptions weren't resonating. I wasn't making sense to them. I could see the certainly my distress was psychological rather than physiological. It was a relief to discover that it was indeed pain—nerve pain and muscles cramping that so many in my interviews described. I continue to see distressed support group attendees mention their pain being dismissed by medical professionals, friends, and family.

Narratives always already reflect relations of power and privilege, and they are always experiential. "I might be able to escape from a narrative I did not write" (Richards 2008, 1721). An added feature to autoethnography is the explicit location of the narrator as the subject producing and analyzing as well as the object under study. And those willing to talk were like me in many more ways than the shared experience of facial paralysis. Applying the reflexive lens, the privilege of having lost something and having a space to articulate that loss is inherently a privileged perspective. Some types of people were so much more likely to have the ability to engage. These people often understood the power and potential value of narrative. Educators, mental health and healthcare professionals, and people who work with people are vasty overrepresented in my sample. There's a working-through that is required, which some people were more likely to be given the space and resources to accomplish. As a result, privilege is enmeshed in access to healing processes, especially those tied to advocacy.

> It's so hard to justify my expertise and my "special abilities" when I feel so broken all the time. But that's what this experience is. An experience of a permanently broken self. [It's] not because of how you look. I don't walk around with a mirror, and I don't see myself most of the time. It's how you feel when you try to communicate, when you have emotion, when you experience life. It never feels quite right again, and it's always on your mind. So here's the reality: I am exactly the person to do this! I did a participant observation dissertation on embodied experience, I've done in-depth interviews and focus groups on a range of subjects, and I've lived this experience. I should feel really proud of the depths I went to, the insights I found, and the way I opened myself up. Instead I feel scared, and broken; when I try to explain it to you, my mouth won't work right. You will just look at me struggling to talk and pity me.

In addition, I had good timing. Advances in research, greater disability awareness, and activism combined with a shortage of advocates meant I was able to participate in academic and advocacy-related events that gave me greater access to people with facial paralysis and their support networks. In turn, this gave greater visibility to my research. Collaborations opened up. I was able to participate in a project involving family members of people with Moebius syndrome, serve on an international advisory board, consult on medical papers, and be an invited speaker at support groups, in person and online. For this type of disfigurement, disease, disability, whatever it is (see chapter 5 for an in-depth discussion), I had good timing.

From "Normal" to "Other"

> I didn't want to see anyone. I basically stayed inside. I didn't go out for two weeks at all. I called in sick; I went on disability. At some point I had to get back out. It's still hard. (Dani S.)

Studying the shift from "normal" to "othered" identity isn't new—the autoethnographies of pain (Neville-Jan 2003), illness (Charmaz 1983; Lefton 1984; Richards 2008; Wheatley 2005), eating disorders (Tillman 2009), addiction (Ettorre 2017), dementia (Saunders 2017), mental health challenges (Martin 2007), and physical disability (Couser 2009; Shell 2005) highlight how identity transitions with bodily shifts or how to understand life as an embodied other. What kind of other is someone with synkinesis?

> The word *grotesquerie* just flew into my mind. I'm not even sure what one is. . . . Yet I have my Hollywood image of freak shows in dark tents. . . . That moment I am marked as "not normal," as "freak," as someone whose appearance is to be tolerated. Mired down by the weight of the fact that everyone "adjusts" to how you look. . . . How do I put that in words? How do I explain that once you notice that someone noticed, it's hanging there. You tell me you don't even notice while you fixate on the corner of my mouth. . . . It's not even at the level of thought—it's that visceral punch to the gut. We learn to move past that moment. But we are always living with it. I am always wondering where on the scale of deformed freak I fall. Always aware that I will be pitied after I leave. And I arm myself with the reminder of our humanness, our shared frailties. And it's hard not to be angry at a system that necessitates I feel this way. It's not something I can just get over, when our culture is continuously sending counterproductive messages about who we are.

As Elizabeth Ettorre (2017) suggests, this type of narrative has historically been devalued and yet is incredibly beneficial. Conducting qualitative interviews with people with facial difference has been an amazing, cathartic, painful, intense, beautiful set of experiences. In almost every interview, one (usually both) of us teared up, if not outright sobbed. Our voices were tight with painful memories then relaxed into understanding. The right to build one's own narrative matters. It matters in the day to day. It matters that we get to be the subjects constructing rather than simply the objects studied.

So much of social science and science has been situated within a quest for an objective truth of experience and, more recently, an authentic rendering. But whether it's the distance of objectivity or the insider stamp of authenticity, a certain privilege is being invoked: the ability to have distance from something is the experience of privilege. To understand the embodied experience of being other, one has to live being other. Being othered is not just navigating more challenging terrain; it is doing so with ongoing physical manifestations and reactions. The sinking feeling in one's stomach, the pounding head, the chest tightening, the sensation of everything seeming heavier are integral to understanding embodied experiences.

Yet my experience is not the only experience; I am a web of axes, many privileged, some not, and my reality is not someone else's. But there are ways our experiences overlap. And there are things I would never have understood if I weren't also living it.

You can't even tell. You wouldn't even notice. That's true sometimes, I suppose. That others don't notice. "Inexpressive" is what people just think. Inscrutable, hard to read. It took many, many interviews of people telling me they were upset about how they looked. Had I not been living it, I wouldn't have realized: it's not about how I look. I can't see myself. And it's not about how I think they think I look, because I know that feeling, and that's part of it, but not all of it. It's this weird feeling in my face: it mimics that behavioral warning we all get when we socially transgress. I am always getting messages from my face that I am socially off. For people without synkinesis, these are useful message reminding you to adapt, to stay within social norms, to avoid shame and stigma. But for me, I get the message regardless. It was not just the expected spoilt identity à la Goffman but the spoilt experience, more akin to Bourdieu's habitus: the ability to enjoy the performance was being disrupted. Even when the external was positive, the internal disruption was eternally troubling. But naming it, understanding it, and talking about it makes it easier.

Embodiment and identity are intimately connected. The corporeal meeting of experience, history, perception, and action that gives meaning to social relations is the point from which we perceive (our source of information) and the thing to which others react (our means of conveying information). But what happens when our ability to convey information is disrupted? What happens when the information we take in reveals discomfiture with our appearance? What happens when experiencing emotion becomes physically uncomfortable? These weren't the questions I necessarily set out to answer, but they quickly emerged as the most salient. "How have you changed?" was an obvious query, but the discussions had unexpected depth. How have *I* changed? Though I may be less sure, less certain, and less able to emote effectively, I think I like the person I am becoming more.

Tools in My Tool Kit

To a large degree, inequity and its consequences can be easily measured and quantified. A wealth of data documenting the impacts of disability already exist. Visible disability negatively impacts income potential (Zarifa, Walters, and Seward 2015) and mental health (short term and long term) (Coulson 2017), and it decreases the odds of achieving a variety of common culturally normative life goals such as getting married (Tumin 2016) or attaining a degree (Zarifa, Walters, and Seward 2015). But even more so, than other marginalized identities, those with disabilities are spoken for and spoken about. More recently, disability identity studies are challenging the assumptions, norms, and the experience of being a disabled object (Darling 2019). A movement toward self-representation is part of foregrounding disability subjecthood (Couser 2009).

Contributing to the disability identity frame of analysis, my project explores a major physiological change. Synkinesis forced me to experience being perceived as disabled in other ways than I was, but to also be disabled and to find a lack of voice for the subject experiencing while being continuously objectified. It wasn't something I was sure could be measured on a scale. There's a process and a period of adaptation. Through this project, I continue to experience and understand how one copes and changes. It was a process of adjusting to being an "other" but also to a disruption of the experience of self. It's profound, and almost no one ever allows us to talk about it or asks questions about it.

Mindful of retraumatizing, I worried about the impact of our interviews. I also feared (re-)creating the "inspirational" narratives that so rankle with implications of exceptionalisms and gatekeeping. Yet it was shocking how quickly rapport was established when they saw I was like them. There aren't very many of us; for more of my participants than not, I was the first other person like them they had ever seen. So people were more than willing to share. They wanted to talk about it—they craved talking about the parts of it that no one acknowledges, these things that make daily life so much harder and that no one seems to understand. Now we are in my wheelhouse: I have years of experience interviewing people who see me as "like them." Previously I worked with co-ed sports participants, female athletes in nontraditional sports, media consumers, various focus groups with social media users, media consumers, and

The Participants

Studying a condition or group of whom one is a member is seen as both an advantage and a disadvantage (Lofland et al. 2006). The researcher already has entrée/rapport/acceptance within the group and understands the subtleties and nuances of communication within the group (Lofland et al. 2006; S. E. Weiss 1994). At the same time, this may leave the researcher unable or unwilling to maintain/obtain enough critical distance for analysis (Corbin and Strauss 2008). One must remain vigilant against universalizing—my experience is not "the experience."

I remain haunted by those with whom I wasn't able to speak. A few folks were shockingly isolated by region or poverty or unstable support networks that indicated failures in medical and social care. I wonder about those who aren't in online support groups or receiving or seeking medical care or attending events, all places from which I recruited. Annie B. was unusual among my interviewees: a cisgendered white woman with a high school education who lives in the rural Midwest. Her rural area is too far from covered medical care to access it. With no car or transit alternatives, she found making several three- to five-hour car trips to set up further care to be an impossibility. She just wasn't receiving any treatment, and she was "uncomfortable." She worked from home and spent her time with her dogs and chickens. She was a little lonely, but a few folks—some relatives, some old friends—visited occasionally, so it was fine. But she just really wanted to talk to someone, someone like her. More voices like this need to be heard.

And this was hard and is hard. Interviewing people who share your trauma is deeply unsettling. I grappled with writing this. I remain deeply invested and deeply distrustful of the open vulnerability of this work. The writing wasn't going well unless I ended up sobbing at some point—my metric for good writing but perhaps not ideal for mental health. At the same time, the experience was cathartic, for the participants and for myself. The support group attendees strongly echoed this sentiment, as suggested by previous research: talking with someone about microaggressions and disabilities in and of itself may be therapeutic (Keller and Galgay 2010) and talking with those who share a disability generally is (Darling 2019). In this case, so many others shared how deeply profound it was to be able to discuss the internal mental state identity aspects of this. It changed the focus of the work. I followed the data, listened to the stories, learned more about myself, and tried to "be better" and then to re-evaluate the goal I am striving toward. I grew and I changed enough to know that "better" is the wrong goal.

Over a two- to three-year period, I interviewed more than 100 people with permanent facial paralysis, a handful of family members, and medical professionals who treat people with permanent facial paralysis. Who volunteered to do an interview alone was telling: though there do not appear to be differences in rates of synkinesis by gender (Bylund et al. 2017), women were far more likely to volunteer to participate (as is common in such studies). Over 80 percent of my participants were female; women significantly outnumber men at every support group I attend. No one identified as nonbinary during the course of the interviews, but my understanding is that this has changed for at least one participant. Research has also demonstrated greater negative approbation of women with disabilities and less access to valued social roles (Darling 2019). Hence, the impact it was having on the experience of self may have been more impactful for women.

The group I interviewed was overeducated and was more likely to have careers in medical or helping professions than the general population. Thirty-five percent of my participants had a graduate degree; another quarter had a four-year college degree. A few had returned to school or were still in school. About a quarter of the participants identified as BIPOC: almost 10 percent of the participants identified as Latine, almost 7 percent as black, and just under 3 percent as Asian American, with the remainder identifying as mixed. It was a little disappointing to not have wider representation, and this will be discussed in subsequent chapters.

As would be expected given that it is the most common cause of facial paralysis leading to synkinesis, Bell's palsy had impacted over 60 percent of my participants. Roughly 10 percent had suffered from an acoustic neuroma, and almost another 10 percent had had a tumor removed. Because disability and identity were central to this project, I had sought out people who had not previously identified as being disabled or having a disability. My participants hailed from across the United States primarily, although I also spoke to a number of people in other countries, and I participate in online support groups centered in other countries. All interviews were conducted in English. Appendix A contains the details regarding my participants.

Certainly, all the ways one would expect social status to matter did matter. The richer, whiter, more educated, more urban one was, the better one's medical treatment was and the wider the range of available options. These also seemed to be the people who were most likely to become involved in advocacy and support, making them the easiest to recruit.

Degree of visible impaction did not seem predictive of coping or willingness to participate. Based on my participants' responses, I suspect that there are many groups whose voices were lost, for a multitude of reasons. I witnessed a range of responses: some of my participants self-presented as successful, but others lamented and highlighted their struggles. Some retreated from more public roles, but others, especially those who became involved in advocacy work,

WHEN LIFE GIVES YOU LEMONS

found themselves far more involved in public speaking or appearing in media than ever before. The value of pets came up a lot. Some actively pointed out their synkinesis, wanted to be on camera, and wanted to see me and others with synkinesis. Some wanted no part of visuals and preferred phone calls. But everyone had a story about how synkinesis had disrupted their sense of and experience of self. Most had rebuilt themselves into someone they liked and were proud of. They (we) had had survived and grown, and are still surviving and growing.

One thing that always stands out in interview projects is how often people tell you that something doesn't bother them, that something didn't upset them, that it's something they don't notice, or it's not important—and then immediately tell you exactly how upsetting, important, or disconcerting that something is. For instance, another professor told me his facial paralysis didn't bother him at all—yet I met him at a support group. Another insisted that he was used to the way he looks—but he sat with the affected side of his face half outside the visual frame for almost our entire interview. I myself have perfected a head tilt that almost completely masks my own obvious paralysis, and I have noticed several others using similar angles. Almost everyone recounted some isolation. One memorable in-person interview began with the participant telling me her social life was no longer impacted; at the end of the interview she told me she planned to seek therapy because she hadn't realized how isolated she had become.

The interviews were semi-structured, meaning I asked everyone a series of demographic and prepared questions, but I also asked participants to tell their stories in their own words. Because each story is unique, the follow-up questions were, too, but I made sure to cover certain aspects of everyone's experience. As one might imagine, the process itself was intense. Someone asked me if it was emotional, and my tongue-in-cheek but true response was "it's only successful if we both cry—and most of my interviews are successful." The participants recounted deeply personal, traumatic experiences in dealing with, as a result of, and sometimes as the cause of facial paralysis. Suicide attempts, familial or peer rejection, depression, and isolation sat alongside stories of support, healing, and newfound talents and abilities. One person described bullying, then a new artistic talent; another spoke of being harassed out of several jobs but going home to amazing support. I wanted to hug some of the parents for the work they had done to support teens. Others broke my heart with their stories of parents who no longer displayed their current photos, friends who cancelled invitations, and co-workers who started to ignore and mock them. Many described the interview process as cathartic; several openly stated that they had volunteered because they thought it would be good for them to open up and talk about it explicitly with someone who shared the experience. At the end of each interview, I gave the participants an opportunity to ask me questions about my own experience. Sometimes the less-forthcoming participants would expand at length after they had asked me several questions through which I established my "disability cred."

During the time I was conducting interviews, I had my second facial paralysis surgery, and I struggled with talking for months—a useful reminder of the more visible aspects of synkinesis. I would see my interviewees have to lean in and struggle a bit to understand me. Often this experience was mutual, and there was a shared moment. The subsequent chapters cannot focus on every aspect of facial paralysis or synkinesis, the experiences of my participants, or my own experiences. I am trying to tell a story about an experience of disruption and adjustment. I know I should write about overcoming, but that's just it— otherness isn't something we overcome. People adjust, move on, and become, but not so much overcome. That's devaluing a part of me, and I don't do that anymore.

Chapter 2 provides the theoretical background for the ensuing discussion. This chapter focuses on social theory, embodiment, and self/identity. Poststructuralism, intersectional feminist theory, critical race theory, queer theory, and disability identity theory are introduced as critical to this analysis.

Chapter 3 explores the experience of being someone with facial difference. Intersecting identities, impacts on experiences, microaggressions, and internalization are central to this discussion.

Chapter 4 is about the fact that *it's the face*. Certainly, any major physical disruption affects our identity and carries moral approbation, but faces are central to our identity, character, and sociability in a very specific way. The loss of the smile as a communicative experience and necessary tool for social interaction is incomparable and devastating. My participants survived and adapted, but almost everyone mourned the loss of the experience of smiling.

Chapter 5 focuses on one of the most puzzling and complicated aspects of facial paralysis, the internal disruption of experience. My participants shared the ways their own internal experience was disrupted continuously, both by seeing the reactions of others and by experiencing "wrong" emotions/expressions. Ultimately, synkinesis disrupts communication with the self and between the self and others. I discuss disability identity, and the idea of a "social" disability is introduced as we transition to chapter 6.

Chapter 6 highlights the active remaking of self in the wake of epiphanic challenges. This final substantive chapter explores how individuals move forward or find ways to cope, personally and professionally, with permanent facial paralysis. Most people not only cope in the long run but also grow as a result.

Chapter 7 concludes with how we not only rebuild ourselves but conceive differently of the process of self. How do we learn and grow through this challenge, and how do we think differently about self and other? How can we all grow and change the way we treat others? How do we change the institutions and ideologies we maintain and endorse? Who do we become through this process?

2

Theorizing Change

Culture, Identity, and the Face

My smile bothers me. My eyes bother me. My friends used to call me "Picture Perfect Peters" because I always had the best smile in all the pictures. I can't smile. This has been a complete . . . it's almost . . . like a death. Like I died. Like I literally had to say goodbye to my face. The old me died. (Jami P., college-educated cisgendered white woman)

I don't wish this on my worst enemy. I would do anything in the world to not have this happen to me or to anybody else. There needs to be a cure for this because it's your face. It's your face, it's your greeting, it's your hello to everyone, and it's affected me majorly. (Maddy D., college-educated cisgendered white woman)

It's a huge event in my life that for the past seventeen years I've had to deal with on a daily basis. (Al L., college-educated Latine cisgendered man)

Sociology of the Body

I really intended to do more traditional sociology: to focus on lost wages, access to care, damage to relationships, and the costs of becoming an "other." But when I spoke with people and listened to what they said, what emerged as central was challenging to articulate. The process of being had been disrupted, revealing the uncertain material and ideological ground on which the self rests. We think we know what the self is—ourself, at least. It's easy to forget what the self as a corporeal being within historically manifest axes of privilege and oppression really means.

The self is simultaneously doing and experiencing. We always think of the self as a separate thing from the body. Sure, the limits and abilities of bodies might shape self-concept or self-identity, but the uncomfortable place where the literal physical limits of self and identity reside is hard to fathom, and it's deeply disquieting to attempt it. To wonder about the physical nature of self and identity is to question some fundamental principles of identity. But we do it all the time. We ask ourselves why we did something. Or we wonder about something

23

we said that seemed "out of character." We recognize that our earlier discontent was only hunger. But the self as one experiences it—and the self as an academic object—has history(ies).

The self (and who is granted the privilege of a subjective self) is deeply entrenched in the history and study of Western thought. There is a history not only of thought about bodies but of what role bodies occupy in the development of thought. There is a demarcation between the selves whose minds rule their bodies and those whose bodies rule their minds. From the enlightenment until recently, social theory and philosophy has been dominated by the Cartesian paradigm of rationality, which foregrounds a mind/body dualism. This meant that mind and body were viewed as separate but interacting entities (Turner 2008). In this view, the self inhabits the body and is generated through rational reflection on the world (Cregan 2006; Howson 2013; Turner 2008). The rational mind is divorced from the body or, oddly, is disembodied. What this effectively means is that the physical/natural/medical was defined as within one set of expertise while the self, experience, the soul, morality, and rationality were "of the mind." The relationship between the body and the mind—and how the widely varying experiences of bodies might produce different takes on knowledge, abilities, thought processes, and physiological reactions—was largely absent. Certainly, this was also mirrored in the field of sociology where, until recently, the corporeal was largely ignored (Cregan 2006; Turner 1992).

The failure of Cartesian views to consider social location—explicitly race (Ozawa de-Silva 2002) and gender (Jagger and Bordo 1989)—has been widely critiqued. The mind/body dualism has operated as a philosophic rationale for using difference to exclude those deemed more of the body (women, children, black, Indigenous and people of color [BIPOC] people), while those of the mind (the scholars defining the categories) use their specific set of skills and knowledges to command the unruly (body). The categorization of "normal" and "abnormal," as in the case of sexuality, further marked some bodies, creating fundamental assumptions about the natural and social world (Foucault 1978). Theorists like Latour (1993) highlight how the boundaries reflect relations of power and privilege, as oppositional poles clearly delineate and limit. Questioning the rights and responsibilities of those in different categories continues to create ethical quagmires and assumptions of human subjects and less human objects.

The body then was not invisible but rather taken for granted as a tool or an object of study (Shilling 2003). The bodies of those studied versus the objective disembodied gaze highlighted differences in power and perception (or the right to perceive) versus that which was perceived and subject to the imposition of the knowledgeable expert. The insights of symbolic interactionists, poststructuralists, feminist, critical race, and queer theorists challenged the assumed dualities and, more importantly, how science is done and what/who counts as a science/tist. Frequently misinterpreted as a discrediting of scientific knowledge, what was being called into question was the ways that the production of knowledge reified specific relations of privilege and oppression. The demand is for a more critical, thoughtful, and less certain science that recognizes a wider range of knowledges and expertise, and prioritizes lived experiences.

Sociology of the body arises in conjunction with these critiques and highlights the absence of a clear understanding of the single instrument common to all investigations and the vantage point from which the social world is experienced. To bring in bodies—as part of a paradigmatic shift in the social sciences—requires the abandonment of dualisms. And as interactionism came to supplant dualism, a very different relationship between mind/body/self was implicated.

In the Cartesian model, the rational mind is not subject to the body; to a large degree, privilege rests upon the assumption that bodies that bear certain traits are able to do this absolutely whereas other bodies are incapable of this feat. By contrast, sociology of the body foregrounds corporeality. Bodies are always simultaneously the site from which we study and the object of study—at once subject and object (Cregan 2006; Howson 2013; Shilling 2003; Turner 2008). The term "bodymind," introduced by Margaret Price (2015) and developed by Sami Schalk, highlights a subject that is the enmeshment of the mind and body, and the impossibility of separating the physical and mental (Schalk 2018).

Concepts like bodymind make visible the corporeal tolls of systemic inequity. This shift in understanding marks a significant theoretical change and challenge to existing relations of privilege and oppression and the system that reifies such relations. Understanding this always already merged state is crucial to understanding a subtle shift in the understanding of power, the social world and bodies that ushered in the transition that opened and shaped this field. Within this view, embodied experience is central to understanding the self.

Symbolic Interactionism, Society, and the Self

Central to the self is the experience of self in the social world. To some degree that is experienced through an internal dialogue/relationship between one's socialized self and one's experiential self. This ongoing dialogue between oneself as subject and oneself as object is captured in Charles Horton Cooley's idea of the looking-glass self ([1902] 2010), and George Herbert Mead's concepts of the I and the Me (1934).

Cooley's concept of the looking-glass self presents the idea of the self as result of a three-phase process. First, we imagine how we appear to others. Second, we imagine others' judgment. This results in a third phase in which "self-feelings," such as pride, shame, or mortification ensue (Cooley [1902] 2010;

Featherstone 1991a; Howson 2013). Mead (1934) added the two-part self, the "instinctual" *I* and the "socially managed and filtered" *Me*. The I is what we do when we do not reflect on our actions; the Me has reflected and constructed a course of action consistent with the managed and considered self. This is not to say the Me is inauthentic; rather, the Me is influenced by aspiration or who we want to be or at least be seen as. It is not simply that the Me is a rational response, but rather that it is an understanding of the self as a social object or an object within a larger social context. More recent studies also note the salience of reference groups, expectations, and identity as process in the development of self (Darling 2019).

Most of us do not walk around with mirrors. The "mirror" is the social interaction, the response we get. Or rather, the mirror is our interpretation of the response we thought we identified. In truth, for me the mirror reveals a far more disturbing set of changes in my appearance than the social response indicates. Over two years of primarily Zoom-based interactions were an especial torment for me. Among my interviewees, the people with acquired facial paralysis more often disliked seeing their visual image. While a few interviews were conducted in person or by audio only, the majority of the interviews were conducted using online programs such as Skype, Zoom, or FaceTime. As a result, generally, the participants (and I) were forced to stare at little images of ourselves during the interview, and the reaction to this became part of the project.

In addition, I volunteer to help facilitate online support groups. Similarly, many avoided having their face on camera. During interviews and support groups the participants often expressed angst or anxiety about the current image they were forced to see as we talked. A few would cover it; some would point out aspects of it as we talked. The most memorable was a man who had acquired facial paralysis as a child: after telling me his face no longer bothered him, he spent the entire interview sitting so that we could both only see the nonparalyzed half (held half off screen). When I pointed this out to him, he shifted his position to continue the interview; after a very short time, he moved half his face once again off camera. I do my own version of this: people often tell me that my camera is set too high, that they can't see my mouth (trust me, it is intentional). As a rule, what people saw in their mirror unsettled, disturbed, and caused distress, so avoiding mirrors, pictures, and being on camera was a common theme. For better or worse, the medium through which I did most of my interviews forced direct confrontation.

The experience, as are all experiences, is an embodied one. We develop *feelings* of pride or mortification. Those feelings are not the dry academic discourse on the page, they are corporeal. Mead used the term "somatic perception" to refer to our making sense through embodied physical assessment (Howson 2013; Mead 1934). Through this process, we are the subject perceiving, the object being perceived, and the self having feelings about perceptions. Part of what we perceive is the response of others, so the process is dynamic, ongoing, and always responsive and generative. These feelings are developed within a social context that gives meaning to the object assessed relative to others. These feelings may not be articulated but are experienced through tension; the expressions "gut-wrenching" and "heart pounding" come to mind. Mead focuses on the reactions to the self in society, and these perceptions arise in a social context. Hence, one receives messages about acceptance, position, pleasure, and warmth that shape behavior. Mead warned in 1934 that increasingly the feedback we receive is coming from mediated commercial sources with profit-based agendas.

Developing these ideas, Erving Goffman's dramaturgical model reveals the performative nature of social life. Roles, norms, and largely prescribed performances dominate social interaction. Certainly, we cannot deny the ubiquity of costume, settings, and the tendency to enact norms. With his concept of dramaturgy, Goffman (1959) highlights the self as a performance, complete with staging, props, scripts, and expectations. The self within it emerges from consensus as to what the performance means within the existing social world. In this view, the self is produced through an active process of negotiation created as one "feels" one's way through social interactions (Howson 2013). This is an embodied, visceral process. By controlling the flow of information, one can construct a narrative that highlights some roles or facets in one setting, and others at different moments. One's feedback on the performance is the in-the-moment visceral reaction by and to others. During performance, one is always simultaneously subject and object. One is always performing a self, and critiquing or reflecting on that performance. Facial difference often leaves us receiving messages that we are relegated to a very limited range of socially devalued roles.

It is important to understand that one's relationship with the self is embodied and experienced as visceral. Goffman (1963) referred to it as a "felt identity." What underlies this is a somatic perception through which we come to understand ourselves as objects (Howson 2013). We reflect on our performance not necessarily as rational, contemplating beings but rather through experiencing a sick feeling in the stomach when we get a look or a response, or dread at having to go back there, or pleasure in a shared moment, looks of admiration, or a flush of pride. The self, then, is an embodied project—a project by the body, on the body, and for the body (Shilling 2003). It seems so obvious as I write this. How much of having privilege is simply not feeling the anxiety of being other. Of walking through the world not feeling the various negatives that come with being in an "other" category or "othered" categories. To always feel one is right, entitled, able. How wonderful it must be to walk through the world without a voice constantly editing and critiquing. Judging. But also how terrible to be so unaware. Through the process of *impression management* we adjust our performance or seek alternate stages to create a self or identity. Goffman's (1959) concepts of dramaturgy and impression management imply an invested actor. Goffman brings in this idea of the self as presented and experienced through the performance of the self. The character is carefully written and constructed, with backstage preparation for front stage performances. Our front stages of the professional world (work or parenting arenas), the quasi professional world (where the obligatory and the social overlap such as at parent–teacher events or networking events), and social interactions are often heavily "scripted." One's ability as a performer is further influenced by the ability to follow the normal scripts or routines of interaction (Giddens 1991). Because a tremendous amount of communication is nonverbal and much of that is facial, people with facial paralysis must relearn normal social performances. One woman, an older, cisgendered, college-educated engineer, noticed she no longer received back the friendly smile she thought she was imparting on her morning jogs. Wondering what others saw, she asked a friend to observe. Her friend had to tell her that the friendly smile she thought she was making looked more like a grimace. Undeterred, she stopped trying to smile and created a "friendly little wave and nod." The "wave and nod" got her the cheery response that told her she was once again conveying what she intended. Compensatory strategies for facial difference (Bogart 2014) like this can be used to create a new performance.

Ascribed characteristics limit the roles one can play. Otherness impedes impression management. It limits the available narratives into which one can insert oneself. Disability limits the possibilities for presentation of self as well as the performances or roles and concomitant status open to one (Howson 2013; Seymour 1998). Goffman uses the term "careful disattention" to refer to the avoidance of contact or full communication with those who have visible stigma such as paralysis or stroke (Howson 2013; Kvigne and Kirkevold 2003). Information management is used to conceal, and the ability to pass is generally valued (Burnett and Holmes 2001; Howson 2013). Certainly, the ability to pass in the facial paralysis world carries with it some complicated benefits and exclusions to be discussed later in this work.

Though performance has some limits, Anthony Giddens (1991) has highlighted our degree of agency in self-fashioning our narratives. As Giddens stresses, individuals may not be able to construct any story about the self, but we have a degree of agency and therefore some ability to construct, reconstruct, and shape our narratives. The ability to maintain or keep the narrative going is the self. One of the more disturbing facets of the experience of facial paralysis is the inability to manage that narrative, especially centered around sociability and the smile. The loss of the smile remains a deep source of loss and grief for most participants (chapter 4 discusses this in depth).

But disability advocates highlight that identity and self are more complicated. "Disability's truth-claims are dependent upon discourses of ableism for their very legitimization" (Campbell 2009, 14). The culturally available narratives for those identified as disabled are limited and generally less desirable. But experience is complicated and contradictory. Embedded in the label is a complicated set of social relations that, despite invalidation, can be a source of pride. As Rosalyn Darling (2019) has observed, stigma and self-perception are complicated. People don't necessarily internalize negative approbation. The development of a disability identity, one's reference group, pre-existing beliefs, and a host of other factors can impact one's sense of self. One key factor is whether one was born identified as disabled or the identification was acquired. Research has demonstrated a greater negative impact to self-esteem and mental health when one acquires a disability compared with being born with the identity (Bogart 2014; Darling 2019). Synkinesis is an acquired condition; therefore, it involves an adjustment or change to identity, a shift in embodied experience, and a shift in performance, reception of performance, and ability to perform.

While symbolic interactionists focus on the way the self develops through performance and interaction, poststructuralists consider how the staging is limited by the time and place of performance. The specific histories of individuals and their perceived identity categories are inseparable. With their focus on practice and institutions, poststructuralists give us the link between embodied experience, self, and the larger society. Pierre Bourdieu and Michel Foucault offer analyses that have a common understanding of power relations as an ongoing process that infuses the social milieu (Lakomski 1984). Both highlight that power is not something imposed as an external force but something constitutive of our beings, something we "do."

Foucault and Subjectivity

Foucault (1978, 1979) theorizes the subject as impacted by systems, structures, time, and place. The subject emerges among relations of power: exercised, experienced, internalized, but not possessed. For Foucault, power is more impactful when it is constitutive rather than coercive, when it is not an external punishment or reward but an internal motivation, anxiety, or pleasure. Bodies and views about bodies are situated within a larger framework of beliefs that shape how bodies are understood, how we navigate systems, and how one comes to evaluate, experience, and present a self (Howson 2013).

Foucault's concept of subjectivity details this as the relationship of the self to the self. How do we come to create knowledge about ourselves? We reflect on ourselves, but that reflection is shaped within webs of knowledge about norms and identities. Relations of power, rather than absolute "truth," undergird these knowledges or "truths." We are reflecting on ourselves as we navigate "normal" life for someone who meets our categorical criteria at a given place and time. Over time and through sociocultural practices, identities are created and given meaning. As I engage in normative practices for my identity, those practices are further solidified as linked to identity categories. The categories themselves give structure or meaning to my performance and experience of identity. Gender (Butler 1990, 1993, 1996) and race (Omi and Winant 1994) provide two examples.

Foucault highlights this process with the concept of the docile body. Foucault argues that modern people are borne of regulations. By this he means "modern" individuals define and create a self in a context of institutionalized normative assessments. The docile body comes to self-survey as an object to meet the expectations of the state and the social order. The rebel body defines itself against that order but is still manifestly shaped by it; its otherness is still defined by how and why it deviates (Foucault 1979). Bodies within privileged or desired categories have reason to invest in the existing systems; bodies outside are tasked with investiture in repair and restorative labor. Foucault highlights the ways that regulation and control of bodies are internalized and become a part of the self (Duncan 1994; Foucault 1980; Rail and Harvey 1995). Critical to this is that it is experienced in a complicated array of repressions, anxieties, pleasures, prides, and the host of mixed feelings that we think of as internal dialogues of the self. *Biopower* refers to the investiture of individuals in the body to meet the edicts of normality, often communicated through formal institutions such as schools (Foucault 1979; Lemke 2011).[1] Designed to meet the needs of the powerful, biopower imposes practices and measurements that validate, legitimate, and exclude.

This biopower leads to the production of docile, disciplined bodies but also makes possible resistance to the disciplinary processes; however, as Foucault notes, resistance always contains elements reproductive of the dominant order (Foucault 1979). Docile bodies are subsequently defined as requiring observation and control through techniques of surveillance (Foucault 1978, 1979). State agencies, such as schools, play a critical role in the exercise of power and authority, acting as key agents in the definition, surveillance, and management of docile bodies. But self-surveillance and the responses of those around us are critical. It's not that others expect our bodies to comply and conform—it's that we do. Increasingly, the needs of the market and private corporations are more central to this process (Giulianotti 2005). Advertising, media, and corporate profits are increasingly central to normative bodily display, practices, and expectations.

Foucault (1978) observes that individuals employ "technologies of the self" and undertake a self-managed quest for improvement. At a more fundamental level, these processes are part of what is referred to as the process of "subjectification" or the development of the self (Foucault 1982). This means such technologies not only shape experience but, more importantly, operate to shape the self that perceives, understands, and makes sense of experience. The self emerges out of reflexive evaluation with consideration of state sanctioned "norms." We, as subjects, understand ourselves as objects through a social lens of norms and practices, a literal embodiment of social relations. Scholars have applied these ideas to beauty and fitness regimes, highlighting how we "become" through practice (Duncan 1994; Dworkin and Wachs 2009; Markula 1996).

Foucault highlighted the role of the state in defining these norms as well as the institutions, such as schools, prisons, and mental health care, that routinize them (Cole 1993; Wright 2009). Foucault's concept of governmentality frames the power of government as a "conduct of conducts," which ties the formation of the state (government) to the formation of the individual subject (Lemke 2011). In modern consumer culture, the role of government and interests of private corporations have effectively become intertwined (Dworkin and Wachs 2009; Giulianotti 2005). Increasingly health, fitness, and basic social needs are tied to consumer imperatives. As a result, appearance is scrutinized as having extreme importance and meaning, and individuals construct an understanding of the self within the context of the ability to meet normative standards of beauty and participation in beauty regimes (Duncan 1994; Dworkin and Wachs 2009).

Bourdieu, Habitus, and the Self

Like Foucault, Bourdieu elucidates how social structure infuses the development of the subject and social life. How does social structure become embodied? Bourdieu (1984; Bourdieu and Waquant 1992) answers this question with practice. Daily routines carry within them social relations, expectations, norms, and the consequences for deviance. What we eat, what we wear, and how we interact with others, all reflect, reinforce, and reproduce our place in the social world and that world itself. In this view, power is exercised through practice and determines what practices are encouraged, expected, rewarded, normalized, discouraged, rendered unfathomable, and carry with them stigma.

Bourdieu (1984) developed the concept of *habitus* to capture the embodiment of social relations. Habitus represents a system of classification that structures what we do (practice), how we do it (technique), how we like to do it (taste), and what we think about it (beliefs) (Fowler 1997; Giulianotti 2005). The habitus evolves through everyday practice or how we enact our everyday lives, which is often done with other people. It is the social world embodied through our engagement in normative practices over time. The habitus is social and biological, developed into an embodied self.

What we do is largely shaped by who we are perceived to be within a larger social context. One's continued engagement in a specific social context engenders a specific or a somewhat limited range of mode(s) of practice or way(s) of physically being. As one "does" or acts out one's social position, one develops a way of being or a "self." Bourdieu highlights that, through repeated practice, one's social location is physically manifest. One's habitus, embodied active self, is the result of and continues to reify one's social location on a myriad of axes of identity. Through taste, embodied knowledge, corporeal presentation, and social connection, one negotiates a position in overlapping fields. Historically, gender provides one key example. Over time, by enacting gendered norms one "becomes" a gendered self. But femaleness and maleness have meaning within a larger social order. As Bourdieu (2001) notes, female and male are defined within a system of masculine domination; to embody idealized femininity creates an inherently different system of benefits and rewards than the embodiment of idealized masculinity. Gender shapes what forms of capital are most valued and the forms of capital to which one has access (Bourdieu 2001; Thorpe 2009; Wachs 2005).

Bourdieu provides further insight into how relations of privilege and oppression infuse bodies in ways that re-create existing social relations while also providing contexts for resistance (Bourdieu and Wacquant 1992). The habitus one develops through daily practice confers a form of physical capital within specific fields, but how translatable that capital is—and the scope and scale of the value—depends on one's social location.

Capital is something of value. It refers to a multitude of things including material wealth (economic capital), cultural resources (cultural capital), social networks (social capital), prestige (symbolic capital), and bodily ability (physical capital) (Bourdieu 1984; Bourdieu and Wacquant 1992; Wacquant 1995a). The types of capital one has access to developing, can exercise, and finds of value depends on the social location of the possessor. Embodied abilities, responses to bodies, and social relations of power and privilege are intertwined (Dworkin and Wachs 2009; Wachs and Chase 2013). Privilege is reflected in the types of capital one has the opportunity and impetus to acquire and in the value of different forms of capital for people in different categories.

Social relations play out in a series of overlapping fields. *Field* refers to networks of power manifest as "objective, historical relations" (Bourdieu and Wacquant 1992). Capital that has value in one field may not translate to other fields or may mark one as an outsider, but the capital of the more privileged will have greater applicability across a wider range of fields. Bourdieu (1984) describes a process by which people at different social locations develop a habitus that is a result of one's experiences at that location, a reaffirmation of self, and a means by which structures and fields are (re)produced. Ultimately bodies and their concomitant practices (taste and developed physical/mental abilities) mark, legitimate, and naturalize the social position of the individual. This status then tautologically serves to reinforce the stigma or privilege assigned to these bodies. This means that bodies at different social locations

THEORIZING CHANGE

possess different abilities and have different tastes. The legitimation of some habitus within the field at the expense of others manifests relations of power.

Status and hierarchy are maintained through what Bourdieu terms "symbolic violence" (Bourdieu and Wacquant 1992). Symbolic violence involves "consent to domination" as part of the habitus of those in specific social positions. Like Antonio Gramsci's concept of hegemony, Bourdieu's concept of symbolic violence involves complicity to social harm (Giulianotti 2005). To put it more simply, the way people simply learn "to be" reproduces their social position; and the assumptions we make about others' ways of being reinforces power and privilege (Bourdieu and Passeron 1977; Lakomski 1984; Nash 1990; Willis 1977). What we accept, expect, tolerate, and assume reflects power operating at the cognitive level. The face—the ability to communicate and its management— is a valuable form of capital that I will discuss in depth later in the book.

Feminist Theory, Embodiment, and Beyond

Intersectional feminists have highlighted the array of filters and challenges that block access and undercut options for people in "othered" categories. Pointing to objectivity as the vantage point of privilege, intersectional feminists have noted how social location shapes the experiences, possibilities, and limitations of bodies over time (Collins 1990; Crenshaw 1989; Dill and Zinn 1996). Embodied experience is foregrounded as the lived reality of privilege/oppression.

Cultural studies, intersectional feminism, critical race theory, queer theory, and disability studies have ushered in a very different view of bodies and selves. Implied in this understanding is that social location matters and that we are all agents limited by structure but with the possibility of praxis (informed action). In this view, how that body is viewed by the society in which it lives; the experiences the body has and its potentials and limitations; what some bodies are encouraged, expected, and rewarded for doing; and what other bodies are blocked from doing—all of this matters.

Subjective Aspects within Being as Object/ Objective Aspects within Being as Subject

Drawing on the work of Foucault and Bourdieu, feminist theorists have challenged the efficacy of dualisms with the complication of embodied experience. Certainly, bodies identified as male or female are both objectified, but cis, straight male privilege has been maintained by partly limiting women's source of power to their ability to be the "right" kind of object. Until fairly recently, nonbinary subjects have been rendered invisible objects, force categorized, or pathologized.

Raewyn Connell's (1987) concept of emphasized femininity problematizes the consent one gives to this process and the ways people invest in these constructions to varying degrees. In other words, it's not an external imposition but an internal reification of social relations. We self-survey our bodies and heavily invest in meeting the dominant standards, for which we are rewarded with social validation. Engaging in these practices is rendered pleasurable, and success is rewarded in social acceptance. Frigga Haug and colleagues (1987) highlight the pleasurable, reflexive, and central-to-identity aspects of understanding and enacting the objective aspects of social relations. In other words, she discusses, how the experience of making oneself into an object as a woman in Western culture contains meaningful, affirming, and pleasurable elements and experiences. Competencies in femininity are part of one's subjective experience, and these competencies and experiences can be quite enjoyable.

Building on Haug's discussion of the subjective aspects within being-as-object, Shari Dworkin and I (2009) highlighted the embodied and reflexive nature of experience as simultaneous subjects and objects within consumer culture. The concept of the objective aspects of being-as-subject points to the importance of bodily display in maintaining, enacting, and experiencing subjecthood (Dworkin and Wachs 2009). With facial paralysis, the experience as both a subject and an object are disrupted so clearly, and the interconnections of those experiences are explicated and complicated. Presumptions about facial difference and overall health provide one example. Though one can be relatively healthy while experiencing synkinesis (at age fifty-three I still try to do a marathon a year, enjoy hiking and biking, and am generally considered healthy), facial difference and ill health are conflated, just as disability and health are.

Disability and Stigma

For social scientists, the experience of difference always has a fundamentally social component. In other words, what it means to be "different," the social and cultural attitudes toward difference, and specifically whether that difference is treated in a way that creates stigma comprise a social issue—they are not something inherent. Those born with a disability often embrace a disability identity (Bogart et al. 2017); however, but those with synkinesis face a sudden and radical change to their identity, acquiring an identity fraught with blame and stigma.

Goffman's (1963) use of the phrase "identity spoilt" resonates so clearly with the responses of the various participants in this study. Many shared their moment of realization that they weren't the person they were before because others saw them differently. This moment of becoming "other" tended to highlight that relationship between the experience of performance and that of audience reception. A middle-aged, white, cisgendered female software engineer shared her inability to maintain the jocular office relationships she had previously enjoyed.

> I love to laugh. I was always coming up with little funny things at work. So my job was having a Halloween party shortly after this happened. So I dressed up like a pirate, and put on a patch, and stuck a googly eye on the patch. And my co-workers just ignored it. Pretended not to see it, basically didn't talk to me. And only one person laughed with me. He's so great; he saw right away that I just wanted to be normal. He was like, "Girl, you are a hoot." That was the only fun I had. The rest of the time, I felt so alone. I used to be able to have such a good time. I thought if people saw me laugh at it, they could see I was the same person and laugh with me. But they didn't . . . they just stared at me. They didn't talk to me. People who used to talk to me mostly ignored me.

Goffman reminds us that a performance requires an audience. It is not only the performance of the self that creates the experience but the reception of or response to that performance. I will return to the importance of internal disruption in later chapters, but I was surprised at how much stigma still resonated within the experiences of the participants, myself included. My son recently found a video clip of me talking about being called a monster by a child shortly after my diagnosis, after I'd attempted a warm greeting. His pain at my story was a good reminder of how difficult that moment was.

Goffman (1963) observes that stigma isn't the challenge as much as the reaction of others that disrupts the ability to have a culturally normative experience of identity. This involves a "discrediting attribute"—a marker of difference and otherness that is linked or tied to something undesirable or problematic. Stigma can stem from one's perceived character ("blemishes of individual character"), physical traits ("abominations of the body"), or group identity ("tribal stigma"). The perceived level of stigma is impacted by visibility (obviousness), publicity (how well known is it), obtrusiveness (impactfulness), and relevance (to that situation). The crux is that the person has something that interferes with his or her ability to be accepted into culturally normative interaction. Stigma "signals" will reveal this facet of identity to others or prevent "passing."

Goffman (1963) notes that those with stigma default to a series of rules for managing social encounters with so-called normals. He clarifies that those with stigma generally assume that "normals" are not malicious but ignorant, and they likely are well intentioned. More recently, Darling (2019) has explored how people with disabilities view their relationships with others, revealing that many experience superficial relationships with nondisabled people. Using Fred Davis's (1961) typology of "fictionalized acceptance," "breaking through," and "moral normality," Darling (2019) argues most fail to move past fictional acceptance. As such, those with stigma are expected to patiently ignore snubs or insults and employ a series of strategies to diffuse tense social situations. Humor or self-mockery is employed, but it is aimed at the marginalized, not the dominant category. Self-deprecating humor has a different meaning when aimed at privileged versus marginalized aspects of identity. One of my interviewees is a professional comedian, and he used a troll character to express his post-synkinesis sense of self. His poignant performance connected with audiences because so many share the fear of revealed stigma and the perception/reaction of others to our universally spoilt identities.

Passing is discussed at length in the next chapter. It refers to the ability to appear as if one is not in the othered category. For those who are not interested in passing or able to pass, the tension of the unknown, the presumed, and the social converge in what Goffman refers to "disclosure etiquette." It follows that, when discussing stigma or disability, intrusive questions, unwanted advice, and the responsibility of putting the so-called normal at ease rest with the stigmatized. Synkinesis is one of those things that has varying degrees of visibility and is likely not to be readily identified correctly. Participants routinely described the tension of disclosure. People were often unsure whether they should disclose, and if so, when or how. Amy D., a cisgendered, Latine, middle-aged, college-educated participant shared that finding ways to manage disclosure had been something that she had worked on for two years in therapy: "I've had this since childhood, and I'm well into adulthood. And after two and a half years of therapy, I finally have the ability to just say, 'Well it's a facial paralysis thing I've had since I was a few months.' It's taken me a long time, but I just say it now."

What underlies this is, as Goffman observed, that those with stigma need to do a tremendous amount of additional work in social interaction to manage or cope. Goffman highlighted the largely socially contingent nature of stigma. Stigma depends on social context and how the attribute is viewed. More recent research has revealed that the perception of stigma can be impacted by the category in which one is perceived (Towler and Schneider 2005), the perception of responsibility for acquisition, visibility, and the impact on communication (Darling 2019; Elliott et al. 1982). Synkinesis has varying ranges of visibility but profoundly impacts communication, as will be discussed.

Those associated with people with stigma can acquire a "courtesy stigma" or stigma-by-association (Darling 2000). Recently a participant in my study shared an incident in which her spouse became the subject of verbal abuse and harassment because of her facial difference. Many were concerned in particular about the impact of their changed appearance on their school-age children. Critiques of Goffman's work highlight the nebulous boundaries of these concepts and the failure to focus on stigmatizers, but his work continues to have profound importance. One key thing Goffman did was to set the idea of stigma apart from the idea of deviance—to recognize the difference in the status of one marked by stigma versus those marked by acts of deviance. He also highlights the interactional nature of a "stigmatized" or "othered" appearance: it's not just how one looks, it's the experience of performing with stigma that is problematic for people. At a recent support group, we had a laugh about being the only people who had loved wearing face masks throughout the COVID-19 pandemic. Returning to a world without masks meant making our difference far more visible—for many of us, our differences had been imperceptible with masks.

Foucault (1999) highlights the role of institutions and structures in defining deformity, normality, and abnormality. It is not simply through interpersonal interactions that difference becomes stigma, but it is within a system of knowledge that gives meaning to associations around difference. Foucault traces connections in beliefs about appearance, behaviors, and identities defined as "depraved" or "abnormal." Questioning the production of knowledge and the concomitant relations of power that arise from that knowledge, Foucault reminds us of the importance of interrogating underlying assumptions.

Disability Studies

Disability studies challenge us to move from a traditional medical perspective that focuses on "healing" or "fixing the individual" to one that understands disability as a social-cultural experience (Gill 1989; Goodley 2014; Hahn 1981; Shakespeare 1999; Tepper 1999, 2001; Wendell 1996). Within the movement, debate may ensue over how disability, difference, and otherness are framed, displayed, discussed, or understood; however, shifting the debate from a characteristic inherent to the individual to a social experience is critical. It is not being disabled that creates the difficulties in one's life; rather, what matters is how the society in which one lives treats a person with disabilities. Although legal definitions for medical treatment, assistance, and accommodation require a certain amount of specificity and operationalizable metrics, the broader experience of being disabled stems from how one makes a sense of self within a social context.

Scholars have noted a cultural shift toward inclusion (Siebers 2010), but the meaning of disability remains complex. The term "people with disabilities" may encapsulate a range of people and conditions, who may or may not view themselves as "disabled" (Watson 2002), and those who experience ableism may not be aware they are being viewed this way.

Disability studies begin with the understanding that the challenge is embedded in the conditions that create the context and meaning of disability. It is also crucial that we remember that disability is not a static condition, either from the perspective of social meanings or in subjective experiences (Shuttleworth et al. 2012; Siebers 2008; Wendell 1996). To a large degree, disability exists to define, reinforce, valorize, and privilege those deemed "normal" (Goodley 2014). Synkinesis meets the standard definitions of disability but hasn't been codified, and those with synkinesis have varying degrees of understanding of oneself as disabled (chapter 5 discusses disability identity in depth). Consumer culture exacerbates these challenges.

Commodification and the Body

The expansion of consumer culture and the importance of visual presentation offer increased expectations regarding appearance and opportunities to alter appearance. As Shari and I observed in *Body Panic*, consumer culture creates body problems and then offers solutions. Expectations of attractiveness and ongoing attempts to eliminate the undesirable in one's appearance are viewed as the responsibility of the individual (Talley 2014). Victorian ideas of visible morality also remain in the conflation of a "fit" appearance and health, which is inextricably linked with axes of privilege and oppression (Dworkin and Wachs 2009).

Through consumer culture, specific bodies, practices, and displays are privileged, normalized, and linked to a host of positive or negative associations that have little to do with health, fitness, or morality. This linkage between what is ultimately the display of privileged bodies and practices and morality is one of power's many insidious effects. The face, as central to display, expression, and communication, receives disproportionate attention. As Heather Laine Talley (2014) observes, "the work of making the body not ugly is a never-ending project . . . a Sisyphean task" (193).

For those with facial difference, the required work to simply appear "normal"—or to produce a normal affect—is added in addition to other expectations. Many of my interviewees noted that aging changed how they were viewed but facial difference added an extra burden. One regular support group attendee, a cisgendered, midforties, college-educated white woman observed, "Getting older, it's good and bad. You become invisible, but that can be kind of nice. But you have time to get used to it—the facial paralysis was instant. And I know I can't look the way I did when I was twenty, but I just want to look normal . . . . I want to be seen as just like everyone else. I've tried so many things."

Putting It All Together

When I set out to do this project, I asked a broader question about the overall impact of facial paralysis on social and professional life. Through the research process, what emerged as most salient was its impact on the experience of self in the social world. Facial paralysis changes one's experience of the world as a social being, and this changes how one sees oneself. But there is another aspect: the deeper frustration with self-expression, communication, misunderstandings with others, and within oneself. This shift in identity and in what it means to go from being viewed as normal to "other" is the focus of the next chapter.

3

Microaggressions, Internalizations, and Contested Ideological Terrain

When we were out in the Bahamas, I heard people commenting. . . . I was with my fiancé, and I overheard people making comments about, "Oh, he must be bringing his sister . . . his disabled sister on vacation." And those kinds of comments and that kind of reaction was very jarring for me because it was the first time I had experienced that kind of reaction. And the way people talked to me, or didn't talk to me . . . you know, people assumed that it was mental disability as well as a physical disability. That, and, I found that the term, Bell's palsy, people think it's almost synonymous with cerebral palsy, so they think you have physical deformity of some sort. You must be completely incapable in some form or another, or you must be delayed, and that was a consistent issue with strangers, and I did not like going out in public for about a six-month duration because it just felt like I was constantly being judged.

Amanda G. is approaching thirty, a college-educated, cisgendered white woman with a satisfying career. She found herself with synkinesis after developing Bell's palsy while planning her wedding. The trip was intended as a family celebration of the couple's upcoming nuptials. The assumptions others made about Amanda, and the assumptions she made, reveal the complex reality of the lived experience of disability. For those perceived as physically "different," legitimation, self-determination of identity, subjecthood, personhood, and existence are experienced as debatable.

This tension between external judgment, internalization, and the experience of self is complicated. Devalued, delegitimated, and robbed of her identity as a sexual and sexually desirable person, Amanda's initial response is to gain distance from the problematic aspects of that identity—to, as Rosalyn Darling (2019) describes, embrace "typicality" (formerly normalization) as identity formation. This means people see themselves as "normal" and may choose to "pass." Those responding to disability in this way may or may not accept stigma, and they may express varying degrees of ableism.

Facial difference is nebulous when considering disability identity (in chapter 5 I discuss this in depth). I focus on the ways difference and ableism infuse interactions and are internalized. For Amanda, the negative assessments embedded in stereotypes and prejudiced assumptions regarding disability led to her questioning being placed in that category, rather than questioning the assumptions embedded within the categorization. Amanda highlights the temporariness of the most visibly disorienting aspects and her "normality," contrasting her situation with those of other physical, cognitive, or communicative disabilities. She reasserts the self she has spent most of her life cultivating, being, and enjoying; she is simultaneously impacted by her ongoing synkinesis and frustrated by the assumptions and judgments. But what is striking is the lack of critique of the systemic assumptions that construct the categories. Instead of questioning the legitimacy of the hierarchical categorizations, she wonders about the policing of their boundaries. Most of us have same instincts because systems self-perpetuate and protect.

Adding a new identity category is not something to necessarily avoid or distain or something that requires distance. People often work toward new identity categories, and many changes are viewed as normal parts of the life course. More recently disability is coming to be seen as a natural variant; however, historically being identified as disabled has come with stigma (Darling 2019). Regardless of how one categorizes the challenges created by synkinesis, the perception of synkinesis is likely to be of disability, deformity, or difference. As will be discussed in the next chapter, facial difference is presumed to signal negative traits such as immorality, maladjustment, or sociopathy.

Synkinesis is acquired, and it thrusts people into a category that is devalued, despite (because of) our enlightenment-infused, well-meant intentions. After spending much of one's lifetime enjoying the ontological surety of a body presumed to be able, the loss of subjecthood/personhood that accompanies assumptions of disability is not something easy to experience. Frankly, it never goes away—it just gets managed. Hence, it's not surprising when someone's initial reaction to being devalued or discredited is to seek distance. Living with synkinesis is living with becoming an "other." This chapter focuses on the experience of becoming an "other" or having another layer added to one's othered identities.

Intersectionality, Feminist Theory, and the Body

Matt E. is a white, cisgendered man who developed facial paralysis after a childhood illness, which also left him with less coordination and some loss of function to his left arm. Though he is now working in his chosen profession and has a meaningful family life, he spoke openly about ongoing indignities and now acts as a mentor to youth with facial difference.

MICROAGGRESSIONS AND INTERNALIZATIONS

As a child, other kids were so bad. We left the valley because of the bullying. My parents were concerned about it. We moved to a small town, which was at the time was about 800 people. . . . I still had a little bit of bullying. But most of the aspects—most of that kind of stopped.

Really what was hurtful was from adults more than the children with me. They wouldn't let me play baseball in the little leagues. They wouldn't wait on me at restaurants, would ignore me. There are just little things here and there that adults would do that you weren't expecting, and I am a very robust personality [laughs] I would say. A lot of people are taken aback by that considering my disfigurement. I got beat up a lot [laughs] because my left arm is not very handy. [They would] call me crooked mouth and mostly names and stuff like that.

My second-grade and my third-grade teachers were really hostile. This was 1956, 1957, '58. . . . We lived in the time when teachers were very intolerant of children that were different. If they caught a Mexican kid speaking Spanish—it happened a couple of times when I was a kid—that kid got slapped, not just a tap. You can see the hand mark on the kid's face for speaking Spanish. They were intolerant of a lot of things, not just my face. But there were a couple of us . . . a kid that had a . . . cleft lip, like, cleft palate. We were both in the same boat. Lots of bullying, and from adults.

Privilege is assumed to be earned, but it is conferred at the behest of power. And it's systemic. We are taught fundamental assumptions, then we take into our body responses and reactions. We learn what to display or reveal, and what to disguise or hide, as we negotiate our "place." Synkinesis is a brutal revelation of how tenuous that position is, how easy it is to slip from the normal into the abyss of other. It's already shockingly difficulty to theorize, to understand, to uncover, and to undo the damage(s) of privilege. We tend to feel rather than think these things. The discomfort is too easy to push away or to blame on others for inflicting. The system is protected by our unease and our desire to avoid, to distance, to cover.

Growing up knowing that you are being tolerated, that your presence is problematic, that there is something you need to hide, or fix, or tame . . . not having that burden is privilege. Black and Latine feminists have challenged feminist theory regarding privilege, oppression, and the experiential and embodied nature of equity to reimagine embodied subjecthood. The personal is political, not only because personal issues are played out in political arenas but because the political is a lived reality. Or to put it simply, the luxury of a minimization of the problematics of embodiment is privilege. The impact of living a stigmatized embodiment on the quality of everyday life and the physical ramifications that ensue are central to Black studies, gender studies, disability studies, and queer studies (Bailey and Mobley 2019). Intersections of identity mean that many bodies carry the weight of a complicated history of meanings, and we are at a moment when we have started to struggle with these complicated intersecting histories. Although some are moving away from the term "intersectionality," many scholars highlight its ongoing usefulness if it is not reduced to an additive model of oppression (Schalk 2018).

Otherness is always an embodied experience. The impacts are lived. They are felt. And they shape corporeality over time. It's not a single interaction but the weight of every interaction and the ongoing trauma of living "other." It is the unspoken history that infuses meaning. The inequity that shows up in statistics and in inequitable income and wealth distributions also shows up in lived experience and becomes part of our hearts and minds. It is hunger, it is fear, and it is anxiety. My interviews with the study participants and my own experience centered on a newfound or increased sense of anxiety, which went beyond impacted communication, and the experience of self. In chapter 5 the physiological and internal aspects will be central. Here, external experience is central: the experience of "identity spoilt" and how it is embodied, with ongoing physical ramifications.

The response to facial difference by others is largely unpredictable and can be highly variable (Hughes 1998). My interviewees highlighted that after they had synkinesis social situations were always fraught. Amy D., a Latine, cisgendered, college-educated woman, has been dealing with facial difference since a childhood accident left her with synkinesis. She, like most of the people who were impacted in childhood, recalled realizing she was "different," and she had wanted to avoid events/moments that highlighted this difference.

> I realized I was different right around kindergarten. It was school pictures, and I remember just hating taking school pictures. And that was a real moment of realization for me, that I was different. Being in the yearbook, that was just traumatic to me, the idea of that. The photographers' responses to me, that was what really told me. . . . It was awful. . . . So, kindergarten, that was my time when I realized I was different. And I just didn't want to be in this situation, to see the photographer response with me and with the other kids.

Similarly, Toni R. expressed a decrease in her confidence. Toni, whom I met in person, was slim, well dressed, and had perfect hair and nails—she exuded a casual elegance. A cisgendered, Black, professional woman with a graduate degree, she shared with me that she was aware of the racism and sexism she had faced, but her strong relationship with family, friends, and sorority sisters had meant she had been resolute to overcome. She saw herself as able to achieve her goals with a valued support network there to assist her.

As Darling (2019) noted, race and gender may be salient aspects of an identity that encounters stigma and oppression, but a positive reference group is likely to exist. That group can mean one finds pride and strength in othered identities, or that one has a buffer that reduces internalized stigma. Those with acquired facial difference rarely meet others with similar challenges, and the popular cultural references are problematic at best. Moreover, the experience of race fractures the disability community such that Black persons are likely to see themselves as having more in common with other Black people than with other people with disabilities (Vernon 1999). To put it more simply, many people who have other aspects of their identity that are stigmatized may not internalize negative approbations because they have meaningful relationships and experiences that insulate them.

But for those with acquired facial difference the protective aspects of that identity—such as a family or shared community—usually don't exist. In addition, the impact of disability has different meanings and material consequences due to race (Schalk 2018). Toni noted the tremendous blow facial paralysis had dealt her sense of self, confidence, and self-concept. She noted that facial difference undermined her self-assurance, and that she continues to struggle with it despite having achieved her career and educational goals thus far. She shared a story that she thought highlighted her change.

> I'm being very talkative with you now because I know you, and you have this, and you know. [She leans in, wraps hands round mug, and a significant in-group look is exchanged. She leans back and continues.] I was always confident and outgoing. That was me. And I need to network for my job—I was always good at that. But in certain situations, I'm not Ms. Personality anymore. I'll say hi to everybody, and I'll go sit down, and I'm quiet. It's harder to socialize, especially if I don't know people. Even in grad school, one of my professors I knew from undergrad, he said, "I want you to work on your confidence because I see that you don't have the same confidence you had in undergrad."

Interacting with people, and especially new people, was almost universally noted as becoming more stressful with synkinesis.

Well understood as a significant factor in physical and mental health, stress has long-term impacts that contour bodies' later responses (Lovallo 2005). The impact of stress is not a single instance of discomfort but a body rendered through ongoing discomforts. And this cost is demonstrated in poorer physical and mental health outcomes (Lovallo 2005; Williams and Williams-Morris 2000). Everyone experiences stress from work projects, impending holidays, or many of life's other challenges, but those in othered categories have a multitude of additional stressors that build up on top of the usual ones. How that stress is manifested, experienced, and expressed is different across axes of identity, but it is physical, and embodied, and costly.

What Is Privilege (and Why Does It Matter?)

Intersectional feminism describes a broad swath of scholarship and activism that shares a fundamental concern with privilege and oppression. To understand this view, we need to use feminist theory definitions of privilege and oppression, not colloquial or instinctual meanings. Patricia Hill Collins (1991) highlights how our identities can be mapped on a matrix of domination, intersecting axes of identity categories on which we are either privileged or oppressed. Kimberle Crenshaw (1989, 1991) used the term *intersectionality* to highlight the need to theorize in ways that take these different axes into account. In so doing, we need a clear way to understand privilege and oppression.

Privilege is generally understood as having access to something that others lack access to through no fault of their own (Collins 1990; hooks 1981; Johnson 2017; McIntosh 1988). These could be "unearned entitlements," things that we should all have but perhaps don't (safety, transit options, right to marry, legal status, etc.), or "conferred dominance," something that gives one advantage or power over another (McIntosh 1997). That power could be obvious, direct, and measurable, such as income differentials by race or gender, or it could be indirect, such as how individuals perceived as more attractive have an advantage in careers that do not require physical beauty (Paustian-Underdahl and Walker 2015). The unique histories of identity categories mean that how one identifies and the meaning of identity categories may be at odds. We may not be seen by others as falling within the category that we believe ourselves to be in, or we may be misidentified. The different costs in disability status for different racial categories and the ability to self-identify as disabled highlight this conundrum (Miles 2019; Bailey and Mobley 2019). Revealing one's disability within one's community may be problematic; and one may not be included in the disability rights community because of other identity categories.

Oppression is simply a limiting of options (Collins 1990; hooks 1981; Johnson 2017; McIntosh 1988). Everyone can recount moments of unfair usage or moments of unexpected advantage. But privilege and oppression are not about individuals. They're about systems and the options open to people within those systems. They're about all the things that define us as who we are, that shape and limit what the world offers us, and defines what are reasonable goals for which we can strive. They're about other people's expectations of and for us and people "like" us.

Multiracial feminists further challenge us to remember that systems of privilege and oppression are structural. Being in a privileged category on one axis of identity doesn't make someone an oppressive person or an oppressor, just someone with some advantages across one axis. Similarly, being in an oppressed category does not necessarily doom you to a life of deprivation, abuse, and hardship. It's very important to remember that privilege doesn't mean you feel happy or are fulfilled, it's that within the system, on a specific axis of identity, you have more or better options (Johnson 2017).

Intersectional feminism focuses on legal and institutional structures. Black feminism, Latine feminism, queer theory, and disability studies move structures into our bodies via lived experience. It's not just that we experience systemic inequity within our bodies but that our bodies come to always already reproduce inequities in our enactments of socialization, in our tastes and preferences, and in our ways of thinking and knowing.

Otherness is complicated. Certainly, to become other in this way is a mark of privilege in and of itself. The next chapter will return to this in greater depth, but for white women the identity cost of this specific type of otherness was a startling shift while other ethnic groups faced a different set of challenges. As noted in existing studies of race and disability, BIPOC women acknowledged that they sometimes felt pressure to simply not be "disabled" (Bailey and Mobley 2019; Miles 2019). One of the first people I interviewed was Dierdre M., a cisgendered, mixed-race woman likely to be identified as Black. She found herself presumed to be an escaped mental patient when she walked into the emergency room with a severe case of Bell's palsy. Unable to clearly enunciate, she was treated as potentially dangerous when she was frightened, vulnerable, and in need of medical assistance. The opportunity to experience the transition and to work through it is an experience of privilege in and of itself. Certainly, having the luxury to interrogate my othering is a sign that I started from a position of relative privilege. By contrast, Viv. V., the immigrant parent financially supporting her family of five, told me she didn't have time to worry about her face—she had to just "get on with things."

Uncovering the multitude of subtle ways privilege and oppression infuse social relations is challenging. The machinations of privilege and oppression show up in things like expectations, responses, assessments, and assumptions. These then shape our relationships with ourselves. Hair provides an easy example. I have curly hair, and the number of times I have read or been advised that straight hair is more professional is astounding, as are the array of products available to me to make it so. Within that view are encoded embedded assumptions that disadvantage certain ethnic groups. It fascinates me how when I bring up this example people often respond, "But it is." Or they highlight the investment in appearance necessary to "do their job." Yet, with a few notable exceptions (I do live in Hollywood), physical appearance has no bearing on what they do. What they mean is that the assumptions people make about appearance will create a barrier.

Speaking as a person with naturally curly hair, the easiest, most practical thing for hair with this texture is washing it, brushing it, and leaving it alone, and depending on the weather, it goes from there. Making it straight requires chemicals, money, and a significant time investment. None of those things will make me more effective on the job—and some of them will make me less so. I have no problem with people who prefer their own hair straightened, but asking someone else to incur significant time and expense to change their natural state to "appear" able to do a job well seems problematic. Also, there are a host of ways these assumptions are raced, classed, and gendered. The politics of hair may seem like a trivial example, but it is not to the people who grew up feeling less capable, less desirable, or just less because of their hair. "Is my hair OK?" occupies space in one's body, in one's head, and in one's response to stress. Do you take a risky stance and rely on hard work, ability, and credentials alone, or do you play it safe and finance the demanded appearance? That additional investment is a burden many avoid by accident of birth—appearance discrimination in employment is well documented (Cavico, Muffler, and Mujtaba 2012). Specifically, for Black women this burden has a range of nuanced dimensions (Prince 2010). Otherness is the ongoing need to compensate, to be a self that is managing otherness, demonstrating enough investment in a system that inherently devalues what one is.

Being an other and the cost of otherness are transmitted to and shape lives in myriad ways. So what does it mean to be other? Quantifiable, measurable costs are the easiest to understand, so we can start here. One of the most obvious and easy to quantify is the financial cost. The financial costs of otherness for race, gender, and disability are well documented. The gender wage gap persists (England [1992] 2017; Monti, Reeder, and Stinson 2014), and race continues to impact earning potential (Bonilla-Silva 2018; Herring and Hynes 2017; Western and Pettit 2005), as does disability status (Rieser 2018). Moreover, race (Bonilla-Silva 2018), gender (England [1992] 2017), sexuality (Westbrook and Schilt 2014), disability (Garland-Thomson 1997; Weiss and Longquist 2017), and the myriad of ways they intersect (Westbrook and Schilt 2014) impact individuals' ability to find employment, limit the types of employment to which they have access, and hinder their ability to achieve positions commensurate with their abilities.

Professional Cost

Disability (Bailey and Mobley 2019; Brown and Maloney 2019) and facial disfigurement specifically (Rifkin et al. 2018) have a problematic impact on income, career, sociability, and mental well-being. The professional cost has been well documented (Brewster 2003; Maroto, Pettinicchio, and Patterson 2019) and is shown to be even more problematic for women, women of color (Maroto,

MICROAGGRESSIONS AND INTERNALIZATIONS

Pettinicchio, and Patterson 2019), and Black Americans/African Americans (Bailey and Mobley 2019; White 2015). Professional discrimination occurs regardless of impairment; disability is always already presumed to be a hinderance (Berger 2013; Linton 1998; Papadimitriou 2001; Siebers 2008). Disability is a nebulous thing. It's a perception set against the historically infused meanings of that identity. Hence, disability can refer as much to appearance as to functional impairment because it is the societal response that creates barriers (Garland-Thomson 1997; Schweik 2009; Siebers 2003).

People with acquired facial paralysis have often experienced a shift in their ease of navigating the professional world, regardless of their abilities, credentials, experience, or training. At a conference, the mother of one of the people I had interviewed approached me. I had found her son to be pleasant, compassionate, smart, funny, and handsome. She shared with me that he had been on a meteoric career track (degrees from top universities, a job at a top firm) when the facial paralysis hit.

> My son was on track. . . . One of the best universities in the world, business school at a top Ivy League. He was on track to have this amazing career, and . . . he's done all right. He's done well . . . but it knocked him completely off his trajectory. . . . And it's simply because of what people see. He won't say it, but he's clearly being discriminated against. . . . I see how people respond to his face. . . . In the world of business, looking different is hard. I saw so many doors suddenly slam shut, and he was the same good, hardworking man.

Intersecting categories can amplify impacts; as has been demonstrated, women's appearance in general has greater professional import for success than men's (Cavico, Muffler, and Mujtaba 012; Williams, Dellinger, and Keister 2010). One interview began with me being transfixed by Miranda G.'s amazing hair. Miranda is a cisgendered white woman, and her hair had been expertly highlighted; it had all the swing, movement, and body that shampoo commercials promise. I stumbled over my opening questions as I admired her hair, which I later learned was a reflection of her chosen career that had been rendered impossible:

> I studied hairdressing, and I was a hairdresser. I did a course which you do here, and then got an apprenticeship, and I moved from the small town to [larger city], and I applied for a lot of jobs, and that's when I really noticed that I was being discriminated against in hairdressing.
>
> Because all the trials that I did, I did a really good job. I was really a good hairdresser, and I did really well in my program and internship. But when I applied to jobs. . . . It's the beauty industry, and they all said, "Look, you're a really good hairdresser. You're amazing. But we're not going to take you on. We're looking for somebody who could meet customers and

48 METAMORPHOSIS

sit at the front of the salon. And we want someone who can smile and be welcoming."

So I retrained in IT, but recently I was forced out of my job when I got a new supervisor and he just kept saying he didn't like my attitude, but what he meant was my face.

I'll keep looking, but . . . it's discouraging. I'm not a bad employee. I didn't have any problems with my old supervisors. They let me stand during meetings so I could hear—I am deaf in one ear as a result of the accident, too. But the new supervisor, the one who didn't like my face, my attitude . . . I explained I had trouble hearing, I asked to stand, I asked for instructions after, when I couldn't hear. . . . He wouldn't help. He wouldn't let me sit where I could hear instructions. If I tried to move, he told me to get back to where I belonged.

I tried to explain multiple times. He was doing it on purpose to make sure I made mistakes and he could get rid of me.

A former paralegal, Angie C. has had graduate training and identifies as a cisgendered Latine woman. She found that despite a successful work history, her experience with Bell's palsy and synkinesis led to assumptions about her work and attitude: "I used to be a paralegal. I had actually been working in a law office for a very long time. But not long after it [Bell's palsy followed by synkinesis] happened, I was laid off. Then it was very difficult for me to get another job in the legal field after that. I think it's because of my face. People perceive or assume I have a "bad attitude." My attitude was fine before . . . I just can't show that."

Complaints about their attitude were a common problem for those with facial paralysis. Facial difference impacts others' perceptions of their abilities and sociability (Bogart 2014). In some cases, people attempted to explain their condition but still faced discrimination. Abby B., a white cisgendered woman with a community college degree and significant impairment, showed genuine distress at her ongoing difficulties as a home health aide. She understood that her clients were sick and vulnerable, so she always disclosed her condition to them. She had developed a friendly spiel to set her clients at ease, and she tried to use it as a jumping off place to relate to their challenges. She mentioned that some of her clients were compassionate, but she often had problems:

I have trouble with new clients. I always tell them about it. . . . I tell them I have facial paralysis and not to think I am angry or unhappy. I really take time to do this carefully. I had one yesterday; she thought I was angry. Then she said I was rude because I was talking out of the side of my face. I get that when I'm out, too. In a store. Or whatever. Nasty looks.

I just try to be quiet and do my job. But it's hard, meeting people. I've had clients look at me and want me removed. One looked at me and called me mentally retarded. She said I was mentally retarded or a drunk, and

MICROAGGRESSIONS AND INTERNALIZATIONS 49

that I come to work drunk because my mouth is droopy. She reported me for coming to work drunk—I don't drink. Another person [was] counting back change to me like she thinks there's something wrong with me. . . . I'm not mentally disabled, stop treating me like I am. It's so frustrating.

Similar to the opening vignette of this chapter, the stigma of cognitive disability loomed over many interactions. It's impossible not to wrestle with the meaning of that, with the ease at which we set the limits of humanity. I confront this issue daily, and I will discuss it more later (chapter 5). But here the focus is on the experience of being discredited. The experience of my study's participants, as suggested by existing literature, was too often stymied career ambitions and employment discrimination. Matt E., who was introduced earlier, found his early career goals and his existing career marred by assumptions about his appearance:

I wanted to be an actor. I wanted to be an entertainer. My grandfather worked for a major studio in Hollywood, and I wanted to be an actor. But I was told right up front that that'll never happen. [He laughs.] Not a really positive influence on a kid. So I went in, and I worked in telecommunications. That's the only job I had until I retired. I had an interview . . . my first interview for promotion. The guy asked me if I have mental issues because of my facial disfigurement. He wanted to talk about why I should have this job if I was mentally unstable.

Jason A., a cisgendered white man with a graduate degree and a career with which he was satisfied prior to suffering synkinesis after experiencing Ramsay Hunt syndrome, described the challenge of interviewing for new opportunities.

Just feeling whole. I just feel like I'm damaged goods. It frustrates me. I had been looking at other professional opportunities, and it made it difficult to go out on an interview. Actually, the second onset with the droopy face came on the day of an interview I had, so I had to go to this interview, and my face was falling off of the vine.

It was a job for which I was well-qualified, and I thought it was a really good fit, having good rapport with the people I had talked to on the phone, and it was just a disaster. We just couldn't connect, and I could see them looking at it, and we couldn't move past it.

As described by Darling (2019), people who are perceived as disabled find that others rarely connect in meaningful ways; instead they maintain only cursory or surface-level connections.

There's something else here, something hard to articulate and talk about that lies in the intersections. That's the thing so many of us have experienced: that moment of knowing you are other, you don't fit, you aren't fully welcome in a space, you lack full citizenship and rights. The gut punch of otherness takes an ongoing toll. Each of us have our unique intersections. How we experience it—the meaning, the options, the reactions—is all carried within our social histories set against unique personal narrations. The devastation of the acquisition of synkinesis has certainly impacted everyone at different social locations in a variety of ways: a home health aide uses antecedent strategies to minimize her clients' complaints, and a tenured professor writes a book.

Social Costs and Challenges: The Right to Public Space

To walk into a public space or gathering and have little concern for one's physical or social safety is privilege. The label of "other" is a different relationship with public space. Through codified laws and enforced norms, those who are classified as other are often perpetually at risk within or banned from public space. Racial exclusion from public space, whether by law or custom, is well documented (Walkowitz and Knauer 2009). The street violence experienced by identifiable sexual minorities (Hanhardt 2013) and women (Bates 2016) serves similarly to limit access to and safety in public space.

Laws like curfews have long been used to limit the use of public space by gender, race, and age (O'Neil 2002). Loitering laws are well understood as existing at intersections of race/class/sexuality/gender control, as are sumptuary laws (Clarke, Doel, and Housiaux 2003; Emberley and Wright 1999). Laws that limit presence in public space are generally aimed at young, nonwhite, and poorer people (Fang 2009).

As with race, gender, and class, disability is policed in public space through formal and informal social control mechanisms (Schweik 2009; Garland-Thomson 2009). Susan Schweik (2009) details the range of laws designed to limit the public appearance of those with bodies deemed to be problematic or unsightly. Although these laws tended to be local and therefore to have different specifics, laws across this nation limited the movements and public appearances of those who could be described as disabled, deformed, or impaired. The "ugly laws" Schweik (2009) has documented are largely relics, but those with acquired facial paralysis experience a sometimes subtle and sometimes not so subtle policing of their appearance in public space.

Although it may be easy to view these experiences as problematic behaviors by the ignorant many, these seemingly unconnected exclusions, devaluations, and invalidations reflect, reinforce, and reify bodies and spaces. Public space means an inevitable reminder of dominant ideology and a reinforcing of existing norms and structures. Regardless of other identity categories, age shapes experience; overt bullying is usually described earlier in life, and among adults microaggressions are more often described. But it's essential that these experiences not be understood as individual; rather, they reflect the lived experience of ideology(ies). They are the daily practice through which structure is perpetuated.

From Bullying to Microaggressions

Otherness is burdensome. This makes daily interactions more difficult, tiring, overwhelming. Microaggressions refer to the everyday indignities that go along with the assumption of otherness. It is a term used to encapsulate all the forms of prejudice one experiences in interpersonal interactions that aren't direct, overt, or immediately identified as discrimination. Microaggressions reveal histories of identities infused with privilege and oppression. With microaggressions, intention isn't relevant; it reveals a social history of difference being stigmatized. Microaggressions expose the fundamental assumptions underlying privilege and oppression. Although individuals may be held accountable, microaggressions are primarily a structural problem: individuals are doing the daily work of structure to maintain hierarchies that may or may not benefit them. Individuals who commit microaggressions are not necessarily those with power or those with privilege. We are all to some extent guilty, regardless of our attempt to avoid them. We all are always reproducing ideological assumptions that support these things. But we can also acknowledge and undermine the structures that produce these relations.

So what are microaggressions? Microaggressions are intended or unintended snubs or discounting (Sue 2010a, 2010b). They occur in everyday interactions and perpetuate ideologies, stereotypes, and beliefs that preserve existing systems (Solórzano, Ceja, and Yosso 2000). Microaggressions are characterized in three ways: microassaults (conscious and intentional actions), microinsults (subtle rudeness or insensitivity in verbal interaction), or microinvalidations (negating the views of the other) (Sue 2010a, 2010b). Microaggressions have been applied to race (Levchak 2018; Sue 2010a, 2010b), disability (Conover, Israel, and Nylund-Gibson 2017; Keller and Galgay 2010), hidden disabilities (Kattari, Olzman, and Hanna 2018), gender (Nadal 2013), sexuality (Haines et al. 2018; Nadal 2013), and various intersections (Lewis et al. 2016). Richard Keller and Corinne Galgay's (2010) work identified eight disability-related microaggressions, which might vary depending on perceptions: denial of personal identity, denial of disability, denial of privacy, helplessness, secondary gain, spread effect, infantilization, patronization, second-class citizenship, and desexualization. Although the impact on individuals is problematic, microaggressions perform ideological repair work for systems, allowing blame for inequity to be displaced onto individuals and categories rather than systemic inequity.

Before we explore the impact of microaggressions, I must bring up that some of my interviewees experienced direct aggression, though this was far less common. Assaults and direct aggression were most often recounted by those who grew up with facial difference. Matt E., who was referenced earlier in this chapter, described an extreme example—a random attack he experienced:

When I was seventeen I was going to the movies . . . to see *Bonnie and Clyde*. And [I] was standing in line, and a guy behind me walks around and looks at my face. And [he] comes around again and says, "What's wrong with your face? What's wrong with you? That son of a bitch, look at him." And I ignored him. He kept asking me what happened to me, and I ignored him because that's what I was taught to do with people with issues, so I wasn't looking. And he slapped me over my right ear by my eardrum, and I went to the ground, and I got back up, and he hit me with a fist, he hit me with open hands.

I was a kid, and he was an adult. I didn't have a real chance, but I tried to hit him back. . . . I don't know what happened to him, but I'm bleeding from the mouth. I was wearing braces at the time 'cause I was going through reconstructive surgery. He damaged my right ear. Damaged my hearing.

Miranda G., who also was previously mentioned, found herself dropping out of high school to avoid harassment from her classmates after having her facial nerve had been damaged in an accident. As a "farm girl" in a rural area, the animals on her farm provided her with the acceptance her classmates denied her. The joys of riding horses or playing with the barn cats or farm dogs offered her solace from relentless bullying:

Because I had a double whammy of not being well off and also being [gestures at face] paralyzed. So I was a funny-looking girl, and they all just got their camps paid for them, and I had to fundraise. So I did what I could. I created a little raffle basket for myself. I've put together a basket, and I baked a cake, and I bought a packet of lollies, and I had to sell raffle tickets.

So raffle tickets, you know? Put some money towards my camp. . . . And I remember the kids following me around laughing at me. Pointing. Making fun of me . . . So it was kind of like a double-whammy type bullying. I couldn't afford camp, and I looked different. So it was a lot of bullying that went on, lot of playground fights.

So I withdrew and became quite, you know . . . rebellious. If I could stay at home and ride my horse, I would. That was the only thing that felt good. So I did the things that felt good, which was—you know, I was farm girl, it was just the animals. So I'd ride my horse and play with my dogs or the cats or a rabbit or anything that didn't judge me for being different, because they don't.

Amy D., who acquiring facial difference as a young child, recounted her brother's support and protection, which prevented similar experiences of childhood harassment. She remains closely connected to her loving, supportive, and

MICROAGGRESSIONS AND INTERNALIZATIONS 53

defensive family: "The first fight—like, physical fight—that my brother was ever in growing up—he must've been eight, nine, or ten—was one of his close friends. His friend made fun of me, and so he got to a fight with him. He was five years older, and I think he kind of defended me growing up . . . to his friends . . . to everyone."

Even some adults experienced direct aggression or bullying. After an online date with whom she didn't feel a connection, mixed race, cisgendered, graduate school–educated Caitlyn Marie reported,

> I have had one guy, I wasn't interested in him. I was polite, just declined a second date. And he sent me some really nasty texts after the date, and one of them was something like, oh, nice harelip.
>
> I wasn't even the least bit interested in the guy, not the least bit interested. In fact, even going on the date was more of a lark for me, just for the hell of it, just to get out of the house. I mean I really was willing to explore him as an option, but I wasn't invested. He didn't take rejection well at all, obviously. He sent me some nasty texts afterwards.
>
> That was really hard for me because when he did that, in the moment I didn't know if he was saying what other people weren't willing to say but thought, or if this guy was just an extraordinary asshole and was looking for the easiest way to hurt my feelings, in the most powerful way. In hindsight, I realized it was the latter. He was just going for the lowest possible blow to make the biggest impact he could because he's not a healthy guy.

Similarly, Ruth-Ellen thought her team at work had her back. A middle-aged, outgoing, cisgendered white woman, Ruth-Ellen had a twinkle in her eye and a willingness to laugh at the funny aspects of stories, despite their painful elements. A successful regional sales rep, she suffered hearing loss and facial paralysis when her acoustic neuroma was removed. She discovered that her co-workers were mimicking her behind her back as she ate while others looked on and laughed:

> So I just couldn't keep working at my job . . . because of the way they [her co-workers] were acting towards me. They didn't say anything to me directly, but the things that they said when I was out of the room was amazing. Other people had told me about it. Just making fun of my face and calling me names, like, "Did you see that? The way she was doing that?" It was horrible because I always from the time I was little I've always been heavy, but everyone said, "Well, at least she has a pretty face," so my whole life I went from having a pretty face and all of a sudden my face was changed. So that was my whole identity, so I had to make a new identity.

Overall, my study's participants related far fewer incidents of direct aggression than they did microaggressions. Microaggressions are relations of privilege and oppression played out in social interaction. It's imperative that microaggressions be understood as fundamentally reflecting macrolevel structures, institutions, and ideologies, in addition to causing individual harm. Earlier in this chapter I discussed access to public space and formal and informal policing. Microassaults often reflect social enforcement of ideological boundary work, as reflected in the right to public space and presence.

Microassaults

Presence in public space is unofficially policed in a host of subtle and not so subtle ways. Just as the "ugly laws" described by Schweik (2009) demonstrate codified resistance to the presence of disability, microaggressions and explicit microassaults make clear the tenuous nature of unequivocal right to public space. Otherness and ugliness are often conflated. Facial difference is frequently used to signify evil or malintent, beyond being deemed undesirable (Talley 2014). Disability is similarly treated and is often used to signify bad, evil, or objectionable (Berger 2013; Talley 2014; Garland-Thomson 1997).

Those with facial difference often found themselves the victim of such microassaults. Microassaults are conscious bias expressed overtly or covertly through statements or actions (Sue 2010a, 2010b). Microassaults tend to take the form of hostile questioning of the right to public space or public shaming. Facial difference and an inability to render appropriate affect is generally viewed as a reason to shame. Several of my participants recounted overhearing comments about their sobriety, competence, attitude, or appearance.

One of the examples that most struck me came from Beverly, a newly retired former counselor. Beverly is a white cisgendered woman who felt bothered by the changes to her appearance and balance; Ramsay Hunt syndrome not only can impact balance but has many other unpleasant side effects. Struggling with paralysis, vertigo, and anxiety about her appearance, Beverly was initially proud of herself for finally venturing out of her home. She was just starting to relax and feel a bit more confident about her ability to resume her daily routines when two women insinuated themselves into her narrative. Observing her trouble with balance, they began loudly discussing her obvious "addiction" and how she should "get help." "She shouldn't be out in public like that!" one said. "Shameful!" the other agreed. They intended her to overhear them, and she went home in tears. "I wondered if everyone saw me that way," she told me.

Elaine E., another affable, middle-aged, cisgendered white woman, recounted deciding to take a nice vacation to cheer herself up after her Bell's palsy failed to resolve and left her with synkinesis. She didn't want her facial paralysis to stop her from one of the things she really enjoyed—traveling and staying at nice hotels. She was thrilled to be treating herself to an extra special trip using her airline travel points. Before check-in, however, she was given an unpleasant reminder of her new vulnerability:

> I was standing in line . . . to check in. And I had booked myself into a nice hotel. I was so happy to be there, and I didn't mind waiting. I was thinking about a nice meal later, maybe a spa service. . . . And this guy in line said, "You don't have to be so angry. You don't have to be so upset." *He* was upset. I was just standing there . . . I'm just standing there, minding my own business. I was happy to be there. And I'm sure he didn't even think twice, I mean, like, about his comment. But I remember it.

Now that she was being perceived as rude or impatient, Elaine E. wondered how to navigate social situations in which her face alone elicited this type of response.

A deeply compassionate, warm, caring, and creative cisgendered immigrant from Asia, Lou C. shared his initial frustrations. He had reached out to me when he heard about my research. He had never met anyone else with synkinesis, and he had struggled for years to have his complaints taken seriously. He shared a wonderful story he had written about his struggles to connect, and about hoping to ask out a girl, eventually meeting his wife, and fulfilling his commitment to his church. He recalled overhearing comments about himself throughout school: "So because of my face, there was some—some impression that I, that others have, you know, that caused them to have sort of look at me as a proud person, as an arrogant person. You know. And they made remarks—I was like that, right? And it was hard to hear . . . that kind of—that kind of remarks. . . . Well they would kind of . . . taunt, right? Make fun of me, and laugh at me. So I just tried to keep to myself and do a good job." I was struck by how extraordinary Lou is. His concerns had been ignored for years, and assumptions were made that he was simply inexpressive—and, as was suggested to him by a school administrator, he simply wasn't good enough. Yet he persisted, eventually receiving a diagnosis almost a decade after onset. And despite the social rejection, he had married, created a career, and was an active and valued member of his church. Lou is funny: his humor is wry, quirky, and charming. His story was beautiful, and he had contacted a stranger over 2,000 miles away to share it. Lou has an impressive ability to connect and express himself, yet he had spent years feeling isolated, lonely, and rejected—not because he lacked supportive family and friends but because of the ongoing negative public interactions that implied he had an internal fault.

For those with facial paralysis, microassaults often carry a presumption of social or moral failing, rather than a physical disability. Shanna Kattari, Miranda Olzman, and Michele Hanna (2018) have described similar policing of those with invisible disabilities.

Microinsults

Microinsults are subtle signs of rudeness or discounting of status (Sue 2010a, 2010b). Those with facial difference frequently experience the invisibility of disability. Scholars have noted the way those with visible disabilities are discounted (Keller and Galgay 2010; Garland-Thomson 2005). People with facial difference described to me an array of verbal and nonverbal microinsults, some that discounted them and others that offered faint praise.

The chapter opened with a classic example of a discounting microinsult: Amanda G's experience on her prewedding family trip. Feeling self-conscious, she had spent the trip using a big hat and sunglasses to try to minimize her Bell's palsy, and she had convinced herself that it wasn't too noticeable when she overheard the first of several assessments—that her fiancé was taking out a disabled sister. I remember her voice cracking and tears welling as she told the story. She spoke quite a bit about what it meant to get married with facial paralysis. She talked about the photos, about wanting to smile, about the echo in her head that she looked more like a disabled sister than a bride. She talked about the fear that someone who looked like her wouldn't be desired or loved. She laughed through tears at the idea that someone would be as openly physical with a sister as her fiancée had been all through the trip. She knew there was no malice intended, but it's precisely because it's the default assumption that it's so hurtful.

Assumptions that those with disabilities lack sexuality and that those who love them are in some way "not normal" are ubiquitous and reveal the depth of the influence of ableism (Loeser, Pini, and Crowley 2018; Keller and Galgay 2010). Dating, sexuality, desirability, and performance are fears articulated in interviews and at focus groups. Most people have had some impaction to the mouth, and the mouth is a sex organ. At support groups people expressed their fear and frustration over assumptions about the limits to their sexual performance and experience. When others gave credence to those fears, the hurt was deeper.

Another common microinsult is what we generally call "faint praise"—a compliment that is undermining. Well-intentioned friends and co-workers so often inadvertently stumble into faint praise when they admire one's ability to cope. Variations on "If it were me, I wouldn't be able to leave the house" or "Oh, I had that for a few weeks, and I couldn't leave the house; I don't know how you do it" are expressed by well-meaning friends, colleagues, and well-wishers. One cisgendered Asian American woman, Vi V., I interviewed expressed it aptly. Bell's palsy during her third pregnancy had left her with synkinesis. A recent immigrant who was the primary income for a family of five, Vi had few options; her spouse was raising their three children while she worked as a nurse. "People were telling me, "Wow, you handle it so well." They're trying to be nice, but it's hard to hear. I'm like, "Yeah. Well, I don't really have a choice. This is just how it is." I deal with it by myself sometimes when I'm having down days. But I don't have a choice, this is my life. But it's hard to hear." No one wants to hear that her life is something others would dread or be unable to cope with, that what is

MICROAGGRESSIONS AND INTERNALIZATIONS   57

admirable about her is her ability to act as if she's still "normal" despite the evidence otherwise. From the inside, we are just being—the assumption that there is something wrong is one of the most common microinsults.

"What's wrong with your face?" The question draws nods and eye rolls from the group at Facial Paralysis Awareness Day. Everyone has heard it. It highlights the loss of privacy that comes with visible stigma (Campbell 2009). Although many preferred to be asked rather than be subjected to an ongoing quizzical expression, the reminder was just as frequently unwelcome. People mentioned it was jarring; the question put them in a position of having to discuss a medical condition publicly that they perhaps did not want to share. Latine, cisgendered Al L. explained the difference between two incidents—one he saw as a caring inquiry, the other as a microaggression: "'Last year somebody just said, 'What's wrong with your face?' Like very bluntly, you know? And that made me very, very uncomfortable because I was around people. But I remember last March on another occasion this older lady had said, 'Hey, I noticed something—well, not at first, but as I look at you more I realize that something's up. What is it?' And I wasn't offended by it, because the way that she asked me was more of with care and interest, not as like, 'Hey, what's wrong with your face?'" These types of interactions encompass a denial of privacy described by those who study disability microaggressions (Kattari, Olzman, and Hanna 2018; Keller and Galgay 2010). The depth of the meaning of "what's wrong with your face?" will be expanded on in the next chapter.

Because synkinesis is tied to health and was most often tied to an acquired condition, an additional form of microinsult occurred: blame. Because facial paralysis and synkinesis are poorly understood, people's condition was sometimes dismissed as of their own creation or fault. It's especially devastating when this sort of microaggression comes from the medical establishment or from those with medical training. Elaine E. is a college-educated healthcare professional who has lived with synkinesis for over three years. She expressed deep hurt at her brother's assessment that her own behavior after Bell's palsy had contributed to her synkinesis. "My brother is a doctor; he actually said, 'You probably went back to work too soon; you did it when you went back to work. You work too much, and you talk too much'—as if you just can control it."

Because most individuals heal on their own regardless of treatment, the endless advice from those who have healed that is offered to those who are not healing may be well meaning but is still problematic. For those with Bell's palsy, the most common cause of synkinesis, over 80 percent will make a full recovery regardless of treatment. Many may believe that alternative therapies "cured" their condition, but spontaneous recovery is actually the norm for Bell's palsy; the insistence that a regime or course of action can alleviate the condition was one of the most painful and hurtful microaggressions my respondents reported.[1] One support group moderator, a facial paralysis advocate, mentioned a specific person who had repeatedly posted pictures of herself as she healed, along with aggressive advice and comments. The group moderator shared that part of the impetus of starting separate groups for newcomers and long-timers was the disconnect between their situations. The tendency for medical professionals to also stress that most heal could be hard for those who did not. Most of the people with synkinesis from Bell's palsy and Ramsay Hunt syndrome mentioned the trauma of being told they would heal—and the implicit blame when they failed to do so. Blame alleviates any need to question stigmatizing social relations.

In addition, I want to discuss the idea of a nonverbal microinsult. In this case, specific types of stares or looks. To return to Goffman's classic discussion of stigma, Goffman notes that stigma is ultimately reified by the reactions of others. Stigma is "the process by which the reaction of others spoils normal identity" (Goffman 1963, 3). Communication is largely nonverbal, facial, and involuntary. What became clear through my research process were the myriad ways that stigma, difference, and otherness were sometimes communicated nonverbally with or without conscious intent. The most common microaggression centered on "the look." The quizzical look, the eyes fixed on the corner of the mouth, the look of discomfort, these were frequently highlighted as a nonverbal reminder of one's difference and failing as a social object. Graduate school-educated, cisgendered white therapist MaryAnn described "the look": "When I first meet people, there's a look they give me. It's something I just notice. Like, maybe they're staring at my mouth or my eye, and then it kind of moves past that. And it's a little sting. And you know, it's funny. You want to say something, but most situations do not lend themselves to it being appropriate to say anything about it." This highlights the problem of microaggressions. Although in many cases the look was inadvertent, staring and looking have broader implications, and communicate unintended messages.

Staring has specific meaning beyond looking. Staring is also an act of power or domination. It demarcates the dominant looker from the "other" upon whom the gaze is fixed (Garland-Thomson 2009). Who is responsible for the gaze reflects differences in status (Hughes 1998; Garland-Thomson 2009). As noted by Rosemarie Garland-Thomson (2009), staring has different meanings depending on the social location of the person doing the staring. For those with a visible difference, the message of the gaze was problematic. Ugly laws prohibit the display of "deformity," not the eye that beholds it (Schweick 2009). Who has the right to look/gaze/stare and at whom reflects power differences in race (Du Bois 1903), gender (Garland-Thomson 2009), ability (Garland-Thomson 2009; Schweik 2009), social class (Bourdieu 1984), and sexuality (Pronger 1992). People are generally aware when they are subject to a gaze or stare (Colwell, Schröder, Sladen 2000; Garland-Thomson 2009), and people dislike being "stared at" (Langer 1976; Rutter 1984; Garland-Thomson 2009)—so much so that it has a negative impact on self-esteem (Garland-Thomson 2009).

MICROAGGRESSIONS AND INTERNALIZATIONS 59

Matt E., who was introduced earlier in this chapter, recounted his dislike of being the object of the gaze:

> What annoys me now is people my age gawking at me. I was like, "What the hell is that all about?!" You know, you want to go up and say, "What the, what are you looking at?" They're just glued to my face and just staring at me. So sometimes when I'm feeling particularly testy, I'll stare back at them, and—or, you know, freak them out. But I know that I've been stared at, and it's not fun, but 90 percent of the time I ignore it. But you can't, you can't be successful if you let every bad apple get to you, you know?

The second vignette comes from a person who is now a leader in the movement and a well-known advocate for those with facial difference. Able to manage her own stigma, the impact it had on her son remained a challenge:

> It was hard when we went out in public on him [her son]. I've had some surgeries, so I'm more symmetrical now, but when I originally had it my smile was very pronounced on the right side. Well, not the right side but the left side would be up here, and then it would be down here. So it was really uneven. Parents would take their kids across the street if they saw me. . . . That really happened. People would point and stare, and it was hard for him. It was hard for me to see him react . . . because his reaction was "I don't understand why these people are acting this way." It became where I kept out of public for him.

The lack of control of the narrative underlies the discomfort. What was so often encapsulated in microinsults was the object status of the other. Other categories make one an object. The potential for threat—social, physical, or psychological—in this situation makes public space hostile and serves to limit access to those with facial difference. Objects are vulnerable and reliant. This movement into status as an object—and a failing object at that—is encapsulated as well in microinvalidations.

Microinvalidations

Showing off her pictures from recent honeymoon, Cathy related the following. "See this picture? This was just a quick photo we took on the cruise. . . . But I knew I was having my photo taken. I wanted to look my best."

In the photo, she's wearing a burgundy cocktail dress, her makeup is flawless, and her hair is beautifully styled. She looks amazing. Her joy is radiant as she poses with her long-time, much-beloved beau. Cathy has had facial paralysis since she was four. "I've looked like this since

I was a kid. So we take a few photos, and I'm happy, and I'm smiling, and [the photographer] says, 'Do you have a problem smiling?' And I say, 'Yes. Don't worry about it.' And that didn't really bother me. He's just trying to do his job. So then he says, 'Maybe try not smiling.'"

Her face clouds for a moment. "I wasn't bothered by the question. I thought he was just trying to do his job. But to tell me not to smile—I know how I look when I smile. It's OK. This is me. This is me happy. It was like me looking happy wasn't good enough. . . . I know he didn't mean it. I wasn't going to complain, he didn't know, I don't want him to be fired, but that hurt."

"Wasn't good enough." I imagined how that moment usually went for brides with a photographer trying to make a sale—the friendly banter, jokes, and flattery. Later in the book, the specific meaning of faces, the smile, as tied to identity and the best and most joyful parts of experience will be discussed. Here, the focus is on the ableism embedded in the idea that some have unacceptable affect.

I have gotten to know Cathy over the years. She is a regular support group attendee, an active member of the community, and her help in maintaining a vibrant network has been essential. She is a beautiful, compassionate, amazing person who has also spent years working to embrace a positive self-image. Several years ago, she shared with me that if she could have an hour without facial paralysis/synkinesis, she would take a million pictures and post them all. She shared her fears about her partner settling, and she has worked to overcome feelings of doubt and social anxiety related to her facial difference. Her brother, mother, and now-spouse shared their awareness of her pain and struggles and their pride in the person she is becoming. Over the years, I've seen a person who has truly come to embrace her experience, her potential, and her self-worth.

Cathy went from second-guessing a promotion that would move her to the front office from the back—to a position where she would now have to interact with clients—to someone who has tips and advice and regularly approaches businesses for donations as part of fundraisers. The assumption that the face she would rather show the world would be a less-expressive one because that would make her difference less noticeable is a painful reminder of a complicated history. She continues to be aware of her struggle, musing on the "normality" that masks had given her during the COVID-19 pandemic and wondering how those who only knew her masked would react in the postpandemic world. She knew the individuals weren't the problem, rather the root is in how people with facial difference are seen. The problem is how anything labeled as different is seen.

Microinvalidations meant, in ways that recall Schweik's ugly laws, that those with facial difference found themselves removed from public space. Recently retired Sarah H. is a cisgendered, college-educated white woman who had expanded her volunteer work to fill her time. She enjoyed the work, feeling like she needed to be useful as she struggled with Bell's palsy and eventually with synkinesis. Volunteering counteracted Sarah's loneliness—that is, until it was made clear to her that her face made her unwelcome. "So I already felt really isolated. I didn't want sympathy; I didn't want people looking at me. I just wanted to be normal. But I wasn't, and probably wasn't going to ever be, so I had to get on with it. I went back to my volunteer work and that helped. But then the team leader suggested I didn't return until I looked better because I was dealing with members of the public. I was crushed. It was a place I felt normal, like I was still useful, and I wasn't wanted because of how I looked." Shanna Kattari, Miranda Olzman, and Michelle Hanna (2010) describe "second class citizen status" as something that happens to those perceived to be disabled. Facial Palsy UK has reported that 76 percent of people with facial palsy face lowered self-esteem as a direct result of the condition.

Without an audience, there is no performance. As noted by Garland-Thomson (2009), looking away is as problematic as staring. A lack of acknowledgment is a statement of public status. Social life is a performance, and performances require audiences because reception hinges on audience response (Goffman 1963). Our imagining of the reaction of the other, moderating the performance of our "me," and tempering the unruly "I," is our performance of self. What does one do with no reaction? What does one do with the invisibility of disability? Ruth B., who was introduced earlier, relates that her neighborhood group of friends simply dropped her after facial difference occurred:

> It was kind of like I suddenly had cooties. I had this group of friends in the neighborhood, and we would hang out pretty regularly, and since everything happened they dropped me like a hot potato, and I have not heard from them. I was there for some of their cancers. . . . And . . . people who I have been friends with and seen every single week . . . we did things together, and all of a sudden, it's like I didn't exist. I made other friends. I have a smaller group now. We hang out. . . . That's helped.

Others found their feelings invalidated or minimized. Patrice D., a cisgendered college-educated white woman, found her friends and family ignored her concerns about her appearance and her feelings about living with synkinesis:

> My smile isn't what it used to be, and that is an unimportant thing, but it's also an important thing. Physically, it is not important. Emotionally, it is. But when I ask for support from family and friends, I get people that say, "Oh, you look the same. You know, you look fine. You look same as you always was." And I told them I feel uncomfortable about pictures, and we'll all hang out. And then, I'll go somewhere and—like just the other day, I went with my sister and two of her friends. We went to have lunch

somewhere, and later we're going to take a picture of us all. So I positioned myself so that my left side is kind of turned in and my right side is kind of turned out, and I have to smile huge because that other eye closes because of my synkinesis. You know it looks weird. . . . And he goes, "Okay, ladies, smile!" He started to take the picture. He goes, "You on the left over there. Smile bigger." I was just like, "This is all the bigger I can do." So emotionally it is difficult still to this day. It's more the emotional part, the effect on your self-image. And no one ever seems to get that it bothers me, that it's hard.

Similarly, Joanne T., a middle-aged, cisgendered, college-educated white woman, noted that people couldn't hear her when she tried to express her physical discomfort:

Sometimes, if I mention it, I have friends—maybe they're trying to make me feel better, but they don't listen. They'll say, "You look fine, nobody can tell," and I'll stop her say, "It's not so much my looks." Just because I don't show it, that it hurts all the time. . . . It really hurts so much. . . . Physically, I mean. I feel physical pain, but, on the other hand, why wouldn't it be okay just to go ahead and also want to look more like I did before? To be able to smile and take pictures without worrying?

People with synkinesis often found their attempts to discuss challenges met with misunderstanding, and they were shut down rather than allowed to share. When they made attempts to discuss their physical, social, or psychological discomfort, they were often reassured that they "look fine." That feels dismissive.

Interestingly, studies have shown that those with facial difference actually viewed their difference as less impactful than others, except during adolescence (Hughes 1998). So we actually don't "look fine," and we know that, but we are probably more optimistic about the situation than are those around us. That's not what we were talking about. We were trying to share something deeply painful, meaningful, and impactful, and it feels as though those closest to us don't care.

A corollary is the lack of acknowledgment faced by those with invisible disabilities (Kattari, Olzman, and Hanna 2018). Those with synkinesis have faced the perception that if it isn't visibly disturbing to others, it isn't problematic, or that appearance insecurity is behind their distress. The response "I don't even notice! You look fine!" when one opens up about facial paralysis elicits laughter at support groups.

Silence

More often an experience of my older participants with early acquisition or congenital facial paralysis and of those for whom additional medical intervention

MICROAGGRESSIONS AND INTERNALIZATIONS 63

was minimally invasive, some people have experienced a resounding silence about their face. Enna T. recounted being told to simply not smile: "My grandmother told me not to smile, so I stopped smiling when I was six. She didn't know. She had a fourth-grade education. She was doing her best. She didn't want me to be seen as different. I grew up feeling like I shouldn't smile. And they never talked about it. If we just never talked about it, it would be like it wasn't there." Enna is aware that no harm was intended, but the deafening silence made it impossible for her to find a voice for her experience and needs. With the best of intentions, that silence sent a message that alienated and isolated.

Denise L. mentioned that her mother had simply ignored her current condition, noting that her mother prominently displayed photos of only her "beautiful family" around her home and on social media. Denise, a cisgendered, middle-aged professional with an associate's degree, spoke with pain in her voice of her sudden disappearance from representations of her family:

> My mother loves to show off my children. She has all her children on the refrigerator, her grandchildren, and I'm not on the refrigerator anymore. All the pictures she has of me are from before. She has friends come over to her house all the time, and she's always showing all the pictures, but none of me. I told my sister about it recently, how that kind of hurts. Then, all of a sudden, when I was at my mother's house last time I noticed that there was a picture of me in a bikini, when I was twenty years old. This was pre-children. That was the picture I guess she thought I looked good in. But she doesn't have a picture of me now. She told me she only likes to be around beautiful people, that she has a beautiful family. I guess she doesn't want her friends to see me now.

My respondents have noted that it was often older relatives who encouraged silence or advised against sharing. This is not to say that individuals behaved this way across the board, but rather to note a cultural shift toward inclusivity and awareness of the impact of lived experience on mental and physical health. Yet, despite the overall dread expressed by others at having to be in our shoes, most encountered a simultaneous minimalization of our experience.

Minimalization of Disability

Minimalizations, which are not exactly a microaggression, occur when challenges or barriers are downplayed, ignored, or invalidated. Minimalizations undermine potential moments of challenge by undercutting a moment when structural critiques could become visible. Overall, there is a pervasive minimalization of synkinesis and facial difference as impactful. Despite the constant threat of imposed self-disclosure ("what's wrong with your face?"), people simultaneously encountered ongoing minimization.

64 METAMORPHOSIS

Matty L. is a white, professional, cisgendered woman in her early fifties who has had synkinesis for about ten years after having had a tumor removed. She has visible facial paralysis and cannot blink[2] or smile. She recounted,

I was at a thing for my brother recently, and this has happened before. . . . I don't know, people were just acting a little off to me. "Oh, you're his sister? Are you visiting? From out of town?" And it's a bigger question—there's something implied. I don't know why, but recently I felt like, I wonder if these people think that I'm not well, like I'm not a fully functional person. Like I'm Jason's broken sister just because of my facial problems.

So I thought I would just say something, explain what it is. So I actually tried to explain about my facial paralysis, and they cut me off. They flat out wouldn't let me talk about it. Everyone said no, no, no, no, no, no, no, of course not, we all have our stuff you know. People like to, to sort of trivialize, like, I'm talking to one of my brother's friends, and why is she was showing me discoloration of her hand and saying we all have our things. You know, I get it's a big deal for her, but for me it's like your hand, it's not your face.

Mandy V., a graduate school–educated, cisgendered white woman who works as a software engineer, expressed frustration that even her closest friends were never comfortable listening to her when she would try to talk about the impact of her fairly severe synkinesis:

So my face is really tight all the time. It hurts; it's contracted. So I tell my friends this, and they all cut me off and say, "Oh you can't really—I hardly notice it now." I'm like, "Well. I know you can notice it." They're like, "No, really, it's not that noticeable. Don't worry about it." I finally got up the nerve to say, "Even though it looks like nothing is going on inside of my face, it is like it is in constant turmoil. It's constantly pulling, and pulling, and it's pulling so hard. I'm in pain all the time. I mean it's pulling so hard it's moving my teeth. My teeth are actually moving. My nasal cavity is collapsing. . . . It's not about you noticing."

The rapidity with which Mandy's self-disclosure was shut down with overassurances of not noticing was telling.

For the person with synkinesis, there are a host of life-altering issues with which they are coping. In a severe case such as Mandy's, recent research has explored the long-term impact on musculoskeletal health (Joseph et al. 2022). And many of my interviewees noted that sharing with family and friends about other health problems elicits compassion and support, but mentioning their synkinesis results in changing the topic and a refusal to engage. Generally, facial paralysis creates medical/physical challenges, problems in communication, and psychosocial challenges. Often the paralysis is not enough to prevent communication or social interaction, or the discomfort may be manageable, but it's always there. It is a barrier one is always navigating—a disruption, a pause, a challenge. This takes a toll: a longer time, a harder time, a more exhausting time.

Eduardo Bonilla-Silva (2003, 2018) has discussed the "minimalization of race" to highlight the discounting of the impact of racism on lived experience. Minimalization, which is derived from critical race theory, refers to the idea or *belief* that race is not having a significant impact on the lives of individuals. Minimalization demonstrates the widespread belief that while racism may have impacted people in the past, and racists do exist, race no longer has a negative impact on the lives of individuals, while ignoring evidence of the influence of racism on structural inequality (Bonilla-Silva 2003, 2018).

Racism and acknowledging the impact it has on people's lives is incredibly uncomfortable. It means acknowledging a system in which we are all complicit, that benefits some at the expense of others. Regardless of consciousness, complicity occurs at the systemic level. "Sincere fictions" is the term Bonilla-Silva (2003, 2018) uses to describe the creation of myths about a past that has been overcome; it highlights moving beyond and assimilating. Color blind racism focuses on cultural deficit arguments or market dynamics to explain racial disparities, rather than acknowledging the ongoing impact of racism (Bonilla-Silva 2003, 2018). Reframing race as a perceived advantage in hiring or school processes is one example. This type of "sincere fiction" suggests ongoing challenges with racism are the fault of individuals or misperceptions. These concepts can be adapted to explore structural inequity more broadly.

Although race, class, gender, sexuality, disability, and other categories may have unique histories, minimalization in different forms is problematic across categories of otherness. Ongoing minimalization internalizes the cost of othered experience. Individuals come to see the challenges they face as their own fault, rather than the direct result of systemic inequity. The sincerely embraced fictive "solution" is self-care or improvement to help that person find a community of acceptance or meditation; the larger systems and structures remain unchallenged. Just as the minimalization of race erases the ongoing impact of racism on structures, institutions, and individuals (Bonilla-Silva 2003, 2018), the minimalization of disability discounts the persistence of ableism and the impact of living with ubiquitous appearance-related discrimination.

People with facial paralysis and synkinesis experience a world in which healthcare providers, co-workers, and sometimes friends and family tend to minimize the impact of their condition medically, socially, and professionally. In a for-profit healthcare system, this minimalization undercuts their ability to receive impactful treatment. One woman I spoke with was a breast cancer survivor; she couldn't fathom why rebuilding her breast was essential to her self-esteem and completely covered by her insurance yet rebuilding her face was not.

Others struggled to afford Botox treatments, which are primarily used to reduce pain and improve communication. A long-time support group attendee showed several of us how his synkinesis was continuing to tighten to the point his neck and shoulders were now pulling constantly; the pain was spreading to his back, but his health insurance wouldn't cover Botox or surgery, claiming they were aesthetic. His condition was worsening, and he was in constant pain, creating a range of physical and psychological challenges. So he had been saving up for medical treatment, and creating a GoFundMe account to accept donations finally allowed him to afford pain relief. My own surgeries took a huge chunk of my liquid savings from twenty years of professional life, a doctor-spouse, and a gift from my parents, but I spend all of my lived experience in significantly less pain.

Fundamentally, minimalization protects privilege. To acknowledge the cost of a loss is to acknowledge the privilege and value of those who have. It calls attention to how the society and culture have failed to provide equity, to meet needs, to provide reasonable accommodations, and to institutionalize compassion. Sometimes the people I interviewed had amazing responses to microaggressions and minimalizations that offered microchallenges and ideological pushback against systemic assumptions.

Responses to Microaggressions and Minimalizations

How do people react to microaggressions and minimalizations? People with facial paralysis (and often the same person) recounted to me a range of responses varying by circumstance or mood. People most often ignored/endured microaggressions, but people also used them as moments to educate. Sometimes people enjoyed using social norms and mores to expose systemic failures by challenging assumptions.

Ruth B., who was introduced earlier this chapter, shared her responses to a few incidents where assumptions were being made about her. After facing bullying at work and the loss of a valued friend group, Ruth started pushing back. In the first case, when a photographer assumed her more muted affect was a personality issue, she gave him a brief glimpse of the impact of synkinesis, something we mostly downplay. In the second incident, she responded to the stage-whispered moral condemnation with countershaming:

> Last summer my nephew got married out here; they live out of state but wanted to get married at the beach. And the photographer he hired starts taking photos and making comments to me like, "grouchy face," "sour

puss," "never smile," "come on you can do better than that," so I just gave him my little controlled smile that I thought would make it look happy. But he kept on, and I knew he wanted me to do a big smile. And I was like, "Fine, here you go, you want a big smile, here. . . . Go ahead, take the picture." He was so stunned that he didn't know what to say or do; he was in shock . . .

I used to ignore it, but with my balance also being impacted and my face, I've had people come up to me in the grocery store and say, "It's a little early to start drinking." . . . I don't walk straight. I don't act right, and I talk kind of funny. And I used to just get really depressed and put on my stuff down and leave my cart and go home and be sad. But I'm not doing anything wrong—they are. They are doing something wrong. And now, I turn around and I say, "I had a brain tumor. What's your excuse for being rude?"

Similarly, many recounted staring back at those who were staring at them until the person would look away, flustered and embarrassed. Turning shame back on the perpetrator was enjoyed by many, and it serves as a microchallenge. Sometimes people choose to use these moments to educate and alter the discourse. This was especially true if the stares or comments came from younger people.

Garland-Thomson (2009) points out that the gaze is also a response of the eye to the unexpected. One learns the social meanings of and uses of staring and whether to stare or not stare in social settings. Children often violate such rules. Similarly, people tend to differentiate between staring and questions by children and by adults. The participants in my study noted that they considered staring or questions by children quite differently than they did by adults. Janice M., a cisgendered white woman who is now retired after her tumor treatment, said she enjoyed providing childcare. The children often have questions, and she simply tells them that her face "broke, because I was really sick, but I'm better now." Janice said the kids usually just accepted that explanation, but more often she found the parents unwilling to hire her as a sitter. Another parent described her daughter's responses to her classmates' questions as a similar situation: "And I think she would say that periodically somebody new would come and say, 'What's wrong with your face?' And she very clearly would just say, 'I had a brain tumor.' And it was just like, 'Oh, okay.' And then, they just kind of went on."

Sometimes people recounted having moments with adults when they were able to meaningfully discuss or educate as well. In the example given previously, Al L. mentioned the difference between microaggressions and genuine inquiries about his face/health, and he shared that he appreciated the genuine inquiry. There was generally positive emotion when people spoke of their ability to educate. Moments of education, advocacy, and action were fulfilling for people. It's a moment of hope, pride, and empowerment. It hinted at the cost of invalidation and microaggressions.

Internalization

Internalization refers to the individual taking in negative beliefs and coming to see the self, rather than response to the self, as what is problematic. Internalization implies that one views oneself as other, with a need to compensate or hide one's challenges. Internalization is a self that has been shaped by a narrative that is inherently invalidating. Much of this process is unconscious; as previously mentioned, having positive support communities who share devalued or delegitimated traits can serve as a buffer (Darling 2019). Al L., introduced earlier this chapter, also shared that despite having a fairly successful career and a close set of friends he still struggles with how he feels about living with synkinesis: "I had my ups and my downs. There are some days that I feel very, very confident, and there are other days that I just can't look in the mirror. It's something I can never seem to overcome. And it's not that it's horrible, but I just feel something inside me, that I don't look right. That I am not right. That I can't and won't ever achieve fulfillment and happiness, you know?"

Graduate school–educated, cisgendered marketing executive Ellie G.'s blunt assessment was shared by many: "It did make me feel initially that I was a freak." The word "freak," references to "freak shows," or the word "freaky" reoccurred with painful regularity in my discussions with the study participants. My own description was I belong in the grotesquerie. What is a freak show to us? Robert Bogdan (1988) places freak shows in a historical context, in which the freak had some agency and value and was to some degree playing the part of an outlandish object to an English-speaking, postcolonial subject; thus, the reference to freak shows invokes stigmatized forced display. One becomes an object of simultaneous fascination, disgust, and pity while having agency, and legitimacy, and humanity stripped away. One is a "me" for whom there can be no nonstigmatized performance.

But from where do we get these views? Microaggressions are daily reminders of embedded social structures. What is normal says something about those of us who face the challenge of not-normal. Microaggressions remind us of our place; internalizing is the cost, as we know that "small slights" have problematic psychological consequences (Meyer 2007; Sue 2010a; Sue 2010b). Internalized racism is a term used to capture the ways an individual's self-perceptions and beliefs contain negative racial stereotypes consistent with dominant culture (Williams and Williams-Morris 2000). Internalization has also been applied to sexism (Bearman and Amrhein 2013), ableism (Campbell 2009; Kattari, Olzman, and Hanna 2018), heterosexism (Nadal and Mendoza 2013; Szymanski and

MICROAGGRESSIONS AND INTERNALIZATIONS

Henrichs-Beck 2014; Watermeyer and Görgens 2013), and intersecting subject positions among categories (Schalk 2022; Szymanski and Henrichs-Beck 2014; Nadal and Mendoza 2013).

Compulsory ableness values passing and devalues signs of difference (Campbell 2009). Similarly, chronic illness and its visible manifestations are viewed as somehow discrediting, and this has similarly negative impacts (Charmaz 1983). People with facial differences may display signs of internalization, specifically around the idea that their appearance and communication are disruptive, unpleasant, or inherently problematic. Both of the ensuing vignettes come from cisgendered, college-educated men who were largely achieving their personal life and career goals, Al L., self-identifies as Latine, and Matt H. identifies as Jewish. Matt shared he offered apologies for his general appearance: "Basically, I apologize to people for how I look. I just apologized up front. But I went on with it. It didn't stop me from doing stuff socially, and I attended a wedding. I was actually part of the wedding. It was a big deal. It was okay. It was on my mind, but it didn't stop me." Recall that symbolic violence is one's internalization and perpetuation of relations of power and privilege through practice. Matt H. undercuts his equal participation in events by noting his facial difference is something that requires redress in the form of apology. By contrast, despite often passing, Al L. shared that it remained something he thought about, managed, and felt concern about revealing:

> I feel that my challenge is more emotional than society-driven because I've been very fortunate to have a regular life. I was a teenager when it happened, but I still played sports, and my career, and college went OK. Nobody ever asked about it. I've heard so many times that "I can't even tell that you have facial paralysis," "I don't even notice." So it doesn't seem like it's a problem for me, but I still think about it. What people are seeing. For my job, there's some public speaking, and that's hard for me. When I have to be in front of people and all eyes are on me . . . it's in my head, all the time. I'm like, "Oh no, they can see," you know?

The identification of one's appearance as disturbing, upsetting, disruptive, or needing to be hidden takes a tremendous toll on one's sense of self-worth.

Internalizations are microaggressions and minimalizations turn inward into shame. As Camara Phyllis Jones (2000) has highlighted, institutionalized and personally mediated discrimination comes from external sources, but internalized experiences come from within, as a result of one's ongoing experiences of social structure. Amy D., introduced earlier in the book, is one of those people who makes an amazing friend. She is the right combination of supportive and honest, and I value having gotten to know her. I see her on support groups sharing advice and funny stories, and she often reaches out to others who are struggling. Upbeat, kind, fun and funny, her interview stood out for me. She grew up with facial paralysis acquired through an early surgery, and she recounts carrying internalized ableism and poignantly shares the long-term cost to her mental health:

> I carried a lot of shame about my appearance. So, meaning I never wanted to bring attention to it. I would hide my smile. I would get tormented by a lot of schoolkids and my neighborhood. I remember [in] fifth grade I had a best friend, and she was close friends with another girl in our class, and that other girl told my friend that she didn't want to be my friend because of my face. So I knew that there were situations like that, and my parents—you know, I didn't have a therapist at that time—they didn't help nurture the skills maybe that I would need to navigate through life with, you know, a condition, with this condition. And so it wasn't something that I really even knew how to address in my life. It was just something I wanted to avoid.
>
> I first became aware of this around kindergarten, like I said. . . . At that time, I was diagnosed with depression. A lot of it had to do with my self-esteem and just how I felt about myself, if I was pretty or not; and it just all came to a head at fourteen. My mom got me a counselor at that time, and so often on throughout my life since then I've been in therapy. And the one that I have now, originally I think we started with my boyfriend at that time, who's now my husband. I started having my own issues with anxiety which I've had on my—since I was fourteen.
>
> Actually, all my life, I can trace it back to kindergarten, me having these anxious moments, but I really needed to help to work through it. . . . And I think partially that's how my depression developed because I kept it all in. And I didn't have anyone to talk to about with it, my situation. And so I would just hold it in, and then when it would get kind of bad, I'd cry and I'd go to my mom or dad and get comfort until the next time I broke down.
>
> So it was really just a quick fix. It was not their words, their comfort, which is a short-term remedy. It really didn't help me get through the feelings I had. I'm still working through those in therapy.

The costs of internalization to mental well-being are well known (Brown et al. 2002; Jones 2000; Williams and Williams-Morris 2000). Microaggressions and internalizations relating to race (Brown, Sellers, and Gomez 2002; Jones 2000; Loue 2006; Williams and Williams-Morris 2000), class (Isenberg 2016), gender (Loue 2006), sexuality (Anzani, Sacchi, and Prunas 2021), gender identity (Arayasirikul and Wilson 2019), and intersections of identities (Moody and Lewis 2019; Schalk 2022) have been shown to impact physical and mental health outcomes. People with visible differences demonstrate social physique anxiety

MICROAGGRESSIONS AND INTERNALIZATIONS

(Martin 2012), thought to originate from experiences of negative physical evaluations (Zitzelsberger 2005).

This is the incalculable toll that otherness takes on the individual. It's not one single thing, but the daily lived experience of otherness that ultimately depresses physical and mental health. Microaggressions are toxic to all of us. What we internalize, what we come to assume, what we come to take for granted in our minds and bodies is toxic. It drives a wedge between us. It makes fearsome and loathsome part of who some of us are, while obfuscating the impact of being treated as such. Internalized entitlement and internalized oppression poison our humanity. The conundrum of passing highlights these tensions.

Passing

> I knew I was passing when people stopped telling me how much better I looked, and how one "couldn't even tell anymore." When people started saying nothing, I knew I was passing. . . . And I mastered a little head-turn smile that works really well. But it didn't change the weird feelings in my face, the better and worse days. It didn't change the impact it was having on me. It didn't mean I didn't have synkinesis. I like passing, but I also don't totally understand it, because in my head I'm not. It's always alienating and confusing.

Passing refers to self-presenting as "normal" or not disclosing or revealing the discredited attribute (Goffman 1963; Hughes 1998). The idea that passing is desirable carries within it the assumption that to be the other is inherently invalidating. Garland-Thompson (2009) describes passing as "an intentional quest for civil inattention in a racist or sexist environment" (42). Passing, in some circumstances and for some people, was a relief. Vi V., introduced earlier in this chapter, found it relieving to know her synkinesis was often unnoticed:

> In the beginning, it was hard to meet new people. I used to get down when I had to meet new people because I would wonder how they saw me, if they noticed. Then I realized they mostly didn't. Now, I'm just myself. Sometimes I still wonder how my friends—how people see me . . . I don't go asking people, but I try to figure it out. Like at my friend's wedding, this one girl she asked her husband, because her husband was "Oh my gosh, Stacy is so beautiful," and then she goes, "Do you notice anything about her face? Can you tell she's got Bell's palsy?" Then a lot of them were like, "No, I can't tell at all." And no one said anything about me. It makes me feel better. I don't know—it used to be always in my mind when I met people; now it's not always at the back of my head when I meet people, now that I know they might not notice.

For Vi, passing relieved her anxiety; many others share her views, using makeup, medical procedures, and physical therapy to more effectively pass. Dani, also introduced earlier in the book, shared her relief that as long as she didn't speak she could pass, as compared with a fellow support group attendee with severe synkinesis. "I know it sounds terrible, but I was just so grateful to not be her. She can never hide it—it's always there. I can pass sometimes. I mean if you didn't know me before . . . if I don't become animated." Passing can drive a wedge between members of a community, between those who can and can't, and between those who value it and those who reject it. Research on people with hidden disabilities or invisible disabilities reveals struggles with "passing" tied to isolation from a community of peer support (Kattari, Olzman, and Hanna 2018; Samuels 2003).

Passing implies that to be discovered will reveal something negative or stigmatized; so while passing might remove immediate external threats, it demonstrates internalization. Amy D., introduced previously in this chapter, has reflected on her complicity in internalized ableism and visibility:

> And even when we went out for dinner—we went to dinner after the FP [facial paralysis] conference—and I remember I told Brad A. and I said, "Your paralysis, it really isn't that bad. Yes, I notice it, but it's very subtle." And that's my honest opinion. And then I just thought to myself, after the fact, that was kind of insensitive of me to say. I just kind of blurt things out sometimes. But maybe to him it's majorly noticeable. And I know he has a tremendous amount of pain, but I forget that because that's not visible. And it's devastating because he used to be able to smile symmetrically. And here I'm downplaying it. So I have a lot to learn in terms of insensitivity towards others that have it as a struggle in their life. And that's just something I have to learn.

Struggling with her own internalized ableism and having the opportunity to meet others with facial paralysis provided an opportunity for Amy to confront her own commission of a microaggression, her internalized ableism, and the boundaries of community. And this struggle reflects how larger social structures are always already embedded in our beliefs, actions, and processes. It's not that Amy is a problematic person; rather, she's navigating a deeply problematic system that has structured her understandings, beliefs, and reactions.

Dani, who values passing, has struggled with feelings of self-worth and depression. She had to change her career after facing discrimination, and she survived a suicide attempt during a period of depression tied to her developing synkinesis. She comes from a family with traditional gender norms and used the phrase "damaged goods" in reference to her current situation: "We had to look good. Oh, yeah. We didn't leave the house without makeup. My grandmother cleaned the house in high heels. Yeah, you always had to look good, always. That was the message I got all the time growing up. That was, like, the most important thing. You always had to look good. You didn't go out and get the mail unless you looked good. And then this happened." She shared the frustration of living in two worlds: one in which she was an educated advocate, and one in which she was expected to slip into passing: using her small smile, tamping down her sociability, and fading into the background. Garland-Thomson (2009) speculates as to the psychological cost of passing and highlights the use of normalizing medical procedures so that one can "pass."

Passing is complicated; it can make things easier, but it feels like an erasure. While some of my participants sought to pass in social situations, others (sometimes the same people) resented the assumption that they should and that not passing was a "failure" or undesirable in and of itself. Several incidents involving photographers are highlighted throughout this book. We may struggle with our photographed image; people seemed to universally resent well-meaning suggestions designed to minimize difference. Cathy, introduced earlier, rejected a photographer's suggestion she smile smaller to hide her facial difference. At many support group meetings people shared their complex emotions at successfully passing and failing to pass, the ambiguity of not knowing whether one is or isn't passing, and the opacity of not knowing how facial difference is "read."

More importantly, Michael Hughes (1998) suggests that those with facial difference are "covering" more than they are "passing," meaning they are "reducing" expression and altering behavior and appearance. In Chapter 5, I discuss the flattening of affect that individuals use to control both the wrong feel within and perceptions of facial difference for others.

Ideological Repair Work

I've never understood the difference between macro and micro—and I am not asking for an explanation. It's just that how social relations are experienced, expressed, resisted, and embodied doesn't seem somehow divorced or separate from social structure. I have always understood it more as that which is micro is the physical expression or manifestation of the macro.

Michael Messner (1988) wrote a piece on the female athlete as contested ideological terrain, which problematized the simplistic idea that female athletic bodies challenged dominant gender norms. Inclusion does not necessarily challenge the existing relations of power; rather, changes in practice, ideologies, and institutions are necessary for change (Messner 2002). Reproducing bodies within neoliberal white supremacist patriarchal structures tends to reinforce existing structures, even at moments of potential challenge or delegitimation. Even when aspects of inequity are challenged, the systemic requirements for and means to produce inequity remain protected (Messner 1988; Hall 1983). Hence, bodies are contested ideological terrain, a place where the ideological webs of power and privilege are rendered material through ongoing practices.

Microaggressions, internalizations, and invalidations are experiences of individuals that do ideological repair work for systemic inequity. Microaggressions are macro ideologies experienced, reinforced, and reproduced. Pierre Bourdieu's symbolic violence reminds us of our complicity in relations, as our embodied selves have an unconscious that acts in accordance with systemic relations of power and privilege. Recall Michel Foucault's concept of subjectivity, how the experience of the self, the inner dialogue, is shaped by these larger ideological structures. Bourdieu reminds us that through daily lived experience, and the management of the self, habitus comes to reinforce existing social relations, statuses, and tastes.

We are complicit in the ongoing systems of our own domination. The participants in my study distanced themselves from the stigmatized aspects of identity, "educated" (again a recategorization strategy), created networks of support, and pursued a host of other microlevel strategies that left the systemic roots of inequity unchallenged and, in some cases, reinforced. However, as people progressed, connected, and interacted, they also began to question their larger assumptions about privilege, access, rights, and subjectivity, as we will discuss in later chapters.

Intersections, Advocacy, and Privilege

Before we move to the next chapter, there needs to be more wrestling with a fundamental dilemma, that of intersecting access, advocacy, and privilege. It's not an accident that overeducated white women are overrepresented in my sample. White, middle-class, middle-aged women were vastly overrepresented in support group membership and event facilitation. Reflecting the nexus of a specific history of gender, race, class, and sexuality, the unpaid labor of women is critical to advocacy and activism, and more often white women have the privilege of participating in unpaid labor.

Understanding advocacy in a specific way is a mark of and an expression of a relatively privileged status. Storytelling as advocacy implies the storyteller is valued. It's important that this problem be understood in terms of what makes access easier for some and what barriers may be experienced by others. The literature on disability, race, class, and health suggests that facial difference, advocacy, and visibility can have different meanings and costs. The historic links between morality and health—and explicitly appearance—highlight the problematics for those who reside at the confluence of otherness. Those in "othered" race and class categories have had health, appearance, and morality conflated (Saguy and Gruys 2010). Hence, health issues and the label of disabled or sick are avoided more often by some communities (Bailey and Mobley 2019; Brown and Moloney 2019).

Regardless of identity category, it's not surprising that many sought ways to mitigate the visual impact of synkinesis. Most had tried, were trying, or hoped for interventions. In *Body Panic* (2009), Shari Dworkin and I note both the objective-aspects-of being-a-subject and the increasing colonization/commodification of all bodies, with gender serving as an organizing marketing tool. Beauty culture and the increasing edict toward normative appearance has been well documented such that the boundaries between elective and necessary interventions are increasingly blurry (Talley 2014). Chapter 4 focuses on the face and the push toward individualized solutions aimed at making one an acceptable object.

4

It's My Face—Why That Matters

"Yeah. It's your *face!!!* And everyone thinks it's vanity, but it's not that. My mom confuses it and tells me, 'You're still a beautiful woman from the inside,' and it's like, 'Oh, shut the hell up.' It's not vanity. It's communication. It's not being able to look happy when you feel happy. It's not being able to show how you feel. What it does is it blocks the you-ness of you. It's what it does. I can't communicate to you who I am. That's the grief." Laura M. is a conventionally attractive, white, college-educated, cisgendered, middle-aged woman. Her presentation is refined and elegant—curated. She is clearly someone who engages with aesthetics and the performance of self; however, she can't give her once-effortless performance of self: "The face is central to identity, and I will never get over the distress of what I see now. It's not that it looks awful. After two surgeries, plus another for a deviated septum, I look OK. Maybe even better in some ways than normal aging would have left me. But just not like me. Not quite right. My father, reflecting on aging, told me, 'You never quite get used to going past mirrors. You're always a bit shocked by that old guy.' It's the same sort of jolt. It's me, but not me."

The impact on communication, sense of self, and ability to interact with others was a challenge for all of those I interviewed. Marcy Louise L, a white, mid-forties, cisgendered, college-educated marketing executive, expressed frustration with her inability to communicate:

> I feel ugly all the time. And that's not just about how you look. Feeling ugly is a feeling about yourself. . . . And I think that the hardest part is the inability to smile. Throughout the total experience, where I'd—you know, it never even occurred to me in my life before what it is to smile. How it makes you feel to smile. . . . How others respond. . . . And now I know it just looks like, almost like I'm snarling.

I tried to, you know, practice. And when I see it, I think gosh, people must think I'm, like, angry. And it feels wrong. . . . Instead of a friendly "Hello," I look mad! I feel weird. I'm trying to say hello or be friendly, and it comes off totally weird.

I think I'm lucky that I got married right before the paralysis began. But I was lucky, getting married, finding my husband and marrying him before it really showed. And I'm luckily married to a very good person who loves me and thinks I'm beautiful anyway. And I feel really lucky because I don't feel ugly with him.

The single most profound experiential and communicative loss is the smile. Multiethnic, graduate school–educated, cisgendered healthcare professional Cara Marie D. highlighted this:

I think it affected me most profoundly in terms of smiling. I know that research has shown that smiling in and of itself can produce feel-good neurotransmitters, because you're communicating to your own body that you're happy. I noticed that when I was in the thick of the paralysis that smiling had the opposite effect for me. Smiling for me became almost a—I was almost classically conditioned to hate smiling because when I would spontaneously smile in front of someone who didn't necessarily know me or wasn't used to—even family, who was used to the way I looked before, I could see in their faces, even if it was just for a split-second, that look of kind of shock, or that look of confusion. They weren't mirroring back to me pleasure, which is what you usually get when you smile. They were reflecting back to me a different kind of look, and that feedback, I mean that feedback was kind of like the dreaded moment, where you knew that your smile was having this very awkward effect on the situation, and it makes you not want to smile. It makes you not want to be looked at. You learn to just avoid, avoid that awkward moment.

The smile was the most often referenced expressive loss and was emblematic of a specific challenge for those who had lost the ability to clearly communicate with their face. Two critical issues were raised by the previous interviewees: the impairment of the internal feelings generated by expressions (which will be covered in detail in the next chapter) and the impact of a changed face on social interactions and experiences.

Those without facial paralysis often try to explain to me that what they see in their friend, loved one, or patient is not what is seen by that person in the mirror or in photos. The impact of facial paralysis on the ability to communicate, or on the self, is not as disturbing or jarring as those with synkinesis imagine. I am frequently reminded that what I see in pictures or glimpse in a

78 METAMORPHOSIS

mirror is always a moment frozen in time that fails to capture the animation of life, that really it's not that noticeable.

It's lovely that you care enough to lie to us. But frankly the normal communicative feedback we receive in daily life clearly tells us otherwise. Certainly the new ubiquity of zooms has made it readily apparent—it's actually far worse than I imagine. For you, perhaps it was a fleeting moment when you remember our smile is different; or your face betrays momentary confusion, which you then forget about. For us, it was another reminder that we carry the weight of stigma. For those with facial disfigurement, social withdrawal and communicative challenges are an ongoing struggle (Hughes 1998). And certainly the compensatory strategies consciously and unconsciously adopted are effective (Bogart, Tickle-Degnen, and Ambady 2014; Bogart and Tickle-Degnen 2015), but they are being enacted to overcome. They are exhausting and anxiety inducing. The next chapter will focus on the internal experience; this chapter focuses on the meaning of the face as part of the presentation of self and the role of face in communication.

Faces are central to identity and presentation of self. They are key to both verbal and nonverbal communication. Effective communication usually involves the face mediating, experiencing, reflecting, and transmitting. Shared expressions are central to this experience. For individuals with facial paralysis, regardless of the cause or degree of impaction, over time the ability to function socially becomes the central challenge (Coulson 2017; Coulson et al. 2004; Hughes 1998). The previous chapter highlighted the role that discrimination and microaggressions play. Here, the relationship between the individual and the face in a market system is central. Faces and the ability to communicate with and through them is a valuable form of learned capital and an important cultural competency. Although its form and import vary by social location, the face is fundamental to connection and the presentation of self. Synkinesis disrupts communication not only by impeding but also by miscommunicating. This leaves those with synkinesis seeking solutions. To understand this process, it's important that we first explore the centrality of faces to communication.

The Face and Communication

Lecturing is not about delivering content, it's about communicating; this was a barrier with which I was struggling.

> As a college professor, this was a big change. I used my face in teaching. To convey emotions, to give information. And I use it not just conveying information but basically keeping people's interest in the subject matter. It was significant in terms of not being able to raise my eyebrows, or smile, show them emotion, encouragement. It's something to which I will always

be adjusting. I started using another way of getting their attention to the issues. So maybe I would make funny comments. I would hide the side of the face that's not working properly and basically half-smile or say, "I'm smiling at you" or "Don't take this as a negative just because I don't smile." Just stuff like that. You joke about it.

So that's not me, but it took me a moment to remember that. Mike H., a southern European immigrant, is also a college professor, albeit in a different field. When I pulled his thoughts on teaching from my notes, I had to take a moment to register that they weren't mine because they resonated so completely with my own experience lecturing. But they also felt "wrong"—not how I would say it, not quite me. Yet the metaphor for the experience of facial paralysis resonated—it's you but not quite you. There's a constant backtalk of not you, not exactly right, floating through your mind.

Along with speech and gestures, the face is at the center of nonverbal communication. Facial expression, conscious or unconscious, is a key transmitter of information and a disseminator of social cues (Hwang and Matsumoto 2016). Facial expression communicates emotion and regulates interaction as we respond to and provide cues (Bogart, Tickle-Degnen, and Ambady 2014; Ekman 1986; Tickle-Degnen 2006). This process is often innate (Bogart, Tickle-Degnen, and Ambady 2014; Ekman 1986; Gifford 2011; Patterson 2014; Tickle-Degnen 2006; Westland 2015). Most people simply react, adjust, or respond.

When humor is not the goal, it's jarring, confusing, or disruptive to communication when there's a mismatch between facial and verbal expression (Preston and Stansfield 2008). That's what synkinesis produces: it's not merely an absence of expression, it's misexpression. One of the most common miswirings is between the eye and the mouth, which are the most impactful areas in nonverbal communication (Ruiz-Solar and Beltran 2012; Hughes 1998). Moreover, the eyebrow is the least likely to recover, and eyebrows are specifically known to be key to regulation of conversation (Flecha-García 2010). Regardless of the compensatory strategies (using extra verbal cues or the hands and body more would be examples), synkinesis disrupts communication because it provides "wrong" feedback. This is very important because even people with less obvious facial difference might still have significant impaction.

As already alluded to, of all expressions the most keenly felt loss is the smile. "Smile . . ." The single facial expression my study's participants discussed the most and with the most heartfelt grief was the smile. And it was deep grief— the grief for a deeply loved, forever lost experience. The meaning and importance of the smile was captured in the perception by so many that they considered their smile to be their "best feature." Three of my participants captured key aspects: appearance, experience, and miscommunication.

Patti D. enjoyed working as a lab technician. A college-educated, cisgendered, white woman, Patti wasn't appearance oriented; she self-presented as low key and relaxed, but she missed her "best feature":

> Because what used to be what I considered my best feature was my smile. You know, how people say, "Oh, you smile just like your mom," and Mom has a beautiful smile. So now nobody says that, and they wouldn't because I don't smile. I try not to smile that big anymore because it just looks so lopsided. But it's much better than it has been ten years ago. It's improved. But it's not going to go away. So what I always thought was my best feature is now my worst. It doesn't share what I wanted to share, and it looks awful, and it's distracting.

Graduate school–educated, cisgendered Latina Angie C., reflected on her inability to emote after the loss of her smile, feeling she was missing out on shared experiences with her friends and family: "It's [the smile] a huge part of, you know, who we are. It expresses us and expresses how, you know, when we're happy or just content. I feel like I can't express how I feel."

Vi V., who was introduced in the last chapter, highlighted the ongoing miscommunication of mood/affect:

> My smile that was my favorite part of my face. . . . You know, when they ask you what's your favorite part about your face, it was my smile. Just, I smiled really big, and now I don't. And everyone always asks, "What's wrong?" . . . My family, my kids, and even at work, people are like, "What's wrong?" I'm, like, nothing's wrong. It's just it's a lot of work to smile. And they think something is wrong with me—I have this, excuse my language, but like a resting b-tch face because I just don't smile all the time. I feel fine, but people keep asking, "What's wrong?"

The smile was referenced as a significant loss by almost every person with whom I spoke. This isn't simply because mouth/eye issues were the most common. It wasn't that the smile really was an objective best feature, as so many asserted. Rather, we must think about what a genuine smile conveys and how it operates in communication. Genuine smiles transmit what we like to think of as the "best" of human experience: warmth, welcome, joy, pleasure, and the positives of social interaction are communicated, shared, and experienced with a smile. Communication is not just about being heard or witnessed, it's a sharing of meaning, of experience, and of moments. The smile is a shared communicative event of the most joyful aspects of human interaction—an exchange of good feeling enhanced through communicative sharing. Synkinesis takes away the ability to share in that communicative event.

Angie C. expanded on the specific importance of smiles for setting a tone or mood for social interaction: "It's like when you first meet somebody. . . . If they

IT'S MY FACE—WHY THAT MATTERS   81

think you look attractive, they think you look nice or pleasant. This is a person I want to get to know better . . . maybe hang out with. . . . And I used to get that [from others], but now I don't. It's like it's weird when I try to smile—my smile is crooked, so I don't give good vibes. I can see it. I have to work harder, you know, to show people, yeah, I'm a nice person."

Mary D. described herself as not a social butterfly but a friendly person. A college-educated, white, cisgendered engineer, she lamented the barrier that the lack of a smile had created in her ongoing short-term communications throughout the day:

It's just an international sign of, like, "Hi. I'm a nice person. Hello, how are you?" You look like you've had a bad day or are mean if you don't, so you smile, just to say, "Hi." But I can't. When I go into the grocery store and somebody smiles at me and I try to smile back, it's almost like they kind of, like, so almost feel like, "Oh, she didn't smile back at me." And I'm like, "No, really, I'm smiling at you. I know it looks difficult, but I smile back." It's just such a—the international hello. Across the board, we may all speak different languages, but that's the one thing that we all speak the same. But it's not something I can do now. I can't share this way of communicating and being welcoming and friendly.

But it is not simply the difficulty in communication when we are trying; inadvertent messages or miscommunications create tremendous social challenges. The previous chapter detailed the microaggressive side of questioning our affect and mood. Here, we consider the communicative side of it. People related to me that, in addition to struggling to communicate, they were struggling to not miscommunicate.

Inadvertent Communication

The problem of inadvertent communication was highlighted in the previous examples in which others questioned my interviewee's mood. One's face is never "at rest" with synkinesis. Muscles tighten in ways that often convey stress, displeasure, concern, or other negative emotions. There's something about active facial muscles that signals emotion; hence, one's resting/not-at-rest face is inadvertently signaling an active emotional state. People have reported discovering inadvertent communication impacted their professional relationships, how friends and family interacted with them, and socializing in general.

Ellie E., who is cisgendered and white, found that in her field as a healthcare worker she now faced an added professional burden:

Actually, there was a client that I'd have for six and a half years. . . . She said, "Are you mad at me all the time?" I said, "No, I'm not." She said, "You look mad all the time." She said, "Your eyes are the same, but the rest of your face is telling me you didn't want to talk to me." I have to work hard to make sure clients don't think this. I noticed other clients are more at ease with me when my Botox is kicked in. . . . Thank goodness that's covered now. Even with it, I have to compensate all the time or everyone thinks I'm mad.

Hence, in addition to her professional responsibilities, Ellie must constantly manage her affect, adding a distracting burden to the process of care.

Similarly, Patti D., who had recently retired after years in a sociable work environment, was looking for a new group with whom to socialize. She became aware that synkinesis was negatively impacting impressions about her—sending the wrong message about her desire to socialize. She described new (and sometimes old) friends always questioning her affect:

People always think I'm unhappy or mad. They would say things like, "Are you mad?" and I would just tell people, "No, I'm not mad." "Oh, well, you just look unhappy." And I'm like, "Oh that's just how I look." And it would be people that I knew pretty well, who knew what I live with, and they would still say things like that every now and then. And they weren't trying to be mean.

And I socialize less. Maybe some people stay away from me possibly because they think I look mad, or unhappy . . . I don't know. They didn't say they were staying away, but you know, maybe you do put off an air like that 'cause you do look . . . the look that you have when you're trying not to smile a lot. . . . You don't wanna smile a whole lot because it's lopsided, and it looks silly.

So you try to have a little half-smile or just a straight face as part of the relaxation technique that they teach you when you're going through the physical therapy. The stuff is to relax your face. But when you totally relax your face, you just look like kinda so hammered down or mad. It's just the way you look. So I work to keep that pleasant look, but it's work.

My study participants described inadvertent miscommunication even with those with whom they were most connected. Mark E., who was introduced in previous chapters, noted his inadvertent expressions triggered hostile responses from his kids: "Yeah, I think there were, and sometimes still are, a lot of problems between the kids and me because they misread my face, and there are a lot more fights because of that. Maybe I am upset or a little annoyed but not really, or [it's] about something else, something from work, whatever . . . and I'll try to be subtle about something, but it just doesn't look subtle that I'm upset. But I guess it looks like I'm really upset, and then all hell breaks loose when it wasn't a big deal."

Cathy R. is a cisgendered, white educator who, despite her relative privilege, found her young children's reactions difficult: "So it's difficult. It was difficult because my one-year-old didn't recognize me from my facial expressions because we communicate through smiles and then I just stopped smiling. It took a while before he would come around me again, which really, really hurt me—my kids not being able to see me like this. I'm not bothered about society; it's my kids seeing a happy mom, that matters. . . . And it broke my heart that I couldn't be that—or even when I was, to look that way."

A pleasant countenance is a valuable form of capital, used in social and professional situations. During an hour-long training session recently, I was reminded at least four times that it is essential to smile. I cannot smile; what they meant was I needed to appear pleasant, which I can do. It's much harder work for me now than it used to me, and it's much harder work for me than it is for someone without synkinesis. At some point I will become tired and forget to manage my face, and then I will be judged.

For many with synkinesis, a relaxed or at-rest face signals displeasure, ill temper, or a bad mood to others, so the face must be constantly managed. Being focused or being intent on something seems to increase both the tightness and the misperceptions. Many have mentioned to me that their mood was questioned when they were focused on work or a task. While we are focusing, we may forget to manage our face, resulting in inadvertent communication. As previously discussed, this can impede our ability to work and to socialize. For instance, clients who perceive their home health aide is "angry with them" may prefer a different aide; students who see my unmanaged face may prefer a different professor. If one's resting face upsets family members, one cannot "relax" or take a break from facial management—ever. It is exhausting. There is an internalized cost to having to always remember to manage one's face to prevent offending or upsetting others.

Synkinesis disrupts communication in problematic ways. Having interviewed those with varying degrees and causes of facial paralysis, and as someone with synkinesis myself, I am in the strange and somewhat unique position to offer a range of insights from both sides. Although my perspective is hardly universal, one thing I observed was that full facial paralysis tends to create a general sense of confusion during interactions. Even with my experience and training, a feeling of general confusion would creep in as a result of the lack of information derived from affect. The anxiety would unsettle me: Is this person unhappy? Wasn't my joke funny? Is this person angry at me? In the back of my mind, the idea that the interaction wasn't smooth or comfortable would worry at me. Synkinesis made the situation even more difficult. Speaking with other people who had synkinesis left me feeling anxious and confused. I was getting contradictory feedback. What was I doing wrong? These people had volunteered to talk to me, and they seemed happy to be doing it, but something I was doing was disrupting our communication—I kept getting this weird feeling.

To really focus on the research, I had developed coping skills. During interviews, as I was listening I found myself almost completely erasing the face and instead focusing on voices, gestures, and tone as the interviews progressed and deepened. As I focused intensely on the interview process, my brain subconsciously was creating a space that protected me from the confusion created by the faces. People often were disturbed by their own face as we interacted (or maybe by mine). Almost everyone who did an on-camera interview with me commented on how much worse their faces looked than they had imagined.

I myself experience this sensation daily during video calls: I imagine myself as normal, and I even feel normal much of the time, but the way I look is disturbing if I don't angle my head exactly right while I speak. One participant sat with only the unaffected side of his face angled toward the camera for most of the interview. When I pointed this out, he shifted his stance on camera—but he quickly reverted after he had watched himself speak. Others acknowledged or lamented how much more obvious or worse the synkinesis was when they were active or speaking; many mentioned feeling distressed by watching their own image throughout the interview. Various participants noted that the unease engendered by our facial difference was mirrored back to them in their daily interactions. During the COVID-19 pandemic, many shared that they appreciated the leveling of the playing field that masks afforded; many have expressed a little regret over the return to necessary facial management and display.

Speaking with experts like Jackie Diels, and Kathleen Bogart clued me in. Facial communication is a complicated process that involves unconscious mimicry (Riehle, Kempkensteffen, and Lincoln 2017). As we communicate with others, we mimic their facial expressions and "take on" the emotional state of our compatriot. Communicating includes a sharing of feeling through culturally normative expressions. This mimicry brings people together, re-creating moments and feelings through shared expressions and ultimately shared feelings (Ruusuvuori and Peräkylä 2009). Synkinesis fundamentally disrupts the subconscious aspects of communication.

This tendency toward mimicry and the problems with mimicking abnormal expressions were captured by Maria M., a Latina with an associate's degree, whose acoustic neuroma surgery had left her with permanent facial paralysis. She commented that others subconsciously mimicked some of her adaptive facial gestures during conversations:

> I notice when people talk to me they tend to do this thing they don't do otherwise: their lips go sideways, like mine. . . . Like, for example, my daughter and one of my clients, when they talk to me face to face, their lip was going sideways talking to me. Two of them actually do this; another client does it, too . . . their lips tend to go sideways as they speak to me.

So I asked my daughter why—why do you do that? She says, "I can't help it. I look at you." And when my lip goes sideways, she said she just does it. . . . It's disturbing. It looks weird. I wish they didn't do it.

As we mirror and share, something is off. It's confusing and disruptive. It makes you uncomfortable and anxious, and that is mirrored to me; back and forth, we transmit vaguely "off feelings." Half my face mirrors back your emotion, while the other half signals stress, anger, pain, or displeasure. My spouse often tells me that he simply looks at one side of my face and ignores the other. It's practical, it's honest, and I hate hearing it. But the reality is that at a subconscious level communicating with someone with synkinesis is problematic. A vague disquiet is the thing we aren't supposed to mention. It's the moment of what Goffman referred to as "identity spoilt."

This tendency to downplay or hide the impact of synkinesis is not out of the ordinary. Those with stigma and those who notice it experience social pressure to hide or ignore it. In the previous chapter we discussed passing more generally; as Goffman (1963) highlighted, the impulse and expectation are that one would hide a "discrediting attribute." It is expected that those with stigma manage it such that it does not burden those without. This leaves people with synkinesis in a situation in which they have a condition that is negatively impacting their ability to emote and communicate, but to remove the burden is to remove ourselves. It is normalized that we believe that we are somehow fundamentally less deserving of social interaction. And honestly, that is seriously f-cked up.

Returning to the idea of "social disability," my participants acknowledged the internal struggle that synkinesis was creating while also lamenting the inability of the social world to adjust, adapt, and assist them. Lois Z., a cisgendered Jewish healthcare professional with a graduate degree, articulated her frustration:

The other thing that is just so-so about this is my face does not animate. There's an animation aspect, especially with my people, you know, being Jewish. When you're Jewish, there's this cultural difference. We're very animated. We are lively, and we interrupt each other, and that's a normal conversation. I can't hear it—you know, I got an auditory-processing thing problem now, too. I can't keep up; I can't animate. A smile barely reaches my face. I have to make a smile very consciously, or it just doesn't happen because the brain connection is broken. If I'm relaxed, people will often say, "Oh, you look tired," or like "You are having a really hard time." And I'm like, "No, I'm just fine, you know, it's just my face. I told you before. It's not a reflection of what is going on with me." So interaction is exhausting, and I end up feeling like I'm not expressing myself. I end up feeling a little left out.

Similarly, Marcy H., who was introduced previously, lamented the inability to share a happy moment: "It's the emotional expression. We've lost that, and that's profound—it really is. It is the inability to share with people that you like them or that you're happy or to be happy with them, and just like to share how you feel because . . . you're always, you're frozen slightly."

There's something in our head disrupting communication, and it's impacting the ability to form communicative relationships. It's not just that we can't express ourselves; it's that we are inadvertently misexpressing and constantly having to compensate for our unacknowledged communicative faux pas. There are layers of stigma and ongoing experiences of microaggressions infusing our expectations. Your confusion and our disability are mirrored in your face, and then my face, and then your face. . . . And now we are both confused, anxious, and frustrated. I just want to go home.

Expression Matters More for Nonprivileged Identity Categories

Feedback from those with synkinesis and from surgeons, occupations/physical therapists, and others who work with individuals with synkinesis has led me to conclude that the impact on social life, communication, sense of self, and identity is something everyone experiences as problematic. However, the scope and scale vary tremendously. Stuart Hall (1983) reminds us of the ways that inequitable systems infuse ideologies that impact how we think, act, and react. The potency of Pierre Bourdieu's (1984) concept of *habitus* is that embodiment is an ongoing process that reifies social relations. Expectations and opportunities shape our skills and capabilities, beliefs, understandings, and ways of being. As our identity changes over time and as the meanings of categories in the social world shift, our ways of being and knowing evolve and adjust.

Internalization is not simply a psychological by-product of relations of power and privilege; it's how they are (re)produced. Physical ways of being in the world are learned through ongoing interaction, and they (re)produce our social locations and the salience of said categories. The exercise of power includes the ability to create context of meaning for identities and behaviors. Whether the smile is most likely to be viewed as inviting, authentic, or smarmy or the lack of smile as reserve, malintent, or ill humor reflects systemic power and privilege. The system creates more believable narratives about some identities, and the concomitant conditions create context. The exercise of power includes the ability to control the narrative.

Synkinesis leaves one perpetually struggling to communicate and inadvertently miscommunicating. The further one's identity is from empowered positions, the more crucial the performance to distance oneself from stigma or invalidating attributes. For example, bias can infuse interpretations of nonverbal expressions, specifically anger (Becker, Neel, and Anderson 2010). What expression means, set against the context of identity, is how power is exhibited in the narrative. Is my anger justified, disproportionate, or dangerous?

Specialists in the field report that women are far more likely to seek surgical or less invasive interventions such as fillers, Botox injections, or fat replacement after synkinesis (one surgeon put the discrepancy at about nine to one). Women also are more likely to attend support groups and be involved in advocacy work. Although these gender differences in cosmetic surgery and support group attendance do exist, with facial difference an additional factor may be at play.

Gender differences in the use of and ability to interpret facial and nonverbal cues (Nelson and Brown 2012) have been noted. Women use facial and nonverbal cues more in communication, while men have been shown to rely more on purely verbal interaction (Gore 2009). Women also tend to read nonverbal interaction more accurately (La France et al. 2009). This may mean the loss of the nonverbal is even more profound for women, who have learned to rely more on these aspects of communication.[1]

The nonverbal is also a key arena in which narratives are constructed: the knowing glance, the eye roll, the inside smirk, the slight pursing of the lips, and the side eye and the modified side eye. With simple eye contact one can signal belonging, inclusion, solidarity, irony, or connection. Synkinesis disrupts the subtleties of positionality in social interaction, in ways that are especially problematic for those not in privileged or dominant categories.

The history of gender in Western culture is that of women's objectification (Dworkin and Wachs 2009). Modern gender roles center around women as nurturers, caregivers, homemakers, and pleasant objects (West and Zimmerman 1987). Gendered expectations that place greater value on physical appeal, congeniality, and amiability still structure social relations. (An unsmiling face has far more positive connotations for a masterful subject than for a gratifying object.) In Western culture, women are expected to do a tremendous amount of emotional labor to maintain harmonious social relations (Bates 2016). To not be able to be appropriately expressive is to not be able to "do gender" for women in Western culture. Recall the microaggressions involving accusations of public drunkenness and ill temper that were described in chapter 3; the perceptions of these behaviors varied by acknowledged identity category.

As I listened to many stories told by people with synkinesis, trends emerged. Expression and the meaning of expression is raced, gendered, classed, sexualized, and tied to age and myriad other culturally relevant categories. Like most interview studies, women were more likely to volunteer, but the differences in response rates exceeded normal expectations. For women and for professional or service-sector workers, the misperceptions of mood and loss of nonverbal communication were especially troubling. Demeanor and nonverbal communication were being used more by this group: they were more essential for their professional life.

88 METAMORPHOSIS

Although it would be hard to generalize about intersections of gender and race, there certainly is evidence that responses to a non-normative affect are influenced by a history of raced and classed expectations. My first on-the-record interview with a person with synkinesis was a multiethnic (probably seen as African American or Black by others) older woman who had returned to school at her local community college. As she supported herself with an online business she also attended classes and worked from home. She recounted having unpleasant encounters with campus security and then being perceived as "insane" rather than in need of assistance when she arrived at the emergency room with severe Bell's palsy.

The perception of "crazy and dangerous" rather than frightened and vulnerable as related to racial status needs further exploration. Microaggressions are known to undermine the quality of care for nonwhite patients (Freeman and Stewart 2018), and we must consider the potential impact of race coupled with a disorder that negatively impacts communication. Those who exist at the confluence of more marginalized, disempowered, discredited, or discriminated against identities will face the most difficult challenges.

Compensatory Strategies

Compensatory strategies are tactics employed to make up for the deficit left by being unable to communicate through nonverbal facial expression. Kathleen Bogart's work (2014, 2015) beautifully illustrates the development of compensatory strategies by those with congenital facial paralysis. Hand gestures, eye contact, verbal cues, and alternative means of expression such as with clothing were all strategies adopted by people as they strove to re-establish communication. Recall the story of replacing a smile with a friendly wave, to elicit appropriate response. What struck me was how clearly people understood what a small smile could communicate—how much we communicate in an unthought expression and how tremendous its loss can be. Another of my participants noticed that others avoided and addressed this with verbal acknowledgments of her facial difference. Lois Z., introduced earlier this chapter, noted,

> Now in public, I'm sure to make an effort to communicate. When I was more paralyzed, I saw how it affected salespeople. I would go out in the world, and I would be there to buy something, and salespeople would look unhappy. They didn't want to interact with me. They mistook this paralysis [to mean] that I was maybe a disagreeable, undesirable person. I would combat that by saying, "You know, my face is paralyzed; I'm actually a really pleasant, warm, and friendly person." Then they would listen up. I tried to show them with my eyes or gestures, other ways, to show them my goodwill. There's that big impact in the world when your face doesn't work.

IT'S MY FACE—WHY THAT MATTERS

In addition to immediate communication, we are all generally communicating through our presentation of self. Bogart (2015) highlighted compensatory strategies such as fashion to mitigate the impact of disrupted identity communication. Two examples among my participants were Vero R., a Latina cisgendered college student, and Teri B., a white, cisgendered woman with a graduate school education. Both had ended up with synkinesis in their teens, Vero from an acoustic neuroma and Teri from Bell's palsy. Both used fashion to rebuild a confident expressive social self. Vero remarked,

> This destroyed my confidence—it changed dramatically. Like it was completely a 180°. I was pretty confident with myself before, but now it's—after it—it was just totally. . . . No one made fun of me to my face, but I heard from friends and staff that people made fun of me behind my back.
>
> So I kind of just forced myself in a way to go out of my comfort zone because I knew my confidence was already shot, so I just wore really outlandish things and created a new fashion for me instead. Just like colorful, like any colors I can find, or have these like really bright—like highlighter-yellow sneaker boots, they were just craziest thing, but they always got compliments . . . [with] a matching, like, yellow-highlighter vest and my bright red lips so people would notice my lips, you know, not the paralysis.
>
> I don't know, it's kind of, like, weird to me, the opposite of before. Before, I wore dark clothes. . . . But because of [synkinesis], I just want to walk around like a peacock. So people would notice that and comment on that rather than the facial paralysis.

Similarly, Teri B acknowledged,

> You know, I always kind of like having a cute outfit—having things that take attention away from your crooked face, you know? Whether, like, having a different hairdo or, you know, like you, like your dress. I've always had, and maybe this is some psychological subconscious thing, but I've always been really well known for my shoes—for having super cute shoes. I have a lot of cute cowboy boots, you know? I wear cowboy boots with skirts. Like, I've always been really famous for the footwear, and maybe I do that for a reason. Like, look down, over there, you know? Like, don't look at my face, look at my feet. All I know is I have really nice hair. It's that, like, long blonde hair naturally, and obviously not anymore, but you know. Maybe there is some compensation with those things.

Several mentioned fashion—outrageous fashion and specifically shoes—as attention-getters, conversation starters, or professional persona enhancers. I have a rather impressive collection of John Fluevog shoes for this reason, and when I have finished this book I will treat myself to the electric blue boots I've

METAMORPHOSIS

been coveting (Sabado boots in blue). And while we all found our strategies, some reflected on going overboard in their attempts to compensate.

Overcompensating

Given the initial shock, it's not surprising that people sometimes overcompensated as they attempted to reforge a social self. With a graduate degree and a successful career as an educator, Latine Abby B. had some discretionary income. However, she recognized that she was attempting to make up for what she had lost rather than expressing who she is, and she adjusted:

> I read in some article, like, "Oh, you know what? Not everyone is just going to see your face. It depends on how you dress too and how you can put yourself together." And so, then, yes, it was then I got super-obsessed with everything else. Like, it must be dialed in, you know? I went on a big shopping spree and then like didn't eat for a whole summer, you know what I mean? And I looked great. We're just, "I'm going to get—everything else is going to be perfect." My clothes, my body, my hair, everything. . . . In the end, it's like, "Well, that's been pretty exhausting." And it was expensive. So it wasn't sustainable. And it wasn't going to fix my face.

Abby still stayed fit and invested in her personal style and appearance, but she no longer demanded the perfection she initially thought was necessary to compensate for her facial difference.

Caitlin Marie, a cisgendered graduate school–educated, mixed-race healthcare professional, mentions feeling pressure to perfect her appearance as a solution to overcoming what seemed to be her inability to connect with some people after a tumor removal had induced synkinesis:

> I don't consider myself a highly judgmental person, but I can read a situation, and I can kind of read when somebody is sizing me up based on my appearance versus somebody who's actually connecting with me. The people that you can tell are very appearance-based, they make me uncomfortable. Or they did—more so in the past, more so when I felt very vulnerable. I don't feel as vulnerable now because I'm taking more ownership of who I am, and I have made much greater peace with my imperfections than I did back then.
>
> At the time, it was kind of like I was thrown into the deep end of the pool, and I was attached to trying to look as perfect as I could. Now I have come to terms with how silly all that is. But when I was in the throes of it before I healed up myself, I was still very vulnerable to how imperfect I had now become. This would be around people; you could tell no hair was

ever out of place, and here I was with my entire face being out of place, and feeling like I had spinach in my teeth or something.

People with disabilities report that most people, even when they believe they are inclusive, are unable to genuinely connect (Darling 2019). People with synkinesis generally have an acquired disability, already have internalized disability stigma, and lack a protective reference group as they restructure their identity. The perpetual feeling of 'always having spinach in one's teeth' resonated.

Given that most of us are not interacting in front of mirrors most of the time, it's not "how we look" that creates problems during interactions but rather the reactions of others. Let us return to the concept of "social death" versus "social disability." To some degree, social death is the macro expression of the micro experience of social disability.

Social death refers to a concept introduced by Zygmunt Bauman (1992) for the experience of those viewed as less than human. Social death hinges on the larger society's perceptions, beliefs, assumptions, and ascriptions. Social death is the creation of a category of vulnerability onto which negative ascriptions can be readily attached. The role of social death in the holocaust and slavery has been well studied. Social death and the treatment of those perceived to be disabled also has been clearly documented (Dell Orto and Power 2007). Michael Hughes (1998) and later Heather Laine Talley (2014) have specifically applied these ideas to facial difference. Talley (2014) describes three criteria that trigger social death as a result of facial difference: (1) indispensable facets of social, economic, and physical life are impacted; (2) social interaction and communication are threatened; and (3) universal human traits are impaired or absent (such as the smile). Although people with synkinesis experience varying degrees of challenges in these areas, it's not social death so much as a social disability that requires ongoing compensatory intervention to manage.

Those with options seek to minimize the factors that allow for their identification with stigmatized categories. The assumptions embedded in the work we do to "compensate" for our disability are fundamentally ideological repair work. It is essential to understand the needs of people within the current system differently from the fundamental systemic challenge embedded within our experiences. This essential contradiction has long undermined and divided movements, as is its role. The logic of the system is the masters' tools.

The Meaning of Disfigurement and the Value of Intervention

I think I'm a very strong woman. Of course, it has affected me. I say I'm pretty strong, but sometimes I look at my old photos and I do cry. I look at it, and it does make me sad because that's a new face. Yeah, you never think after you turn thirty you get a brand-new face. So it's really hard to accept. It makes it easier to joke about it, but when I'm by myself and think about it, it does hurt. When I have time, I can use makeup to make it look more symmetrical, and I like that; but it's expensive, and it takes time. (Vi V.)

Disfigurement exists as a social category or designation rather than a medical or diagnostic one (Foucault 1972, 1999; Talley 2014). *Deformity* refers more often to a congenital difference whereas *disfigurement* generally refers to conditions that are acquired (Hughes 1998). People who are deformed or disfigured are obscured and simultaneously hypervisible for overlapping and interrelated reasons.

Deformity carries the social stigma of being viewed as not fully human status whereas disfigurement carries the tragedy of formerly human status, embedded with fear and blame. As Talley (2014) puts it, "the specter of disfigurement . . . saturates our collective imagination" (11). Historically, freak shows monetized visual difference (Bogdan 1990), ugly laws shaped public visibility (Schweik 2009), and informal social norms communicated the objectification of the disabled and disfigured (Garland-Thomson 2009). Certainly, people with facial paralysis recognized their membership in a cultural category linked with a specific set of negative associations.

About a month after my own onset, I traveled to Costa Rica for a trip with my partner. Trying to enjoy myself despite dealing with slow healing, I smiled at a child as we explored on a hike. Terror filled her face, and she ran crying to her family about "la monstrua." Even if I didn't have a basic knowledge of Spanish (which I do), I would have understood. It was jarring and crushing. Negotiating postcolonial imperialism as a tourist is challenging enough; to be the monster who frightens children is a major self-image adjustment. Nor was I alone in this. Hilary S., a successful and attractive cisgendered white artist who had just turned thirty, still recalls the pain of hearing from another artist that she was indeed a freak, a monster:

I had a friend when I first got Bell's palsy. And I was thirty and attractive, but I didn't really think about it. This friend of mine—well, not really a friend after this—said, "Oh, I am going to film you. I want to make a movie about you. It's so weird what happened to you. This is so weird and how you transformed. . . . You were normal, and you've become a monster before our very eyes, and I want to make a movie about it." And I couldn't believe it. You know, these kinds of reactions from people were so horrifying. At that time, I was thirty, and I was a beauty . . . and then all of a sudden I was a real freak of nature. To be told I had become a monster. . . . That was . . . [she trailed off shaking her head].

Our cultural imagination leaves few other options for those with facial difference. The power of ideology is that one's transformation is channeled toward understandings consistent with the existing relations, norms, values, meanings, actions, and beings (Hall 1983).

Why is this shift such a devastating change? Why are we so driven to extinguish that which marks the other? Within our current ideological framework, what does our otherness do? The market creates, and solves, our problems within a specific set of logics. Within racial capitalism, the other occupies several necessary spaces. The labor of the other is infinitely exploitable, and the other's presence reinforces the value of not being in that position (Robinson 1983). But the other is also a means to generate consent and consumption, to valorize daily practices that serve systemic needs (Dworkin and Wachs 2009). We demonstrate our moral rectitude through our performance of that which is not other. In my previous work, Shari Dworkin and I explored the creation of gendered bodies in which "deviance" is exorcised with exercise. "Deserving" bodies demonstrated their engagement via a host of practices designed to create appropriately gendered bodies dependent on consumer-based enactments. The market created and solved a host of gendered bodily failures, creating and then assuaging anxiety. Conflations of health and fitness with appearance, regardless of actual health benefits, was a key finding.

Where we are most vulnerable is where cultural indoctrination is most impactful. What appears as "common sense" reflects consent to, engagement with, and action through social structures (Hall 1983). "Looking different" in ways associated with disease, immorality, vulnerability, and social devaluation, especially in a society increasingly monetizing appearance, is problematic. Disfigurement carries an additional burden of deeply internalized blame and guilt. For individuals with Bell's palsy, failing to recover when 71 percent do make a full recovery (Peiterson 2002) often prompts additional self-flagellation: people routinely cited "faults" like working too hard, a stressful lifestyle, and even karma for not being kind enough to others as tied into their condition. If it was the result of a personal failing, couldn't we fix it by fixing the failing? Or fix the failing by fixing this? Shouldn't we be doing or trying *something*? Most people had tried a range of things—some medically prescribed and proven, some not, and others potentially harmful. But doing "something" was framed exactly as one would expect in our current system.

It's not surprising that a neoliberal market system would offer entirely individualized consumer-based products and services. Synkinesis is a rare condition and very poorly understood. The obscurity of the condition, the advocacy necessary for coverage of treatment, and the limited number of people with expertise leaves most paying out of pocket for all but the most basic treatment. Botox (botulinum toxin type A) injections are the most common treatment for pain and asymmetry. Even with a doctor spouse who could throw around medical terms, my own doctorate, and several childhood friends who worked for my healthcare provider, it took me years to obtain the right care and coverage for my pain management. During that process, I experienced lots of useless visits and an unnecessary spinal tap, with subsequent complications. All but one of my surgeries (turns out I had a severely deviated septum and couldn't breathe either!) were paid for by me; though I may not be able to retire on time now, I can sort of smile about it. More importantly, I feel only mild discomfort as opposed to the eternally tightening muscles in the side of my neck, face, and jaw.

Herein lies one of the most disturbing things I encountered. Because the condition is not well understood, myriad "treatments" are recommended, most of which involve paying out of pocket. There's not enough clear evidence at this point to render a judgment about their efficacy. Some treatments may alleviate discomfort, and others may enhance appearance; some may do both, and others do nothing. A few of those I interviewed noted that a treatment might or might not be working, but they found the practitioner to be a skilled sympathetic listener and therefore a worthwhile short-term investment.

For me, a combination of neuromuscular retraining, surgeries, and Botox gave me back some functionality, the ability to pass if I don't speak much, and a significant reduction in my constant discomfort, pain, and tightness. Given the pain and stigma, many have reported spending a considerable amount of time and money attempting to return to "normal"—or at least attempting to be in less pain, communicate more clearly, and feel less disturbance. They found a world of proffered treatments, with little guidance about their efficacy or appropriateness. It seemed that what constitutes treatment varies tremendously within and between medical professionals, patients, and kin. The trade-offs between addressing functionality, aesthetics, communication, pain, and long-term structural problematics can be difficult to navigate. There is a lot of snake oil out there, even well-meaning practitioners may be inadvertently selling it. As a result, many of those I spoke with felt abandoned by healthcare providers and taken advantage of by homeopathic practitioners. Several recounted filing for bankruptcy after insurance failed to cover their treatments, but their pain and appearance still led them to try whatever they hoped might work.

Although most patients with acquired facial difference and synkinesis desired or were engaging in some types of interventions, some had found family and friends resistant to their treatment attempts. The medical interventions that also improve appearance were often viewed as some sort of unearned entitlement. A noteworthy number of participants reported at least some resistance in their support networks to even the most mundane and standard of treatments. Jen P., a white, cisgendered woman working in the entertainment industry, found her friends were shocked at the price tag for the Botox injections that she considered a necessity to provide relief from pain and to enhance her ability to communicate:

> "1,500 dollars for corrective Botox? Why? You look fine." "You look fine! Why would you spend that kind of money? Oh, that's silly." "Ah, 1,500 dollars? I can take my family on a trip. Jeez." "Really, every three months you're going to do that? Why bother? You look fine. You must not care about money like me."
>
> I get that, you know. It's a lot of money. But I'm in pain. And I feel awful about how I look, and I slur my speech . . . I wish it was covered.

We had a laugh over the fact they were telling her she looked fine *with* Botox, not without it: if she looks fine and is communicating effectively, *the treatment is working*. It's *not* something she doesn't need.

I try to imagine the same conversation about a treatment that, say, eliminated a limp so someone could walk effectively and without pain. I imagine a friend would be shocked that my healthcare provider was failing to cover my necessary treatment in that situation. One of my participants drew upon her own experiences to highlight this disparity in treatment. White, college-educated, middle-aged, cisgendered Emily A. was a breast cancer survivor with synkinesis. She shared her ongoing frustration at the unwillingness of her healthcare insurer to cover procedures to restore symmetry to her face, despite having her postmastectomy breast reconstruction fully covered by the same provider. Restoring her breast after surgery was essential to her self-esteem she had been assured. With disbelief she recounted them denying her any surgery to restore her facial symmetry: "This I could hide [she gestured to her breasts]. This everyone can see [she gestured to her face]. How can this not be a health condition negatively impacting my self-esteem?"

The study participants in the United States found that their insurance often considered treatments for synkinesis "aesthetic" rather than functional and refused coverage. Meanwhile, the main complaints at the support groups involved pain and problems related to vision, dental, and communication.

Given cultural ideologies that valorize overcoming or rendering disability irrelevant (Clare 2017; Davis 1995), why is the face viewed with more ambiguity? Facial difference, damage, or deformity is conflated with moral degeneration (Bogdan 1990; Schweik 2009; Talley 2014). In addition, dominant ableist ideologies result in disability being viewed as discrediting and isolating (Wendell 1996). To be disfigured is to deserve disfigurement. Both my study participants and those around them sometimes spoke in terms of guilt or blame. The ongoing use of popular culture using facial difference to signal malintent, mental instability, or evil has rendered visible a history of classism[2] and ableism. For those in for-profit healthcare systems, such as in the United States, obviously the goals of healthcare providers are always at odds with ideal patient care, yet even beyond the failures of market systems the covered treatments were especially inadequate. Given the ubiquity of microaggressions, discrimination, blame, and heightened unwanted visibility, it's not surprising that many sought out treatments that would make them both feel and look as they had before.

Research has demonstrated that when an individual is initially psychologically healthy, facial reconstruction can improve self-image and reduce negative feelings (Hughes 1998). Although many in my study had experiences with ill advised, poorly applied, or inappropriate treatments, most who sought medically sanctioned treatments from recognized experts were satisfied. Botox injections, surgery, and occupational therapy or physical therapy with someone specifically trained were the standard treatments for synkinesis. Generally, my participants had a combination of three goals when they did seek treatment: improvement in function (communication, eating, eye management, and so forth), reduction in pain, and returning symmetry to their appearance. However, most faced challenges in receiving treatment even for pain management.

The High Cost of Normal

Increasingly, visual investiture is an expected necessity. The heightened visuality of postmodern consumer culture engenders a centering of specific presentation of selves. Having a "different" appearance is something defined within the larger cultural context and is a social structural issue. The boundaries of "difference," and who is included, and which areas of identity are annihilated in complicit silences remains a site of struggle. Consumer culture includes a strong emphasis on display of simultaneously normative and "authentic" selves (Featherstone 1991a, 1991b; Shilling 2003, 2016). Regardless of identity categories, faces, eyes, and smiles are perceived as central to our genuine display of self. Victorian conflations of health, morality, and appearance reinforce class status and provide ideologies that stigmatize physical differences (Garland-Thomson 2005; Hughes 1998). In my previous work with Shari Dworkin, we noted the copious amount of consumer connected body work that goes into an "authentic" or normative presentation of a physically fit, gendered self (Dworkin and Wachs 2009). Consumer culture generates anxiety for our failures to meet expectations and then offers market-based solutions. Obviously, these "solutions" remain too costly for some and inaccessible for others.

Even for those without facial difference, aging and natural asymmetries can be "corrected" through cosmetic surgery. Social media usage appears to be exacerbating image concerns, especially among young women (Tiggemann and Slater 2013). And appearance concerns are profitable: it's estimated that over their lifetimes women spend almost a quarter of a million dollars on their appearance; men spend about 22 percent less but still almost $200,000 (SWNS 2017).

In 2018, Americans spent over $16.5 billion on cosmetic surgery (American Society of Plastic Surgeons 2018)). Although men are using more body products, cosmetic surgery remains something women are more likely to pursue: in 2018, 90 percent of facelifts were performed on women, and only 13 percent of invasive and 8 percent of minimally invasive procedures were performed on men. Beauty (cosmetics) is a $42 billion a year industry in the United States alone, and sales are rebounding after mask mandates and the global pandemic led to a dip in sales during 2020 and 2021 (Souza 2021). Use of cosmetics by men is increasing, and online tutorials have demonstrated the potential for transformation. Although video filters may make one's online image more palatable, people are now seeking surgeries to achieve the look "in the real" (Kelly 2020). What constitutes "damage" and expected investment in facework is expanding (Talley 2014), and current conflations of appearance and social usefulness recall eugenics, phrenology, and physiognomy.

Appearance justifies classism. One of the key ways that power is symbolically maintained is not through shows of force but through displays of wealth and luxury (Veblen [1899] 1994). Beauty is a way of displaying advantage in a way that seems to justify or explain one's position. Hence, the tendency for family and friends to discourage actively paying for treatment reveals the complexity of a society that highly values appearance but eschews the social climbing implications of "investment" in appearance. Recall the conflations of "health" and "fitness" that infuse moral legitimacy into some bodily practices commensurate with privilege.

The Face and Physical Capital

Appearance is a valuable form of physical capital. In the previous chapter, facial difference as a marker of stigma was highlighted. Individuals with facial difference tend to experience some social isolation or discrimination (Hughes 1998), and the participants in my study were no exception. Social discrimination is predictive of internalization and negative impacts on self-esteem (Brown, Sellers, and Gomez 2002). As I have discussed, it becomes difficult to align a positive presentation of self with an abnormal facial presentation/function unless compensatory actions are taken (Bogart, Tickle-Degnen, and Ambady 2014; Bogart and Tickle-Degnen 2015). But it's not only about internalizing stigma—faces are also useful and valuable, and the loss of facial expression is frustrating.

The face is a critical part of the performance of self and a way to display socially desirable attributes (Goffman 1967). Talley (2014) highlights the face as metaphoric in the "saving face" way (25), but it is also of direct importance in terms of the growing centrality of facial appearance in Western culture. The face serves as a valuable biosocial resource and is a form of physical capital in appearance and functionality as a medium of communication (Talley 2014). Recall the concept of capital introduced in chapter 2. Bourdieu (1984) introduces the idea of a range of valuable resources or different forms of capital. The term habitus is used by Bourdieu to highlight how social status or social location is embodied. Taste provides a critical example because it creates a shared experience and reproduces existing social relations.

Loïc Wacquant bridges the gap between capital and habitus with the idea of physical capital, which is the value of our developed physical abilities (1995a, 1995b). One's developed habitus is a form of capital. The professorial mode I unconsciously adopt as I step onto campus is a physically different self than is present in other places, but that self commands attention and respect, and I can pull it out when necessary in any situation. To chit chat, schmooze, or socialize is a learned, acquired, embodied physical skill that varies depending on context, and how one uses one's face during that process can be critical. A pleasant or affable demeanor is a valuable form of capital, that many, especially those in service professions, have honed. Regardless of whether one is a lawyer or a home health aide, each role has a specific facial language that facilitates it.

Moreover, the face can grant one access to other forms of capital. For example, the face is a valuable tool in the acquisition of social capital or connections (Talley 2014). It's not just that a pretty face is valuable, but that knowing how to use one's face to communicate or not communicate, to share or elicit expressions, is a valuable form of capital. As we code switch between salient identity categories, we demonstrate facial competencies for different identities. For many of those I interviewed, suddenly losing a resource—having it become instead an impediment—was devastating. It's not just that I am not as attractive as I once was but that I can't participate socially in the same way. I can't draw on innumerable expressive gestures, honed over years of social interaction, to get the appropriate social result. And that is an enormous loss.

Laura M. works in marketing. After developing her networking skills in college, she lamented the loss of a valuable asset: the ability to use her face.

> It's like a tennis player breaking a wrist and [not] being able to play tennis anymore. And that [was] a thing that gives them joy. And it doesn't ruin his or her life overall, but, like, the tool in the toolbox that makes them happy, that makes one's life [gestures expansively]. . . . And the smile, my face, for socializing, for work, for all sorts of things. . . . When it's gone, you know, it's like it just—it felt like one of these essential tools in my toolbox was gone. And also like an essential piece of who I am is gone.
>
> It's not that people don't talk to me anymore or that I don't make connections. . . . Maybe I'm the only person who even gives a shit. In our meeting last week, it was like nobody cares, nobody cares that I don't smile. Nobody cares, you know. Maybe they do, I don't know, but once they know me . . . nobody cares. The only person who cares is me.

> So it's not that other people aren't talking to me or that I don't have good friendships or that I wasn't, you know, I am able to get a job. But the heartbreak has to do with, like, how I move inside my own body [and] how I use the tools of my face for connection and communication were lost, and it's so much harder.

Certainly, professional women, especially those who work in service occupations, are vastly overrepresented in this study, but this is also the group for whom this loss of capital may be most impactful. I think/know/live that going from being relatively attractive, with a well-organized set of expressions designed to elicit positive responses, to having an appearance that may range from vaguely disquieting to rather noticeably disfigured is jarring. Recall that gender differences in the use and understanding of nonverbal communication do exist (Nelson and Brown 2012), so perhaps it's a greater loss for women. Also, women may be more aware of others' mixed and complicated responses.

Communication Capital

Communication capital is our learned and developed ability to communicate. It varies depending on social location and is a valuable competency; many people code switch between different styles. Faces are a form of investable physical capital. The ability to maximize socially normative facial aesthetics is a valuable resource (Talley 2014). Those with facial impairment are at a significant social disadvantage, especially with initial meetings and first impressions (Hughes 1998). As social, cultural, material, and technological changes have combined to foreground visual display, those with facial paralysis are disadvantaged for a critical means of identity enactment. An easy example would be the centrality of appearance to elections since the advent of television (Croteau and Hoynes 2019).

Unfortunately, visible disfigurement or difference is conflated with blame and stigma. The idea that immorality is written on one's visage is a vestige of Victorian sensibilities and has been carried forward in cultural depictions (Foucault 1999; Hughes 1998). So often villains in popular movies carry some marker of facial difference. One exception would be Deadpool, the visibly scared antihero—who was initially a villain. Two-Face, the Batman villain, has a face that is described as normal on one side and disfigured with acid on the other; after his face is restored through surgery, he is no longer a villain, but he reverts to crime after redisfigurement. The James Bond movie franchise also has long symbolized evil intentions with facial differences.

The discrediting nature of visible difference means an immediate removal from the category of normal (Foucault 1999). Not being considered normal generally removes one from access to certain rights and expectations

METAMORPHOSIS

of competencies. The idea of a social disability foregrounds the ways in which the individual is left to seek solutions, with relative privilege gatekeeping access. It also provides a point from which to unify and organize. More often, members of the community are registering their displeasure, speaking up, organizing campaigns, and providing alternative examples to challenge how people with facial difference are being presented and understood. But communication is also an experience of self; most have shared a poignant struggle with adapting to an altered internal experience, which is the topic of the next chapter.

5

Disrupted Selves

I just lost that ability to be me and to be happy. I was this happy, confident, outgoing girl that, you know, everybody loved and . . . I wasn't Ms. Popularity, I didn't need to be the center of attention, I was just friendly. I liked to have a laugh with people . . . I loved it when everybody was laughing. . . . I was happy with who I was, and . . . now I feel like I'm so hidden. I don't feel like the same person.

Like I said, I wasn't the center of it all, but I was friendly. Now I'm not that same outgoing person anymore . . . I don't even want to try. . . . Before, I'd always say smile at everyone. Connect. Like, you could smile at somebody that day, and you could do something good by being nice, by connecting. Like, prevent something, like, they might they have the worst day of their lives and that little smile could be a little moment of connection. Maybe cheer someone up who's having a bad day . . . or just make someone smile back. But connect. Show people you care.

And now I've lost that. I've lost that ability to make other people smile back, to connect, and I miss laughing with my boyfriend and stuff, and I just I miss the old me. Who I was, who I liked, it's not me anymore. (Carrie R.)

Because I think it's mostly when you're laughing with people and stuff, it's supposed to be a happy feeling . . . you know, a happy moment. . . . And everybody is feeling happy and stuff, but then occasionally there will be someone new to my life or whatever, and they notice when I'm laughing and I notice, and that kind of takes the happy moment away from me. And I feel it pulling . . . so like I can never be fully be happy in that moment. (Vero R.)

Carrie R., a cisgendered, white, home health aide, and Vero R, the Latina college student introduced in the previous chapter, share the difficulty of experiencing synkinesis, and they highlight two of the critical themes of this chapter: disruption to the experience of self and miscommunication with the self. As someone living with synkinesis myself, it took me a shockingly long time to understand that it's not just about the way you "look." And it's not just about how others treat you; it can be easy to forget about how you look when you aren't receiving feedback. The previous chapters focused on external feedback, but sometimes the feedback isn't external. It can manifest as anxiety about how we look because we don't have other ways to explain it, to process it. I see the annoyance in my spouse and friends. You look fine, they say. It's hardly noticeable. No one notices. (But someone does notice. Always. You can't escape it. That someone matters.)

It took me awhile to figure out because it *feels* like it's about how you look. It *feels* like stress, it *feels* like anxiety, it *feels* like prickles of awareness that come with tension, fear, trepidation, warning, foreboding. It *feels* like something's happened to tighten my neck and jaw—that tightness in the face, always a harbinger, a warning, setting one on edge, a prelude to nothing good. Synkinesis is always forcing one into that state. There is always something distracting from experience, filled with traditional physical manifestations of risk, anxiety, or stress. As hard as a communicative disability can make social interaction, the most troubling, gut-twisting, heart-wrenching, break down and sob about it 'cause it can't be helped or fixed thing is what it does *to the experience of self.*

It's important to recognize that the self is not something one is, but rather is something one is always doing. It is an ongoing series of experiences performed, with ongoing feedback from a complicated, confusing, and often paradoxical social world. That is how we experience self. We spend a long time learning and practicing and mastering our "authentic" performances. It is often pleasurable, and we take pride in our abilities. But synkinesis f-cks all that up.[1] It's more than being launched from an identity of normativity into that of an experience of disability/disfigurement (which may or may not be experienced to varying degrees). Rather, it disrupts the experience of *doing* self, and it undermines the pleasure of *being* self.

Having developed Bell's palsy twice in a six-year period in her twenties, during and after college, Amanda G., who is now in her early thirties, shared that synkinesis impacted her sense of confidence and self in ways she had not experienced when Bell's palsy had fully resolved:

> I mean, most people have some degree of vanity or confidence when they're young. I was very confident with my appearance before Bell's palsy, and even after my first case I didn't have any noticeable residual effects, so I was just as confident after as I was before. With the second bout of Bell's palsy, I was constantly afraid of going out; I didn't want to be seen. I am consistently anxious about my appearance. I don't like it when people notice it. I don't like it when it's called out or attention is drawn to it, and I go out of my way to try to hide it. But it's not just that. It's always in my

head. I can't keep it out of my thoughts when I can feel it all the time, so . . .

Similarly, Maria M., a Latina participant introduced earlier in the book, lamented: "It changed my whole attitude. I was always a bubbly person, I was always laughing, always making people smile, doing funny things to make somebody laugh. . . . And I can't get that back. I tried. During the first year, I was determined to be me again. I was like, I will be me, I will laugh with them, make jokes, still be the person who does something to make someone smile. But I just didn't feel it. I lost part of myself. My mom says, 'You're different, and I don't know why.'"

To some degree, it is the synkinesis. It's a hard thing to express. It took me years of reading theory, interviewing experts, talking to those with synkinesis, and living it myself to gain only a small understanding. Hence, people tend to resort to the only language we have, that it's about how we look. But it's not. It's about disruptions to the fundamental experience of being. And to some degree, that is a really weird statement to make. Although I would like to believe that my unique history opens me to insights, it is also my privilege that leads to valuation of my expression. What does that mean? As a person living with synkinesis, a former athlete and ongoing workout enthusiast, a person with a specialty in the sociology of the body, who has the privilege that education, class status, racial privilege, and a safe childhood confer, I am in a somewhat unique position to compile, articulate, and share insights relating to synkinetic experiences of identity disruption. Yeah, go me! This is a very long way of saying, "About some of this, just trust me." But also understand that privilege infuses all narratives in problematic and contradictory ways.

The self is an embodied thing. It is experienced from a specific subject position, with social relations made material through practice (Bourdieu 1984), and subject locations internalized (Du Bois 2008) and reified through enactment (West and Zimmerman 1987). There are our material selves and our biochemical responses, shaping and shaped by experiences. And there is us, in there having that experience, making meaning and coping. The body is not the self, but the self and body are intertwined. Bodies are imbued with, possessed by, and possess the self simultaneously (Shilling 2012; Turner 2008). The body and the self are experienced and understood with and against a history of social relations that reify (make material) identity categories (Shilling 2012; Turner 2008).

Categorized bodies have norms, roles, and expectations conventionalized and institutionalized (Foucault 1971). The categories reified by the experiences of bodies within webs of identity-based relations shape bodies with experiences, options, opportunities, designations, actions, and reactions. The histories of gender, race, sexuality, class, and other identity categories carry expectations that make material the social relations within our bodies. We become in a world of possibilities, and we don't become things rendered inconceivable.

Assigned categories shape and limit, and these categories serve to make "nature" reflect relations of power and privilege.[2] As we perform identity, there are ever-changing and sometimes conflicting role expectations (Adler and Adler 1991; Goffman 1959). We develop our sense of self with the pride or mortification based on perceived reception (Cooley [1902] 2010; Mead 1934) and the internalization of social location (Bourdieu, Du Bois). Our resistance to it (Foucault) makes our self inseparable from the social world around us.

But it is also us.

The body is something that we simultaneously have and are, a site of being and becoming (Merleau-Ponty [1962] 2012). Acquired disabilities are known to generate feelings of loss of identity, which may be exacerbated by the ableism they (we) have likely internalized from our larger culture (Smart 2009). Erving Goffman (1959) discussed *role strain*, the tension between incompatible norms in our competing roles. For example, when deadlines at work and family events conflict, we experience role strain. Disability is often erroneously assumed to be incompatible with many of the roles that are most meaningful to our sense of identity (Siebers 1995). Sexuality, productive capacity, and social value are largely denied to those living with disabilities as a result. Cultural depictions tend to vary predictably—exceptional savant, vehicle through which a lesson is delivered, psychotic killer—but rarely do they include full integration into daily life.

Synkinesis creates a disruptive internal experience, a disquiet in the performance and experience of our lives. It disorders the ability to understand, validate, and experience the performance of self. It does this in a series of ways. Synkinesis disrupts (1) physical experience/sensation and the processing of experience/sensation; (2) self-expression and participation in *communicative events*; and (3) communication with/of/to the self. There is the additional weight of trauma as the internal experience of self creates physical discomfort and triggers feelings of fear, loss, grief, and exclusion.

Physical Experience/Sensation and the Processing of Experience/Sensation

Coming from a sociable Latine family, Guillermo M. now works in finance:

> I guess the hardest part for me now is just eating, going out and socializing with people. . . . When I go outside to dinner and . . .
>
> Because I'm constantly self-conscious of my eyes tearing, which to anybody else may not sound like a big deal . . . but it's a constant reminder of what happened and that my face still feels like it doesn't do some things sometimes. . . . Like I can't make expressions, and my eyelid is not as strong to squint, so my face kind of feels scrunched up on this

side all the time, like when there's a lot of light and everything. But it's all the time.

So it's mostly just me constantly being aware of it. No matter what . . . if anything, that's where my focus goes because there's always this kind of—discomfort. I'm always physically uncomfortable, but it's like in where I'm me, and I'm not sure how I look, what they see . . . I feel like I'm spaced out sometimes when I'm trying to talk to someone because I'm constantly thinking about what does my face look like right now. But I can't ignore it because it hurts.

Synkinesis disrupts the process by which we experience and process sensations tied to emotions. Emotions are experienced, and part of that experience is facial display. But with wrong feel, emotion becomes confusing and problematic. The disruption of information combined with misinformation muddies experience, even if one can sort it out in the end; the spontaneous or in-the-moment nature of experience is forever lost.

In addition, some have experienced disruption or changes to basic sensory data. As has been found in other studies of facial disfigurement (Yaron et al. 2017), many of those I spoke with emphasized changes in their baseline senses or gathering of sensory information. This is a hard one to fathom because it's not the same as vision loss, hearing loss, or normal age changes. Although changes to taste, hearing, and brightness were all referenced, the specific complaints tended to focus on challenges with *filtering*. Whether light, noise, or taste, many noted challenges to sorting out sensation. It's not that one's hearing or vision is measurably better or worse, but that the ability to focus has changed—on discerning a voice in a loud, crowded space, or picking out what you want to hear and tuning out what you don't, or being outside without sunglasses, or holding off motion sickness.

I noticed it first with the color blue. The sky was brighter. Contrasts seemed more extreme—not unpleasant, not upsetting, just *more*. The difference wasn't necessarily worse or better, but it was an adjustment I had to make. Many of my interviewees highlighted a number of challenges. Common complaints pointed to things like filtering noise in social situations, filtering light while driving into the sun, and feeling "not quite right" with one's prescription lenses. Vertigo or challenges with balance was another common complaint, especially among those with Ramsay Hunt syndrome or an acoustic neuroma.

But these challenges were manageable. It was the loss of shared sensory experiences that rankled. Shared social experiences are a deeply felt loss. One key, visceral loss some experience is the ability to enjoy food. Beyond the tremendous anxiety generated by eating becoming a challenging activity in which one's disability is "on display," some experienced a change to taste. There was a moment during an interview when a participant described something I had also experienced—it was so visceral, I could taste it: the weird metallic/fish taste that so often seems to prevent me from enjoying food was synkinesis.

At that moment, a kinetic energy traveled through my body and exploded in a silent rage: to be robbed of something so basic—the ability to enjoy the taste of food. And I was not alone. James A., a successful marketing executive, had loved hosting events. He lamented, "I really miss enjoying food. I miss grilling steaks on the barbecue. I always said, if I was on a deserted island and I only had one food I could have to live on, it would be chips and salsa, and I can't eat that stuff anymore. Can't chew right. Can't even enjoy eating it. Doesn't taste the same. Doesn't feel the same. I very much enjoyed the textures of different foods, and I want that back. I miss enjoying food."

Experience is the amalgamation of sensation, perception, and interpretation (Braun and Clarke 2008; Yaron et al. 2017). Synkinesis disrupts one's experience of all three. It's not only that one's intake of sensation is problematic, one's experience of sensation becomes disrupted and confused by the experience of synkinesis. As a result, one may experience "wrong feel" or wrong emotions.

Expression and Communication Are Disrupted

Synkinesis disrupts an individual's embodied experience in a very specific way because it impacts the locus of expression, or the experience of expression and communication. Recall that as we communicate we mimic or take on and share the expressions of those with whom we are communicating (Blairy, Herrera, and Hess 1999; Hess and Bourgeois 2010). Synkinesis disrupts this from both ends, interjecting wrong expressions/feels throughout the interaction.

Imagine that you are feeling confused or are not understanding the directions someone is giving you: your brows draw together in a traditional gesture of confusion, but as they do your neck tightens, your jaw hardens . . . a flash of. . . . What is that? Annoyance? Fear? Anger? Oh no, it's synkinesis—so you consciously relax the muscles. (Now where was I? Did they see it? Do they think I am angry? *Argh*, I was supposed to be listening!)

Now imagine laughing: you are waving goodbye and start to blow a kiss—but your mouth is wrong, and your eye tightens. Your friend looks confused, and the cheery wave back momentarily pauses. So you wave instead.

Now imagine your friend is telling a funny story, and you laugh together—but your eye tightens, your chin hurts, and your neck pulls. OK, so you adjust adjust adjust. You replay the joke, and you can laugh again, but smaller this time.

One is always interpreting and managing the communication and interpretation methods that were mastered early in childhood development. It's not just that the unconscious mimicry of communication is disrupted such that communication with others is more challenging; it's that the experience of

DISRUPTED SELVES

communication is lessened without it. It's less shared, less evocative, less fulfilling, and less satisfying—it's less. Interaction is now filled with facial management, anxiety over miscommunication, and grief for the inability to not be disrupted in the moment.

Communication is shared meaning. The depth hinges on the degree of shared understanding. The ability to generate appropriate sensations, perceptions, and expressions, to share meaning is disrupted by synkinesis. Regardless of age, gender, ethnicity, or other characteristics, most my participants reflected on this change. The first quote comes from a gregarious woman, Maria M., and the second from Lou C., both previously introduced. Both highlighted how disruptive to communication synkinesis can be.

> I definitely don't laugh as much as I used to. . . . I don't think it's just because when you laugh, it makes the face look worse. . . . And I do hate to see that reaction, that look of shock. I definitely laughed more before, and then I physically laughed . . . out loud . . . I've never been a big, boisterous laugher anyways, even if I didn't have *this*—you know what I mean. I've always been a quiet laugher even before this, but now I'll put my hand over my face to . . . sort of like you're holding your face . . . I do this all the time when I'm laughing, my hand immediately goes to my face. Because it pulls down this side, and it feels . . . not right. And my eye will not feel right. . . . And the mouth that starts to look funny. . . . So now I even laugh with hands; I hold my face and cover it and use my hands. (Maria M.)

> Yeah, sometimes when I'm talking to someone like my boss, for example. I feel this huge tension on my face, [and] I'm just wondering, "Does he notice it?" you know. You know, "Does he notice a huge lump on my face or not?" [He laughs.] That kind of—some sensation that leaves me wondering if he sees it, right? Because I feel something and I'm talking to him, right? So that kind of feeling, right? It makes me a bit, like, I'm not so confident when I'm talking to him, you know. And I am distracted. And I have to think about my face. (Lou C.)

A shared spontaneous moment of communication now involves management and planning. Pride and accomplishment are undercut by distraction. Lou C. was good at his job and proud of his work, but he could never fully enjoy the accolades he received. Spontaneous communication is too often physically uncomfortable and anxiety inducing. But it's not only communication with others that is being disrupted—it's the experience of self.

Communication/Experience of the Self Is Disrupted

As the previous participants revealed, much of what has been disrupting communication for them is centered on their internal experience. Corrine C. enjoyed her middle age, with a satisfying career and family life. Yet synkinesis has interrupted her internal experience:

> Well, I feel like I'm always thinking about my face . . . I'm always aware of it. It's always in the back of my mind, as opposed to thinking about what I want to—like, I can multitask. I can certainly do more than one thing. I can be noticing my face and working with the family, or noticing my face and making love, or noticing my face and working in the garden, whatever it is, right? I think I can do more than that. But I'm aware of my face, which is an odd thing, right? It's a constant distraction. It's always interrupting the moment.

I have this memory of the old me. I am leaving a co-worker/friend's office, laughing, and we're pulling faces as we relive a funny moment we've shared. As I head back down the hall, I smile at colleagues, greet students: a few words, a big smile, raised eyebrows and a nod for someone else, the front-stage performance of personality. I so enjoyed those little moments of comradery. I miss them so much. It's not that I don't visit friend's offices to share a quick story about our kids, pets, students, or life in general. It's not that my small smile and big wave don't also convey the same warmth of greeting. But there's no way to remove that weird tension near my eye, in my neck, or the fear of miscommunication that accompanies it, or the weirdness of filtering out the misinformation it brings, or the management to hopefully "look normal." It's so much more work. It's so much harder, and concomitantly less satisfying.

What does that mean in terms of sense of self? It's not merely that shared moments or aspects of experience are lost; it's that something fundamental to how we experience is eternally disrupted. Misinformation is constantly having to be "tuned out" or "managed." Having to consciously tune out misinformation about one's emotional/psychological state is detrimental to one's emotional/psychological state. It adds to the social fatigue so often described by those with synkinesis. Socializing is so much more work, not only due to misinformation in the communicative process but in our own reactions and feelings.

Our expressions are part of our emotional/psychological/corporeal existence. Embodied experience, specifically facial expression, impacts high-level comprehension and social experience (Davis, Winkielman, and Coulson 2015). To put it simply, we experience life and emotion in part through their physical manifestations of those things, and synkinesis disrupts this process. We are both receiving/feeling wrong things and having to be conscious of this experience and adjusting. Even the use of Botox can impact social emotional processing (Havas et al. 2010). Those with synkinesis frequently use Botox as a treatment to manage pain, wrong movement, and wrong feel. It is an adjustment; people consistently mentioned having to "adjust" to Botox and to it wearing off. They feel they are always adjusting, always coping with a layer of misinformation.

DISRUPTED SELVES

This is confusing, disruptive, exhausting and frustrating. It's also triggering. As one sorts through miscommunication and misinformation, one is always having to confront that one has and is managing synkinesis. This "reminder," as so many described to me, takes you out of the moment. It undermines the spontaneity of life: undercutting joy, magnifying sorrow, reiterating grief. Mike H., the college professor previously introduced, lamented the loss of self that comes with synkinesis:

> But previously I was a more vocal person, more expressive . . . I used to express a lot with my face. I used to use my face to a considerable extent—to communicate, to be funny, to share a laugh. . . . Now, I just try to tone it down. I control it and try to keep it a little more calm. Yeah. It's a continuous effort not to show too much with the face. Always holding back what I want to express.
>
> So it does affect how I express myself . . . how I feel. . . . I consider the way I express myself with my face all the time. It's now a part of my character, who I am. And I always am thinking about it while I'm trying to make my point. I can't not think about it. It's like it's poking at you. So, yeah. It does affect the way I communicate, how I interact with people. How I present myself. Who I am.

A successful educator, athlete, and parent, yet he is always operating with a little voice in the back of his head reminding him to manage his face in ways that feel unnatural, calling to mind the internalized stigma of ableism.

The ubiquity of this experience manifests in people's grief for the experience of smiling. As mentioned in the last chapter, this was a profound communicative loss. It's also an acute loss of self. Samantha H., who had recently retired from a professional career, reflected on how smiling now makes her feel: "I feel very sad when I try to smile. *Very* sad actually. I feel sad because I'll be unable to smile and you take it all for granted. I can smile, but when I do, for like a second, I feel happy, but then I feel it pull. And it hurts. It's uncomfortable. The minute I do smile and feel happy about something, I then get this reminder of what I'm not happy about. So it's almost like a punishment for being happy." That one experiences excitement, joy, and companionship yet always with a physically, emotionally, and psychologically difficult trigger is difficult. Most with acquired facial paralysis experienced its onset as distressing—a profound understatement.

The experience of synkinesis usually begins with a traumatic incident. The aftereffects remain an ongoing reminder of mortality, stigma, fear, and pain. Given that Bell's palsy is the most common cause of facial paralysis and synkinesis, it's not surprising that those with synkinesis from Bell's palsy or the more serious Ramsay Hunt syndrome comprised almost two-thirds of my participants. The majority had arrived at emergency rooms in distress. The second most common cause was as a potentially unfortunate side effect of removing an acoustic neuroma (or similar skull tumor). Just over 20 percent of respondents had had a tumor removed. First learning that one has a tumor in one's head, then undergoing tests and surgeries, the entire experience is difficult, painful, and traumatic; many faced single-sided deafness in addition to synkinesis. The condition for a few of my participants was the result of physical trauma (vehicular accidents, gun violence, or animal attacks). It's a constant reminder of, as computer specialist Bob H. described it, a time of "uncertainty and scariness":

> Because to me this is a reminder that I have Bell's palsy, and I would like not to be reminded of it every single day. But I am. It was a bad experience. It is very uncomfortable, and it's scary because they say you're gonna recover and mine was on target to recover. . . . And just the uncertainty of it, so. . . . And there are physical deformities or—I call it a deformity—physical things you can hide. . . . Other things you can't hide, but there's not much you can do with your face unless you want to stay inside all the time. Never socialize.
>
> So I think it's particularly onerous to people, and I don't think why—one of the reasons why I'm talking to you is because I don't think enough attention is paid to psychological aspects of it. It's not just how people treat you, it's doing things to you, to how you feel. Like I got no support from doctors—I got nothing from them about "How is this making you feel? Does it make you depressed or whatever?" I think that's completely missing from the treatment. There's not enough support or coverage. There's a lot of uncertainty and scariness. And even now, I get reminded of that.

Many expressed dislike for these reminders of the changes it had wrought on their lives, but even more profound was a sense of a lost self.

Alienation/Self-estrangement

Previous studies have found that disruptions to perception and sensation create "self-estrangement" or alienation (Svenaeus 2000, 2015; Yaron et al. 2017). I heard many variations of "I don't feel like myself." This was never a positive assessment. Hilda S., a college-educated, middle-aged white woman with a fulfilling career in the arts, described the experience as "I felt dreadful. I felt—I think I felt like I didn't know myself anymore. That I have lost a portion of myself." Though she does feel more like herself now, she described it as an ongoing adjustment.

In a classic Marxist sense, *alienation* refers to becoming alienated from (1) the product of one's labor, (2) one's activity of labor, (3) one's own humanity, and (4) one's community of fellows as workers within the wage labor system.

Theorists later broadened the idea to explore identity. Understanding the self as a process, and synkinesis as creating alienation in this process, provides a useful metaphor. Synkinesis creates an experience of self-alienation. One is alienated from the product (display of a social self), the activity (the performance of a social self), the internal experience of the social self (being "me"), and the shared experience of a community of fellows (easy interaction with others).

Alienation from the Me (Display/Performed Self)

I've already described in depth how synkinesis makes nonverbal communication and display problematic. People often expressed dismay, shock, and discomfort with images of themselves. "I didn't know I looked like that when I talked" was a common refrain from those who hadn't spent much time on video conference calls. Others asked to do phone interviews specifically because they found watching themselves problematic. Many of my online interviews and support groups included real-time discussions of dismay with the thumbnails on the screen. One person blurted out, "I had no idea I looked that bad when I talk. . . . Oh, man." Similar to my participants, I found myself sometimes sitting partially off camera or resting my face on one hand after COVID-19 resulted in full days of Zoom calls. This indicates a fundamental, problematic disruption to the ability to display and perform not only a normative self but the normative self one used to display. One's affect is perpetually "off." The inability to find a socially acceptable normative self for many remains an ongoing challenge.

There is simply an inability to perform. Many facial expressions are off-limits for me: they cause discomfort, or they are shocking in their asymmetry, or they are simply impossible to attain. A response that implies confusion, awareness of difference, and adjustment to my otherness ensues. That feels bad. So you do less: you make fewer expressions, and you tamp down your affect. You fade a bit.

Someone once told me, "I simply thought you were inexpressive," and that was heartbreaking to hear because I had once so enjoyed being a person I could no longer be. It's not simply because I can no longer produce a flawless performance; it's that the performance is no longer gratifying or effective. It's physically uncomfortable. It's shame inducing. The tendency to flatten one's affect, and by extension the self, is a consequence of alienation.

Alienation from the "I" (Experience of Producing/Displaying Self)— Experience of Producing a Self

The I is your individualized, spontaneous response. When you are among your people, the I moments are shared. Spontaneous laughter, shared moments of joy—together the I and the me combine. The problem with synkinesis is your I's perpetual disruption. There are no experiences that don't include reminders of faux pas, pain, loss, trauma, and grief. It's that your I is forever experiencing a stigmatized "me"—or mortification rather than pride—simply in the attempt to

112 METAMORPHOSIS

express or "do" self. It's not that I'm perceived as not right; it's that I'm constantly receiving internal feedback that I'm not right. I don't mean negative self-talk, imposter syndrome, or the fears and doubts so many experience. I mean the basic way I understand the messages my own face sends me about social interaction. I mean the basic experience and process of communication with others and myself. My "being-in-the-world" is a never-ending challenge. And it's tiring.

Alienation from Subjective Experience (from Experiencing Joie de Vivre)

People sometimes lose the ability to do things they enjoyed as well as the ability to experience unrestrained joie de vivre—or to stay in a moment of joy. Experience is a physical/thought interconnection; it's where they meet and reify. It's the merging of physical sensation and mental interpretation.

To a certain degree, the quest for authenticity is that of experience of a satisfied I and me. Those joie-de-vivre moments highlight the best of what it means to be alive and human. Whether it's hearing your favorite song performed live with an excited room of like-minded fans, or connecting with the friend who always knows exactly what you mean, or snow-boarding down a hill in fresh powder, or riding a bike when it almost feels like flying, or running in the early morning as the owls call, or listening to my kid's outside-the-box analyses that tell me he is thinking critically about the social world, or laughing with family and friends at something ridiculous, or dancing at weddings . . . these are my moments. Yours are unique to your own brand of joy. But there is overlap to how we experience expression and materiality, which is an embodied self.

Synkinesis messes up this experience. We're often told to just ignore it or to pretend it isn't there or to get used to it. We do. But something can't be had/ is always lost when the moment requires letting go of conscious management of self. Imagine your own perfect moment. Feel that smile creeping across your face? What if, as you felt that, something else that signals stress or discomfort or displeasure also fired in your thoughts, and you had to push that irrational, wrong emotion away to stay in the moment? Now consider that you must do this all the time.

Imagine a belly laugh, a moment of pure joy. The feeling that is the best of being—I don't know the word for it—it's the thing that starts the smile; the slight curve in the upper lip, tightening the cheek balls, the face pulling into the mask of us happy. That reason we all say our smile is our best feature, is really a feeling. It's when we feel our inner and outer selves aligned. Now imagine that it didn't. Imagine that that your eye closed against your will, that your face is pulling the wrong way, and it's painful and disturbing and confusing. Every single time. Scholars use the term "being-in-the-world" to denote a confident sense of self (Leder 1990; Yaron et al. 2017). Shared experience with one's most treasured allies involves an easy unthought shared "being-in-the world." Our "being-in-the-world" is severely disrupted, and the social aspects of it, permanently require management. Reading this to myself, I had the realization, sometimes I go to sleep, just so I don't have to mis-feel my face anymore, because it's so exhausting, and inescapable. It's heart rending, to never share that feeling again. This experience ultimately creates a barrier between ourselves and others.

Alienation from Shared Social Experience (Community of Fellows)

"It was heartbreaking. I lost my way of connecting, my way of communicating. In its way, my physical smile died. My ability to communicate my joy and happiness. My ability to feel happy, to share being happy. . . . To be happy with other people." Laura M., who was previously introduced, shared her devastation at the loss of spontaneous shared joy. Similarly, Janice M., a regular attendee at support group meetings and an advocate, shared her frustration with group photos. Everyone else could look joyful, but her own joy wasn't reflected on her face. She spoke with love of friends who posed with serious expressions so that the moment could be captured as shared. As I think of Janice—her infectious energy, her warmth, and the love she gives to everyone around her—I smile. Then it happens: the wrong pull, the wrong feel, the pull in the platysma muscle and across my chin, and the weird feeling of my eyeball. (Botox is due in a few days, so it's extra uncomfortable today.) My warm memories are interrupted as the wrong expression drives my emotions in wrong directions; then I feel the frustration of being unable to just feel, and the heartbreak of the permanent loss. I dig a little deeper, I am resilient, and . . . I'm always managing.

As a result of managing synkinesis, we become /feel like outsiders. Al L., who was previously introduced, described the impact of managing his affect:

> I have to manage my face. I can't let my guard down. I let it slip a couple of months ago. We're sitting in a birthday dinner, and I was sitting across somebody who didn't know. I was actually talking and laughing; I was in the moment, I wasn't managing my face, and I saw her smiling, and then I saw her kind of do a double-take. And when I saw that, I felt it [he gestures at his face], and I just stopped, and I corrected myself, and just like that, I raised my shades again. I was controlled again.
>
> I couldn't just be in the moment talking; I had to manage my face. So it was just an unspoken thing that you just feel, that pause in the air. I hurt myself if I dwell on it, so I . . . and they just . . . they move on. I don't know if later in the car on the ride home that person asked the person they were with, "Hey, I noticed this." [It's] something you know, but I know I have to be open to what people would say, ask, you know, or see that. But I try not to dwell on it too much.

It's not only a management of one's appearance, but also one's feelings about being other. The management, and the feedback one receives regarding facial interaction, reinforces as sense of otherness. As previously discussed, when people sought support or tried to articulate their challenges, quick reassurances that one "looked fine," undermined, dismissed, or hid the lived experience and reinforced separation. Matti L., who identifies as a cisgendered Latina and has a satisfying career in medical administration, related that, despite having a supportive family, synkinesis generated a profound feeling of loneliness: "There's a real feeling of loneliness that I think we all experience sometimes. It just happens because you don't ever have people around you with this problem. I always feel like am I the only one going through this. And it's a lot. And no one wants to hear me if I do say anything." Given the external and internal disruption, people with synkinesis must adjust.

So What Does That Mean as Lived Experience? Shutting Down

Expressions are both managed and spontaneous. A faux pas is the unmanaged/ mismanaged expression at the wrong moment. And synkinesis is always already walking into communication preparing to correct failure, both internally (self-miscommunication) and externally (managing face). I am now disadvantaged relative to others in regards to a key way I obtain and transmit communicative data. When my eye tightens, I can't tell whether you see it and think it indicates something, or I am just feeling it. I don't know, but it's confusing and distracting and unpleasant. We are always alert for signs of miscommunication and the need for adjustment, and nothing can fix that. Surgeries, neuromuscular retraining, and ongoing Botox treatments can mitigate the issue, but it can't be fixed.

But there was an adjustment that many made: people engaged in a reduction in expressiveness. Flattening of affect was an almost universally adopted strategy to avoid unpleasant reminders seen in the responses of others and the internal physical cues—to reduce the negative experiences of self *through* expression. Kevin S., a cisgendered white man with a background in performance arts and a graduate degree, detailed his own transformation:

I used to be really, really social. I had lots of friends; I found it easy to insert myself into a conversation and meet someone new. I was always dating someone and having a whole lot of friends, and that was me. That was nothing; that was easy to me. Same as like smiling and laughing. I was a really funny guy; I loved to laugh out loud. And that got hard.

I found for a while I shut myself down because my smile is not the same smile anymore. . . . It doesn't feel the same. It feels wrong. And laughing, you know, the more emotion that I feel—the more sort of distorted my face can get. And especially when I laugh, it feels so tight and uncomfortable and wrong, so I started to shut down my laugh.

And it's only recently that I have just accepted it more and more, that I can just push through it and force myself back to the moment. And if someone is looking at me and their reaction is difficult, I learned to look away . . . if someone is looking weird at me. . . . Sometimes I just shut my eyes, so it feels less pull; and if I shut my eyes, you can't tell that they are looking at it.

Patti D., a cisgendered white laboratory technician, similarly reported, "If I start laughing hard, then I know . . . I still laugh, and I'll still have fun and just be laughing with people. But when I do, I'm thinking about how my face is wrong. I know that only one side of my face is laughing and all the pulling. . . . So anytime I show strong emotion, I cut it short. I'm more reserved. I laugh less, I smile less. Definitely, a lot less than I'd like to. But it has to be less, or it's a problem."

People like Brad A. and Erika B. noted the negative impact that reducing their affect had on their experiences. Brad A., the previously introduced entertainer, noted the heartbreaking impact on joy:

> The problem with synkinesis is that you are just aware of it all the time. It's like a background noise . . . this ongoing conversation. If you are out having a great time, you have to just think, OK, don't smile. Or you smile and it feels wrong . . . so you just shut down mentally, from the inside-out. You don't allow yourself to get fully immersed in things, so you never have a genuine moment where you laugh or smile or you just enjoy things without thinking about this.
>
> I try not to let myself get too happy because when I smile or laugh genuinely, that's when it pulls the most. It hurts. . . . You laugh, [and] there goes your neck and your eye. . . . It's the constant reminders that wear you down. After a while, you just try to find reasons and ways to not have that happen. You feel less, you express less.

Erika B., who identifies as a Black, cisgendered woman, has a supportive family, an associate's degree, and a career in technology. She reflected on how reducing her affect has impacted her overall personality and experience of self: "I was a much happier person before. I had issues, but I think I was so much happier . . . I think it made me more introverted. I'm just less. That's the biggest thing."

Illness, debilitation, and disfigurement are often described as discrediting. In chapter 3, I noted the internalization of systemic dehumanization with microaggressions as social experience does systemic ideological repair work. The cumulative and varying impacts of overlapping, intersecting, and opposing identity categories, with ensuing microaggressions, have consequences for our experience of self. Here, we focus on synkinesis, but I commend the scholars who have highlighted the many ways that experiences of otherness impact bodies.

Self is fundamentally an embodied experience. We experience self through the body, and we only understand the world through our own embodied state

(Campbell 2009). What people are expressing is that communication with oneself about embodied states and experiences is disrupted in ways that undermine existence. My participants grieved for their social self, the person they used to be but weren't anymore. That's easy to relate to: people often lament hobbies they may no longer be able to enjoy because an injury, their age, or their location has made it impossible. But it's harder to express a lost experience of social self. It's like one has a permanent killjoy inside one's own head. The word *fun* came up a lot and the loss of the ability to have it.

Maddie D., a cisgendered white event manager with an associate's degree, shared with me her heartbreak at not being able to cut lose and party anymore. Her job included networking, making people feel comfortable and included, and keeping conversations going. She just wasn't as adept at that as she used to be. But what frustrated her more was her inability to connect in shared unadulterated "fun."

> This kind of makes me like want to cry. [She paused.] I used to be the life of the party. I've kind of been nicknamed "The Purple Dragon." There was this little restaurant on our honeymoon. . . . So we had a destination wedding and honeymoon . . . and I had drunk so much that day, and we tried to get over to this little restaurant down river called the Purple Dragon. . . . I just had too much fun that day, and I couldn't handle it, and in the end my husband had to drive me home with a boat.
>
> I was partying, and having so much fun, and going crazy, and everyone was having fun. So it became this inside joke; all of our friends were always like, "We're going to see the Purple Dragon tonight." And I haven't really been the Purple Dragon since this happened. . . . I don't know if I will ever be that person again. [She teared up.]

There's that spontaneous, authentic, in-the-moment sharing of expression and experience encapsulated in the word "fun." I've already discussed the self-alienation that comes from wrong feel. It is tremendous work to constantly manage the face/self while internally correcting wrong feel and adjusting to cues from others. Shutting down reduces the work burden but also diminishes the experience of daily life, and it leaves one grieving for an experience of self, something lost inside, invisible, and deeply painful.

The tremendous effort that ongoing management of synkinesis requires is largely invisible when one is successful, but moments of slippage are highlighted. Those failures, combined with wrong feel, are disruptive and exhausting. The next chapter will highlight how people overcome, cope, and adjust; but as with any loss, grief marks the passage of what was once experienced as valuable, joyful, necessary, and completing—and now permanently lost. But one grieves the dead, and I'm not.

Social Death or Social Disability?

While alienation from one's social world is an ongoing challenge, the social death predicted for those with facial difference also seems an overstatement for many with synkinesis. Because most do cope. Although my interviews revealed struggle, heartache, rejection, isolation, bullying, suicide attempts, and self-harm, ultimately people did survive. They got help, they did the work, they challenged themselves, and they grew. I was left impressed by their resilience, adaptability, endurance, and compassion.

Recall that Heather Laine Talley (2014) describes three criteria believed to trigger social death: degree of impaction, threats to social interaction and communication, and absence or impairment of universal human traits (such as the smile). Overall, those perceived as disabled may find that some people cannot form meaningful relationships with them (Darling 2019). As a result of their/our ongoing experiences, people with visible facial differences exhibit higher rates of anxiety in social interaction (van Dalen et al. 2020).[3] Synkinesis certainly can be visible and startling. It impacts nonverbal communication, presentation of self, and comfort/ease of communication; one's smile is altered, rendered nonspontaneous, and sometimes functionally absent. But much of that can be managed or hidden; though, as discussed, this comes at a cost to the individual.

But social death? Outside assessments are always not quite right, are always invasive, and are always a little cruel. For me, the reminder of my loss of social status always came/comes like a sucker punch, out of nowhere, brutal and swift. I am always unprepared. I was caught unawares by a book about dogs. An offhand comment of the inevitability of social death for those with facial paralysis was a sickening jolt. Reading Khaled Hosseini's *The Kite Runner* (2003) while recovering provided a similar slap in the face: the person with facial difference was rendered incomplete and less human in description. I have no interest in seeing *The Phantom of the Opera* again.

The presumption of isolation for the facially disfigured, the pathologization, the dehumanization, the failure to consider how class, social position, and other factors might shape experience, and the assumptions embedded are all indications that those with facial difference are never considered fully human. Facial paralysis, a face like mine, has been enough to explain and to justify social exclusion. To show compassion, interest, or kindness to someone like me is considered an act of mercy. To the paternalistic norms and assumptions embedded in our system, I say (and not for the first time), F-CK YOU!!!!!!!! F-CK YOU and your dispassionate assessments and assumptions. F-ck you with your assessment of my experience and my life. F-ck you for thinking you know and can help—by knowing, by helping, by pitying, you create my cage.

I hadn't planned for inevitable social death, and I don't intend to live it. I expected and still expect to be a functioning member of society. I wasn't aware that my presence created a burden and gifted you with status for your tolerance of my presence. And much as I would like to believe I am "exceptional" (as I often say, "you're special, just like everyone else"), the need for those with disabilities to be exceptional in some other way that justifies their (our) existence and normalizes their (our) narrative is intensely problematic. And there it is: a social diminishment comes with facial paralysis, and with disability, and with otherness more generally. The same rage at ongoing rejection, self-management, double-consciousness, code switching, and stigma percolates up in narratives that center on race, disability, documentation status, gender, religion, and the plethora of ways identities intersect.[4]

Beyond the personal struggle to acclimate, to mitigate, and to move past, there is that social experience of not being good enough, and the weighty history of what is done to those in that category. But who is *they*? Who is doing? That generalized other represents the norms of social structure bolstered by systemic ideologies, reinforced/policed with microaggressions, salved with purchased panaceas. There is no they, but they are also everywhere and everyone. It is inside ourselves, and we are them.

Is Facial Paralysis a (What Is a) Disability?

"There is another sort of blow that comes from within—that you don't feel until it's too late to do anything about it, until you realize with finality and in some regard you will never be as good a man again . . . [it] happens almost without your knowing it but is realized suddenly indeed" (Fitzgerald [1936] 2017). In writing about illness and disability, Mark Lefton (1984) highlights F. Scott Fitzgerald's lament. The shock or frustration of losing capabilities is a painful reality that aging allows some to experience, but there is also a deep internalization of ableism. At its core is the belief that physical differences weaken you, make you dependent, and make you less. Your value to humanity comes in quantifiable, tangible, productive forms, and productivity is measured in specific rational quantifiable ways.[5] That's one narrative. But maybe being someone who has learned what it means to live without what's presumed to be "normal" or has lost an ability—who now has insight into what is gained instead—has value. That value is not only reserved to ourselves; it can be shared with institutions and organizations and can shape how we manage/organize/shape our public spaces and policies.

We make meaning out of our personal biographies within a social world that provides current and historical context. The context given to process disability identity and visible difference is problematic. How do people with synkinesis understand this experience with regards to the larger community of people with disabilities? Is it a disability? A disfigurement? A personal challenge? The core of that question is unanswerable. What is a disability? At first the answer seems obvious: it's when someone needs accommodation. But where is the line between normal variant and alternative accommodations? We all need accommodation. For example, the university where I teach is thirty-five miles from my home; without the accommodation transit provides I would be unable to make that commute on a potentially daily basis. I am 5′3″, so I don't have the same reach as taller people. Both my parents wear/wore glasses, but I don't really need them. Accommodations are only viewed as such when they deviate from a socially imposed norm. Those norms may change for a host of reasons. What was considered a visual impairment a hundred years ago is easily "corrected" with surgery or glasses today. Similarly, what was once considered quirky may now be an "invisible disability."

Despite one-fifth of Americans having a disability, and this being an identity category that anyone can presumably join, disabilities are heavily stigmatized (Campbell 2009; Garland-Thomson 2005, 2009; Olkin 1999). People who are born with disabilities may have protective reference groups, but people with acquired disabilities are more likely to internalize negative self-images (Darling 2019; Smith and Sparkes 2005). Western cultural tropes of disability highlight what Fiona Campbell (2009) refers to "enduring vulnerability," precipitated by "compensatory initiatives and safety nets" that reify (dis)ability as financially dependent and inherently limited (disabled). The narratives and identities open to those with disabilities reflect these underlying assumptions about humanity, value, and rights.

But we also have to ask larger questions about narratives. Why are so many narratives problematic? Michel Foucault (1979) reminds us of the power of the defined, institutionalized, investigated norm around which knowledge is produced. Being or not being disabled is a function of place, experience, and a combination of social and individual characteristics. There also are assumptions embedded in the category. It is the experience of a social category of stigma (Hughes 1998). The assumption embedded in disability is that one is not just different but less than; one is burdensome, problematic, unproductive, and should be grateful for inclusion. The dispassionate idealizations embedded in market systems of producers and consumers render disabilities only valuable as niche markets or inclusive virtue signaling.

Within the social sciences there has been a larger movement that challenges seeing the world and ourselves through the ontological and epistemological lens of colonialism. Disability studies challenges this fundamental model and frames disability as something tied into a system of social (in)justice (Siebers 2008). In this view, disability is an identity or an experience of otherness (Seibers 2008; Olkin 1999; Wendell 1996). The challenge is in how the larger society perceives, treats, and judges those viewed as disabled.

Research has indicated that the context has a significant impact on how identity and self-esteem are impacted by disability status (Barnwell and Kavanagh 1997; Brooks and Matson 1982; Craig, Hancock, and Chang 1994; Nosek et al. 2003; Walsh and Walsh 1989). In my own project, whether my participants saw themselves as impaired, disfigured, or disabled revealed how disability continues to be stigmatized; but it also foreshadowed impending change. Scholars and activists are coming to expand our understandings of ability, needs, rights, and accommodations. Crip theory has expanded the experience of disability to include a wider range of bodily experiences and challenges and provides a space for wider advocacy (Schalk 2018).

One-fifth of the population in the United States identifies as living with what our larger culture views as a disability or an impairment.[6] But what is viewed as a disability varies widely from person to person, and internalized ableism means that many choose to disavow or fail to acknowledge such conditions (Kattari, Olzman, Hanna 2018). I explicitly asked my participants whether they viewed themselves as disabled, and whether they considered facial paralysis/synkinesis a disability more generally. Among those with facial paralysis and/or synkinesis, some rejected the idea that facial paralysis is a disability. Others indicated that it could be a disability, but they rejected disability status for themselves. Some viewed the impact of facial paralysis as disabling. And, finally, some did embrace a disability identity.

"It's Not Like Losing an Arm or a Leg": Rejection of Disability Status

Previous research on those with *acquired* facial difference has indicated a rejection of disability identity (Watson 2002). Kathleen Bogart and colleagues have found that those with congenital facial paralysis are more likely to embrace a disability self-concept than those with acquired difference (Bogart 2014; Bogart, Rosa, and Slepian 2019). Many of those I interviewed did not see themselves as disabled per se, nor did they internalize a disability identity. Kevin S., who was previously introduced, noted he had changed his views to not see his acquired facial paralysis as a disability: "I used to think because . . . this is a disability, half my face doesn't work, that's a disability. But it isn't. Like, I realized, 'No, it's not.' Like, a disability is that you need a crutch; you need help to do something. Either you can't see or you can't hear or you need a wheelchair or something like that. So no, this is not a disability. I can talk, I can walk." Cara R., a cisgendered, high school–educated, home health aide, similarly highlighted her mobility and personal productivity as leading her to reject the label of disability:

> I was really upset when I see that people labeled it a disability, because I do support work for people with disabilities. I look after people with disabilities, with learning disabilities, mental health disabilities—children

DISRUPTED SELVES

and adults. I've seen it all. I am in the community. I'm not in that situation; I'm working, I'm making a difference, [and] I'm helping people live a better quality of life. I don't think it's a disability now because it's—you're lacking your communication, but now it's debilitating but it's not a disability because I'm still able-bodied. I can still do things, and I've seen disability and it's not that.

Comparing the experience of synkinesis to that other disabilities was among the most common distancing strategies. Participants who did not view themselves as disabled frequently noted the lack of mobility challenges or lack of cognitive challenges. It was almost a conflation of the standards for disabled parking and disability. I'm from Los Angeles, and more than most am I willing to consider parking as a metric or standard, but in the case of disability this struck me as more a reflection of larger cultural views of productivity and, ableism than lived experience. The desire to distance oneself from others demonstrates how systems self-perpetuate. Given the stigmatizations of difference and disability in postcolonial racial capitalism, it's not surprising that many simply rejected disability status and did so by highlighting traditional measures of productivity.

Many of the same people who disavowed disability status mentioned challenges doing basic things like eating and speaking or having issues with vision; some highlighted experiences resulting from visible difference. Given the proliferation of challenges and the prevalence of stigma, the majority of those with whom I spoke tended to view their condition in a more nebulous way, classifying it either as perhaps a disability for others but not for themselves or as being disabling, but not a disability.

Disability—but Not Me! And/or Disabling

Those who viewed their condition as perhaps a disability for others but not themselves, and those who did find it disabling were similar in that they acknowledged the impact of facial paralysis, either for themselves or for others, but they didn't exactly categorize themselves as disabled.

But Not Me!

Angi C., the previously introduced Latina, mused, "Do I think of it as a disability? Yes and no. . . . With it came all these psychological factors, anxiety, social phobias. . . . But physically, am I able to work? Of course! So it's not really a disability. Maybe for others." Here was an interesting acknowledgment of the negative impacts coupled with distancing.

One person noted that despite the pain, loss of function, and ensuing mental health impacts, she could work. She contrasted her own situation with that of others from an advocacy event, and she highlighted one woman who had very noticeable synkinesis: "In her case, it's a disability. It's what everyone is going to see. . . . You can't ignore it." Maybe this type of self-protective understanding is necessitated by systemic internalizations of what disability encompasses. It allows one to talk about the impact of synkinesis from more of a distance, to highlight how it could impact people rather than how it is impacting oneself. This is sort of like interviewing over a hundred people and writing a book about it. Others used descriptors such as disabling or disfiguring rather than labeling it a disability.

Disabling

Highlighting the tension between internalized ableism and the importance of advocacy, some distanced themselves from the label of disability while acknowledging an experience that required redress, or that was *disabling*. This usually was acknowledged in two ways, the psychological impact of facial difference, and the social stigma of visible difference.

The psychological cost was ubiquitous. To a large degree, that is the focus of much of this book. Many recognized that facial paralysis had created a real and tangible mental health burden. Corrine C., who was previously introduced, reflected on her experience with synkinesis as disabling rather than a disability:

> I don't know if I would call it a disability, but it was disabling. I think that there's this emotional burden for me; I think that there's emotional baggage with it. That there's weight with it that played into. I feel like my capacity to be my best is lower, and to be as super functional. Right now I'm rebuilding my private business, and I'm so fortunate that I don't have to work forty to sixty hours a week, right? But part of me feels like I don't even know if I can do that. Do you know what I mean? I have all this doubt I didn't have before.

Elaine E., who was previously introduced, similarly mused on the social burden:

> I don't know if it's a disability. . . . It makes people look twice. . . . It's not like having a stroke, is it? I don't know. When people have a paralyzed limb, that's a disability. . . . People notice something is different: Oh, okay, something is different. And now . . . people do know that something's different, I guess. I don't know if it's disability, but I am constantly aware that there's something different. I wish I was able to forget sometimes, about me being different. . . . That's more the burden, the always feeling different.

Moving the boundaries of disability or minimizing the impact was a critical way people distanced themselves from painful labels and experiences. Amy D., a cisgendered Latina professional, has lived with synkinesis since a childhood accident. Creating a boundary between the condition and herself was part of how she had developed a positive self-concept:

> I see it as a medical condition. I don't see it—for myself, it has not impaired my ability to learn and has not impaired and in some ways, it's—I mean, it's brought amazing things to my life. It's added a lot of character. I think I have more empathy and compassion for people now. You know, that's something I learned because of my paralysis and what it did to me mental health wise.
>
> It's certainly been an issue and a factor, but there's that it's not a sole issue. It's just a part of who I am, and it doesn't . . . I used to think it defined me. I lived my life as if it defined me, and that's why I was really shameful about it. But it doesn't keep me from driving. It doesn't keep me from living independently. It doesn't keep me from holding a job, from having friends, from having positive relationships.
>
> So there's been no impairment other than just not having the ability to move the left side of my face. Everything else about me functions fine.

These were strong, capable people, whom I liked, and they showed genuine compassion toward others. So to now start talking about their ableism feels like a betrayal of them and of myself. It's not up to me to decide what it means for individuals to be disabled. I am not the arbiter of categories; it's not up to me to determine what it means to understand or to embrace or reject categories.

But the categories are telling. They reveal deeper assumptions at play in our social, political, and economic structures. They show the demarcation between cognitive and physical disabilities, between impairments and disabilities, and between disfigurement and disability, revealing our social biases. This is at the heart of where ableism infests: who is a valuable member of society versus who is a dependent, less-than "other." Daniel Willingham (2010) writes about his daughter with Down syndrome, highlighting her capacity for care, her work as a home health specialist, and his recognition that she will be the child who cares for them in their old age. . . . Again my own ableism is showing. The cognitively disabled as valuable only when productive in a measurable monetary labor-based way reveals the core toxicity of our existing system. Only when providing care, rather than receiving care, can someone matter. That is ableism, and that is what we must confront within others, within ourselves, and within our society.

Ableism is deeply embedded. The boundaries of disability allow many to distance themselves, to turn away from a potentially stigmatizing aspect of identity. The frustration with misperceptions of cognitive disabilities highlights that, even within communities, hierarchy and ableism can create fractures. Crip theory has struggled with gaining broader visibility and acknowledgment for people who traditionally are not identified as disabled or who have what are euphemistically referred to as "invisible disabilities" (Schalk 2018). Within this framing, disability becomes a standpoint of advocacy and experiential wealth in a self-constructed narrative.

Disability Status

> The presence of disability upsets the modernist craving for ontological
> security. (Campbell 2009, 13)

The increasingly outdated medicolegal model defines a person with a disability as someone with a physical or mental impairment that limits major life activities or is perceived as doing so. What is central is that the person with the disability is somehow limited, less than, deficient, or in need. Although they are problematic, the medicolegal views of disability do provide an initial space from which to advocate. The three examples that follow demonstrate the importance of addressing the impact of a visible facial difference, pain management, and reasonable accommodations.

Diane L., a white, cisgendered, middle-aged office manager, is obviously impacted by synkinesis, and sometimes she has difficulty speaking clearly. She sees herself as disabled and is open about the many challenges, physical and social, she now faces:

> It is a disability because I can't go into any situation the way that I used to. It's going in with a disability. It's going in with a handicap; that's the way that I look at it. Some days it's worse than others. Some days, my eye is more closed. Some days, my mouth just won't do what I want it to do, so that my speech is more messed up. I'll be out and asking someone a question in the supermarket or somewhere, and they're not getting the question. They're not understanding what I'm saying. And it's not comfortable. It doesn't feel good. It's not easy to live with, but what am I going to do? I have no choice; I have to live with it. I live with a disability.

One feature of nerve damage that is difficult to explain to someone who has never experienced it is the pain. While healing from Bell's palsy I remember it always felt like I had been beaten a day or two before. I always felt sore and uncomfortable, punctuated by random shooting pains. Sometimes it felt like my head was being snapped around, hard. And when I mentioned this to medical personnel, I was told, "Bell's palsy doesn't hurt." So I stopped talking about it, and stopped complaining. But I didn't stop hurting. Synkinesis, on a bad day, is like having severe muscle cramps that cannot be eased—and it hurts.

Jen P., who was introduced previously, detailed the impact of chronic pain on her life: "I definitely think it's a disability. Not just because of the physical pain. It's constant pain, constant tightness in your face. It's like for having a horrible, horrible toothache which you can't take an aspirin for or something. And that's pretty much physical, the physical discomfort that you don't look right or whatever. I understand that's general physical discomfort. But the pain is affecting my ability to concentrate and focus. I can't focus, I can't concentrate, it's hard to sleep."

Chronic pain needs to be understood as disabling. When treatment was possible, my interviewees sometimes found their workplaces were unwilling to accommodate them. Marnie V., a graduate school–educated software engineer, noted that her employer was unwilling to accommodate her with a more flexible schedule: "I would say that it is a disability because it did take away my ability to work the way I normally would work, even if it was just I need to go to [physical therapy] or appointments. They didn't want to deal with that. And it changed people's perception of me. It changed how they treated me, how they saw me. They wouldn't work with me at all. And that's what made it hard." For Marnie, some minor adjustments to scheduling and her work environment would have made the impact of synkinesis almost negligible. The refusal made it almost impossible to succeed in the job she had valued and at which she had performed well for over a decade.

A few people reported rather significant workplace bullying, unresponsive medical providers, and public hostility. My American interviewees were able to protect themselves at work, obtain financial and/or medical support (if necessary), and receive accommodations through the Americans with Disabilities Act of 1990. Ruth B., the cisgendered, college-educated woman who works in marketing, shared how she had reached out to human resources (HR) at her job to deal with bullying, and she now advises others to do the same.

> There's quite a few people that I worked with privately online about contacting their HR department and sitting down with the HR because there's more things that have been said, and the way people act in their workplace that is just not right. I work in HR, and in HR we used to have a meeting on how to handle disabilities, and things you can and cannot do. This can apply to bullying.
>
> By rights with the ADA, the Americans with Disabilities Act, you can actually get that other person removed if you want to because of the way they're bullying you and how they're acting. They can lose their jobs. And I think this can help the whole workplace.
>
> A lot of people don't know how to deal with it [bullying] or what to do, so to help the whole workplace it's good to have an expert at it and talk about how to deal with disabilities. Not just this disability—how to deal with any disability. Questions to ask, ask if they're willing to talk. . . . Or something like, "Would you like to talk about it, or would you rather I not ask?" It's simple.

I would much prefer that than the staring or the talking behind my back and making fun of me, and dressing up for a Halloween as a half-faced clown and when people ask about your costume, you say, "Who am I? I'm Ruth B." You know, that sort of thing. . . . It helps everyone with a disability to have it understood you can't do that. That it's not allowed.

In the various interviews, differences from country to country were understood and referenced, and some lamented the lack of protections where they live. One person, facing a manager refusing to make basic accommodations for her single-sided deafness, who also had expressed negative assessments of her appearance and "mood," noted that where she was "it's different—you don't really have rights about things like this." These protections are an imperative first step.

Disability identity focuses on the lived experience from the position of the subject (Siebers 2008). Ideologies about disability rather than physical difference are problematized. Foregrounding experience generates what Siebers (2008) refers to as a theory of complex embodiment, or one that considers the social and cultural meanings of disability in conjunction with other aspects of identity. This offers a way to advocate for collective interests and "fundamental democratic principles such as inclusiveness and participation" (Siebers 2006, 25).

Not surprisingly, having a disability identity is linked with higher self-esteem (Nario-Redmond, Noel, and Fern 2013). It gives a subject position to the person living with disability, rather than defining as a problematic object. People who embraced disability identity acknowledged social, professional, and physical challenges, but they also do things: seek medical care, advocate and educate, and fight for coverage. But there's more to it. So often it was part of healing and growth.

Previous research on facial difference has suggested that the amount of stigma one faces and the degree of impact or severity is predictive of self-identification as disabled (Bogart et al. 2017), as is the condition being congenital versus acquired (Bogart 2021). But there's also something to this moment. People are finding the existing systems and structures aren't reflecting our needs, our desires, our goals, or who we want to be. The dominant worldview and the traditional ideologies of success, normality, progress, and civilization are being called into question. Histories of colonization, inequality, and conquest underlie much of our current worldview and belief systems, and those things are being eroded.

There's a tremendous pressure to achieve "normality" in a colonized world. The cost of failing to achieve the norm is high. In our past worldview, to be different was to be less than, burdensome, and problematic; one strives to rectify this through appropriate displays of self as producer and/or consumer of the accoutrements of value. This larger worldview is being called into question in complex and interrelated ways, one of them being the challenges posed by disability studies.

DISRUPTED SELVES

Disability studies are about owning it. Owning it is so much more bearable—to just stop worrying about the burden you may be inflicting on others, to stop hoping to hide it, to stop pretending, and just to be a person with a disability. To be disabled. I have heard lots of good semantic arguments, and I don't have a clear answer for the labels. But it's not about the label; it's about letting go of shame, and at the core of internalization is shame.

While I was writing this book, I learned my son lives with autism and attention-deficit/hyperactivity disorder (ADHD); although he can sometimes pass, both conditions impact his life. After poring over books, I couldn't help but notice how clearly the descriptions of autism spectrum disorder (ASD) female adults fit me. The one that described knitting, running, and science fiction–identified girls is the last line of my academic biography: the author enjoys running/hiking, knitting/crocheting, and reading (science fiction). When they threw in pouring glasses of tea that you forget to drink because at first it's too hot but then you get distracted. . . . I had the weird feeling its writer was standing behind me and judging my three half-finished mugs.[7] And confronting my own internalized ableism on two fronts simultaneously revealed how deeply entrenched it is. Reading lists that rank "being like me" (either through facial paralysis or neuroatypicality, which rates well below losing a limb) is hard to process. Because I enjoy being me. And I want my kid to enjoy being.

Laura M., a college-educated, cisgendered white advertising executive, similarly expressed her frustration with how people perceived and treated her because of synkinesis. Yet rather than using other disabilities to distance herself, Laura M. made connections. Employing the same strategy of highlighting known disabilities by contrast, Laura M. drew parallels: "It's a disability like a limp is a disability. It's not like losing a leg or an arm, but it is a disability. It is a challenge. Some things just don't work as quickly, or you might have to figure out another way to do something. You have a process of learning to adjust or adapt." As suggested by disability-identity models, the challenges come not from the disability but from the larger society. Although few of my study's participants embraced disability identity, the idea of a "social disability" resonated with many of them, regardless of their disability identity.

A Social Disability

Social disabilities impact an individual's ability to communicate with self and others, especially in social settings. Social disabilities are not limited to those with facial differences and would include many other overlapping challenges.[8] The shortcomings of the medicolegal model become immediately apparent as one struggles to understand costs, reasonable accommodations, and medical interventions, appropriate for the wide range of social disabilities with

128   METAMORPHOSIS

which people are faced. The boundaries are murky, as are the impacts to the
individual.

Synkinesis as a Social Disability

Synkinesis, as a social disability, includes internal miscommunication and external misunderstandings. Isolation and internalization are the impact of social
disabilities. Previously introduced Amy G., a college educated, cisgendered,
white woman, found her second experience with Bell's palsy left her with synkinesis and an ongoing feeling of anxiety, an internal manifestation of synkinesis
as a social disability.

> I was . . . I mean, most people have some degree of vanity; I was very con-
> fident with my appearance before Bell's palsy. And even after my first case
> I didn't have any residual effects, so I was just as confident after as I had
> been before. With the second bout of Bell's palsy, I was constantly afraid
> of going out, [and] I didn't want to be seen. I am consistently anxious
> about my appearance. I don't like it when people notice it. I don't like it
> when it's called out or attention is drawn to it, and I go out of my way to
> try to hide it. But just how it feels makes me anxious.

Lou C. commented on his social isolation as a result: "Social isolation, that's
been hard. Yeah, you don't want to meet people, [and] you don't want to be in a
setting where you got to talk to people, that kind of scenario. You don't want to
be in the limelight, you don't want to stand in front of a room and give a speech
or talk. You know, those kind of scenarios I go out of my way to avoid, right? So
that kind of thing and then as a consequence, yeah, you become a bit of a social
recluse, right? Someone that doesn't like to mix around." What struck me about
Lou C., who was introduced in chapter 3, is that the man who was telling me he
is a recluse was not. He was married with children and active in his church;
he had found me online and shared short fiction he had written about his
experiences. His initially seemingly inexpressive features hid a man who loved
to laugh and to make others laugh. He enjoyed socializing. Yet his face had led to
isolation, to diminished life expectations.

"Otherness" is internalized. Otherness is a "social disability." The discrimination faced by visible others varies by identity; however, there is an overlap in
the internalization of the negative experiences (Jones 2000). Otherness is
something that creates a thing one is always negotiating, managing, and
double-thinking. Du Bois (1897) introduced the idea of "double-consciousness"
to highlight the impact of what we would come to call *internalization*: the impact
of looking at oneself through the negative lens imposed by the larger world on
those in your category and the necessity of managing that while being aware of
it. The ongoing cost of this experience has been well documented for race,

DISRUPTED SELVES

129

gender, sexuality, disability, and the intersecting spaces where identities overlap (Darling 2019; Lui and Quezada 2019; Ocampo 2022).

Synkinesis creates the experience of otherness through facial difference, magnified by the symptoms of the condition itself. But we are at a moment where people are struggling with these categories, what they mean for ourselves and others, how they help and harm, and what we can change in how we treat people.

Struggling with Internalized Ableism

This experience has challenged me to think more deeply about *isms*. Like retired scientist Patti D., many struggled with internalized ableism and their current condition:

> I sometimes wonder what people were thinking. 'Cause sometimes people have thought that I had a mental disability. I actually have a younger brother who is profoundly retarded. I don't know . . . I don't know what the correct term is now . . . but when he was diagnosed, that's what it was. . . . But he's fifty-three to fifty-four years old, and he's always . . . people can tell. So I'm very familiar with the, you know, the way people look at him, the way people treat him. Yes, I just don't want people to think I was retarded. When they are looking baffled at what's wrong with me, that's definitely crossed my mind. That was a big part of what I've gone through, you know . . . I don't want to be seen that way. . . . People don't treat you as fully human. But there's also my brother. He's treated like that, and he's a person. Certainly, that's in my head too.

So where do I fit? How do I see myself? These are obvious questions after that discussion. The answer is, I don't know. Some days disability identity feels like a wonderful refuge, sometimes like a prison; sometimes fraudulent, sometimes creating community, sometimes, alienating. Some days it just feels sad. Sometimes I forget about it, and I just am. Some days a weird pain is distracting.

The reality is that it's an ongoing process. It's a struggle. It's an opportunity to confront myself and my colonized mind. Where the proverbial rubber meets the road—where the most discomfort, fear, and need for clear boundaries and reassurance emerged—was in the demarcation between physical and cognitive disabilities. Here was my own confrontation, a place to struggle, to change, and to grow.

Rachel Simon's *Riding the Bus with My Sister* (2002) captured it for me. She describes her quest to better understand a sister who has a cognitive disability, and in so doing she confronts ableism. The opening vignette shares a tension of not wanting to be othered that completely, but also feeling a strange

130 METAMORPHOSIS

sense of betrayal, of abandonment. There is something different about those in that "other" category that allows for their dehumanization. With that boundary, we reject what is contemptible to us, what terrifies us, what it embodies, and what it threatens. We reject what our body could become. But more often people find ways to reforge identity and empower and advocate while questioning existing structures. The penultimate chapter centers on rebuilding, challenges, and growth.

6

Someone I Would Rather Be

For me the hardest part was having to reforge my identity. I likened it to having an arbitrary new name imposed upon you that you have to get used to, and that some people will understand and some people won't. Don't worry about explaining it to the people that aren't important to you. But that it definitely takes time, and you have to cultivate aspects of your identity. (Cari M.)

So here one is, stuck with a medical condition that impedes the ability to express self, to communicate, to perform identity. As discussed, there is a shutting down, a loss, a grieving process, but most of those I spoke with were able to reforge identity and find ways to embrace an experience of self. In the last chapter I discussed the loss of the performative self (communication to you), experience of becoming a successful object (me), the spontaneous experience of subjectivity (I), and a shared communal experience (we). Wrestling with disability identity is central, and here I focus on how people reforged their identity and their place, and ultimately on how they challenge assumptions about difference.

Communicative Performance

To some degree, one has to alter the performance to communicate effectively. I trained to be a professor. I thought standing in front of people to convey information was a valuable, learned skill. I spent years developing this. I took drama, dance, music, and other performing arts. I learned stage presence, manner, and how to give the right facial expression, to convey mood, emotion, and tone through expression, to make small changes to affect. The deadpan delivery with a wink, smirk, or raised eyebrow reveals the intended meaning.

At first it all seemed no longer as useful—or at least that was my initial frustrated-angry-hurt-embarrassed-ashamed-afraid response. But stage acting is often about using body language, props, and scene to convey what might not be visible to the back row. A head tilt can convey the same as a knowing smile.

As Kathleen Bogart, Linda Tickle-Degnen, and Mathew Joffe (2012) observed, nonverbal communication can be demonstrated in other ways—effectively, impactfully, and self satisfyingly. Social communication is always fraught with tension, and we all code switch and adjust as we read rooms, situations, and moments. Interpretation of the same performance changes drastically and radically based on perceived identity.

Most of my study's participants figured out eventually how to communicate effectively. Whether it was substituting a wave for a smile or giving a verbal cue, people figured out how to create satisfying interactions. What made these little interactions satisfying were the brief moments of connection, communion, or warmth, not necessarily the smile. This isn't to say that the frustrations of misexpression, misfeel, or misperception were now absent, but they were being effectively managed. To some degree, adjusting to changes in communication as our bodies grow, develop, and fail is a normal process. Synkinesis amplifies or complicates this process, making it more exhausting and more difficult, and restricting roles and performances but not eradicating them.

Me—The Object Produced

The *me* is the object produced through social performance. In the last chapter, the difficulty of producing a me that could elicit "pride" rather than "mortification" was discussed. The concept of the me not only captures a feeling within the self but highlights relations of power and privilege. Looking and being looked at are deeply intertwined, as discussed in chapter 3. Implied is the right to look and assess (the subject position of the "normal"), and the object position of that which is under scrutiny (the "abnormal" other). Regardless of whether it is for pleasure, amusement, or abhorrence, being the object is not entirely a disempowered position. The object can choose to enact or manage the performance in specific ways. Performing/doing self isn't about creating an object that "pleases" others; it's about a performance that conveys. But one cannot perform any "me," and some performances are more powerful. Social locations of privilege and oppression limit the mes from which one can choose. Some mes are closer to our I, some protect our Is, some render us vulnerable, and some feel disingenuous.

Synkinesis did not enhance one's appearance as an approachable, likeable object. Everyone knew it. Everyone knew their physical capital had dropped, their approachability had lessened, and their social desirability had diminished. Certainly, existing social location impacted one's perception of the meaning and the cost or risk of this, but it was universally acknowledged that synkinesis negatively impacted others' evaluations of us and our ability to manage that (such as provide a warm smile). Several noted how it had negatively impacted their looks in ways that hurt their career; others said it had impacted their ability to appear welcoming or friendly; some said that family or friends had misinterpreted; many said that it had simply created moments where folks seemed to "notice" and wonder. In each case, one had that moment of seeing the self as an object and confronting the brutal impact of synkinesis on that assessment. Erving Goffman (1959) gave us the example of the "faux pas" for moments when impression management is blown; synkinesis is forever failing at impression management.

The faux pas provides such a potent example because it's so relatable. Let's stop for a minute and think about what it means to fail at impression management. The cost or stakes and the reactions of others are what makes it devastating, not the actual moment of immediate failure. If we feel safe, it's funny. We all laugh uproariously at faux pas when committed within our circles of trust. My overly literal childhood friend and I often explode in mirth at the many faux pas created by both of us sharing this trait. My spouse and I bonded over the humor we find in self social failure. With friends and with kith and kin it's not really embarrassing—it's funny, it's you. But what if no one laughs, or the laughter is cruel, derisive, and alienating rather than shared?

The threat is in what one stands to *lose*, not that one is imperfect. What one stands to *lose* is actually the systemic problem of privilege and oppression manifest in personal discomfiture. The cost of a faux pas is very different depending on one's existing subject location. How one internalizes moments of social imperfection and the costs is relative. What is discrediting, disqualifying, and problematic for those in some subject locations may have no cost for those in other locations. The initial assessment shapes the interaction in ways that may make it likely to be satisfying, alienating, shaming, or even deadly. Being mistaken for a "Karen"[1] versus being mistaken for an assailant—that is, being viewed as less capable rather than as a threat—carries different risks, meanings, and impacts.

Regardless of individual identity, something is different, more challenging, and more difficult. But does it have to be a loss? In our current system, yes. Hierarchies and tyrannies of norms infuse identities while privilege and oppression enforce values. Our existing ways of understanding bodies and selves suffer terribly from the damage we do to ourselves and others with that belief and the larger systems of beliefs in which we are entrenched.

It's not just pride or mortification. The impact on bodies of the differences in our relative safety, access to meaningful care, respect for bodily autonomy, and what it means to live with vulnerability cannot be underestimated. Having a me impacted primarily by mortification, rather than the other potential impacts of historic relations of privilege and oppression, is privilege.

In my previous work with Shari Dworkin (2009), we discussed Frigga Haug's subjective aspects-of-being-as-object. Haug highlights the pleasure of making oneself into a desirable object, and the experience of subjecthood embedded within that experience. Shari and I explore the commodification of our processes of creating embodied gendered/heteronormative, raced, and "not" classed bodies. The market creates never-ending flaws that one then works to address or solve, deriving satisfaction from one's hard work toward an unachievable ideal with some tangible goals improved upon. Investing capital in the self yields short-term pleasurable experiences and successes, and people are quick to share imagery of goals met and statuses achieved, displaying a morally validated self.

But we don't have equitable access. The pleasures we are offered, that are normalized, that are valued and validated, are part of the perpetuation of a hierarchical market system. Our moments of pride, of shared experience, of display, and of humanity are increasingly shaped primarily by a commodified me. George Herbert Mead (1934) observed from the genesis of the concept of the "me" that invasion by the foreign symbols of advertising—feedback that was market infused rather than community based—was problematic. Because your me is still you: it's not the actual judgment of others, it's the system in your head structuring your investment, shaping your daily practices, beliefs, hopes, and desires.

What does one do with problematic feedback? The people I spoke with tended to cope in a variety of ways. Often the same person might employ different strategies depending on the day, mood, or audience. Avoiding, educating, or ignoring were the three most common and obvious ways people dealt with the inevitable assaults to the self that synkinesis creates.

As previously discussed, some dealt with challenges, negative feedback, and dehumanizations by avoiding contact with new people, public presentations, and/or withdrawing from social interaction. Although there is a tendency to see withdrawal through a lens of problematization (and as discussed in chapter 4, it can be problematic), it can also be self-protective and liberating. Some of my participants highlighted cutting back on some things, appreciating the freedom to do so. Others realized that some relationships, workplaces, and even some family members were not supportive or compassionate, and they didn't need to tolerate that treatment. Some found it gave them the excuse to not do things for which they weren't well suited regardless of synkinesis.

One lovely woman whom I had the pleasure of meeting at the Pacific Northwest support group shared in our interview that her family, especially one person, was extremely invested in appearances. They cycled through denial and hurtful statements; for them, her facial paralysis was never about her but always about how it reflected on the "family." Struggling to regain a positive self-image, she'd always part from that person feeling like "damaged goods." She found the realization that she could limit her time with that person—or avoid her entirely on days when she didn't feel up to the meeting—was liberating and self-protective.

Another participant shared how her once reasonably sociable workplace suddenly became a place where everyone still laughed—but at her, and with cruelty. Witnessing her co-workers' mimicry, she was initially devastated. But she remembered she'd had always thought that clique unkind and had avoided their meanness; now she didn't really want to be around them or in a workplace that tolerated that. This theme re-emerged with some regularly in discussions, support groups, and online: some people, places, and events just weren't worth bothering about, so why put oneself in that situation?

Similarly, some did nothing. In this case, they were aware that people had noticed their face, but they decided to simply leave it up to everyone's imagination. Much of the time they saw someone "notice" and then the moment would pass by unremarked. They viewed it as a minor faux pas—their face communicated something nonsensical, jarring, startling, unusual, or whatever. They could see the audience respond, briefly confused, offended, bemused, annoyed, troubled, shocked, curious, or whatever. But the moment always passed, and there was enough interest in the content of the conversation that the moment was forgotten in the miasma of information communicated. Or maybe they didn't forget, but why worry about it?

As Julie G., who has lived with synkinesis for twenty years, recounted, after she had met some new people she noticed one of the women staring at her mouth. She observed, "I don't know if they asked about it in the car on the way home. . . . I thought about saying something, but the moment passed, and it wasn't that important."

Kintsugi, or kintsukuroi, the Japanese practice of re-creating broken pottery as art with lacquer and silver-, gold-, or platinum-infused dust, is the oft-used metaphor for embracing damage. The beauty and elegance of the new piece highlights the surviving damage. Although the metaphor is beautiful in its simplicity, much is overlooked. The repair is an action, but it's also an ability, and it is so much easier for some. In some cases a few simple cracks are filled—elegant, achievable; but other pots are shattered, stepped on, or already chipped. Similarly, by accident of birth, some people are better equipped materially, physically, and psychosocially for survival. Having the privilege to (re) create the self through advocacy, through education, and through outreach gave some the opportunity to re-create a satisfying experience of the subjective experience of being-as-object. But not everyone has the same access, needs, or desires. For those who are rebuilding, advocacy for self and others was often an important part of their experience. Advocacy and education could take place

136 METAMORPHOSIS

in formal, or informal settings. Formal advocacy took the form of support groups, volunteering, awareness days, speaking at events, or speaking to groups or schools. Many recounted sharing with schools, workplaces, and other groups.

Gina C., a white, college-educated, cisgendered entertainer, found ways to use public performance to embrace and accept her postsurgical facial paralysis. She observed, "Becoming a performer, and bringing it into my performance gave me power over it, instead of it having power over me. Me being able to laugh at it, to laugh at myself, with others. . . . Instead of feeling bad about myself or hiding." Similarly, Amy D. mentioned always being happy to answer questions from strangers: "Educating people is really empowering. It's a good example to set. People shouldn't be ashamed to be who they are. And you feel better about yourself."

At the essence of subjecthood is self, and it is critical to have some ability to shape the narrative. In that shaping, there is opportunity for cultural challenge. Who tells the story of our categories? At a deeper level, as Michel Foucault would assert, the epistemic core of our culture is revealed in these categorizations, the machinations of power. There is nothing wrong with my face. There is nothing wrong with anyone's face. There may be lots of things "wrong" with me, but it's not about my face. It's the histories of tyranny that colonize my knowledge, the cruelty of norms, that is what's wrong. But it's not my face.

In consumer culture, the body as project is central to our displays of morality, security, and success (Featherstone and Turner 1995). One must confront what one now is, and how one will be seen, but also what one is taught to think and how. To some degree the reflexive project of the self under late-stage racial capitalism is a commodified quest for desirable normativity, with adherence justifying privilege and deviations validating failures. Disability identity inherently challenges that by undermining the quest with alternative cultural valuations. One of the days I was working on this section, my neighbor asked about my eye. He's a lovely man; despite our obvious political differences (I ignore his lawn signs, and he ignores my T-shirts), we chat about dogs, our kids, and neighborhood happenings. Without thinking, he asked if I could see normally with both eyes, and then immediately he was aghast. I could see that he wanted to backpedal and was worried he had offended; he immediately apologized. Certainly, there's always a pang with these reminders of what once was and now is, but is that wrong? Is that something I shouldn't feel or hold? I turn it over in my hands like a smooth stone, running my fingers over it, and finding comfort in its solid presence: I can drop it, or skip it across a lake, or hurl it far away, or put it in my pocket.[2] It is what I was, and what I am, and who I am because of what I was, and what I lost, and what I gained. I can put the stone back, or I can hold it, squeeze it tight, and take comfort in its solid reality.

I answered my neighbor honestly and openly. I shared that I was writing a book; I had synkinesis, the result of Bell's palsy, and that my vision wasn't impacted, but others might indeed have some issues. Advocacy feels good. It makes one an expert. But the interaction highlighted the other side: we aren't supposed to ask. But why not? Why is a physical difference always assumed a failure about which it would be rude to inquire? When someone changes their hair or gets in shape, we ask about it and we comment because we view it as a positive change. Though synkinesis is rarely seen as a physical improvement, what we may have learned and how we may have grown might be. With synkinesis, the potential privacy of bodily failure is rendered obsolete by its visibility. Advocacy puts one in control of the narrative. Of course, we can't control others' judgments, beliefs, kindnesses, or cruelties. But the narratives I share, those can be mine.

Advocacy puts into doubt who is committing the faux pas. Because what makes it a faux pas is the assumption of failure and shame. Advocacy is about removing shame. Disability, as a social construct, is hurtful; advocacy mitigates the pain. It gives one a satisfying, meaningful, and useful role in interactions. We set aside the underlying cultural assumptions embedded in useful and meaningful social roles and the ableism. But no, that isn't right either—that's exactly the problem. It's there, in all space, and in our minds, and in our selves. It's already embedded in our feelings of self-worth, pride, shame. To live in a body that fails to approximate the norm is to always be a body that isn't being right. It's to always be an object—scrutinized, wondered, pitied, and discounted.

It's so easy to forget that one is also always a subject. And it's very easy to be angry. Angry at them for not understanding. angry at me for being this way. Angry that it can't be different. Angry that it can't just be. Angry at the world. Angry. Advocacy feels so much better, like a step closer to I, a step closer to controlling the narrative. But it's deeper: it's about a refusal to demand approximation to a norm, refusal to be less than—for anyone to be less than. There is also a looming conundrum. We should be accepted as is, but may also require medical support to rebuild or reconstruct. That is our choice. That's what "being seen" means.

Effective/Authentic Performances of Self (I)

This is it. The one that hurts the most. I want to be me (I), without this distraction. This is the one that's impossible. It's always there, disrupting my I, festering at the edge of consciousness. It's inserting itself, unwanted, into experience. There is a something lost, a spontaneous appreciation of being, as detailed in the last chapter. But perhaps something's gained: the wisdom that comes with loss. Knowledge, valuable and terrible, is in the price. But "I" is "I." A disrupted synkinetic challenging experience is the authentic embodied experience I now have.

So how do I turn that experience into an I that better fits? How do I change the conditions by which the me is evaluated?

In some ways that experience of the I is lost, but the necessary introspection is something gained. Like therapy, it forces you to think about the why of the I. One needs to reflect deeply, and often on feelings. Irrational moods signaling impending illness are obvious to me now. Forced to sort through irrational feelings in my face or head, a recent flu surprised me by how aware I was of very slight changes in my body temperature, manifesting in inexplicable frustration and irritability.

Adapting to sorting through physical sensations that don't belong manifests necessary introspection. Maria M., introduced previously, shared my observations, noting how her experience with synkinesis deepened her understanding of the connection between mental and physical health:

> I don't want to get sick again. I've had to learn how to manage my anger. To not let things get to me. I'm not saying I have no feelings whatsoever, but I just learn not to let it get to me as much, even though it hurts or whatever. . . . I just remind myself I am going to get through this . . . I don't have to be angry. I can be OK, whatever happens. Because I don't want my face to droop again. I don't want my face to get like it was before. So I learned how to control my emotions. I learned how to control my anger even though, like I said, whatever I'm going through it may hurt, it may not hurt, I may shed a couple of tears then I was like, "OK, you're fine, don't worry, you're good. Keep going." And it's easier to feel good.

Many people cited a greater mind-body awareness, appreciation, or management as something they gained. A shift in a sense of self was conjectured; people shared an awareness of our embodied fragility, which terrified and emboldened them.

The other key positive people noted was growth. There was a challenge that forced confrontation with some of the -isms of our society—ableism, faceism, neuroatypicalism—in others and in ourselves. We were forced to look at what we believed and why, and the fears and validations behind it, and to come out the other side as kinder, more compassionate, and perhaps wiser. The realization of the fragility of identity entrenched in hierarchy and privilege, of the limits of the ontological security of normality, is more than changing one's views on disability. Disability identity is about challenging the ontological foundations of self in Western society. It's about fundamentally questioning the binaries that place some into the privileged norm and others into the stigmatized category of other. Increasingly, people are pushing back against the categorical imperative of a tyrannical normal. The bridge between the theoretical and the embodied remains in practice. The process of rebuilding and reconciling the self can be part of a shared communal experience.

Creating Shared Experiential Community

Through my healing process, it reinforced my beliefs about caring. I think that the most therapeutic thing you can do is to care about other people. But at the same time you can't give up yourself. When I did the psychotherapy with people, with groups, or gave talks, it's a lot of things to balance. On the one hand, you want to care about other people and be altruistic. On the other hand, you also balance that, you have to love yourself enough, that you're not dependent on the approval of other people. You have to have that balance. You have to be OK with you. And other people have to be OK with themselves, and finding ways for us all to be that way. To all be OK. Maybe better than OK.

Sandy D., a graduate school–educated, cisgendered, white mental health professional, observed the necessity of community and acceptance. A shared experience means something different in the world emerging. The larger community of people, one's community of choice, and the disability identity/synkinesis community all mattered in different ways to people. The most challenging was the larger world and especially new people or large groups.

The larger world was the space of microaggression, stares, bullying, and less success. Meeting "new people" was challenging; public presentations and speaking were now more often avoided than embraced. A disproportionate number of participants in my project and in support groups were those who could not avoid public space/performances. Teachers, entertainers, service providers all discussed having strategies for addressing what would be a barrier to establishing communion.

And although negative experiences certainly reoccurred, persistence revealed communities of acceptance. Care and compassion could generate deep feelings of connection and community. Several people highlighted being invited to speak at schools, religious services, or to groups about their experience. Through advocacy, larger communities became more tolerant and accepting. And, as an educator, sharing my experiences with students has resulted in several recounting their own experiences or that of valued family. Being open and vulnerable in public spaces has resulted in others being more open and vulnerable in response. And the weirdest thing is that being vulnerable somehow creates strength.

Amy D., who was previously introduced, highlighted how her childhood friend had attended a support event with her and listened carefully to her concerns regarding photographs. She noticed her friend thence forth always took special care to ensure she was feeling good about sharing any photo taken. She noted that her friend's unasked for gesture was deeply meaningful, and she strove to extend that same compassion to others who might face different, but equally daunting, challenges.

Another long-time participant at support groups, Meagan T., a cisgendered, middle-aged, college-educated woman, was working up the courage to try dating after a divorce and synkinesis. Commiserating with a dear friend, she was reassured by her friend, who highlighted the ways all their friends' bodies were becoming more difficult as they aged. Rather than pretending it wasn't noticeable or impactful, her friend commiserated with her, sharing her own concerns of how her body would be viewed after cancer. She had remarked that anyone their age had some body problems, just some were more immediately visible than others. That genuine honesty combined with care—the ability to make it an "us" through the shared fear of rejection and frustrations over inevitable age changes—is community, and she recounted feeling stronger as a result.

But there is something unique about the experience of synkinesis. Something about the depth of the experience and that loss of and rebuilding of the "I" that craves kinship with the like. The single most common statement at support groups was the importance of simply being with others who shared this rare experience. Disability as a source of community because of shared experience can be as much a source of identity and community as other forms of identity such as race, gender, or sexual orientation (Baker 2011; Berger 2013; Bogart and Hemmesch 2016; Martin 2007). One of the many exceptional people I met doing this research was Lou C., who was introduced earlier in the book. He found me—he'd emailed me after finding me on a website and looking me up to ensure I was legitimate. He had accurate intel: he noted I had mentioned it was harder to find male participants, so he then reached out. He sent me a short story and a blog post he had written as an introduction before our interview.

Probably contracting Bell's palsy in his teens, Lou's ongoing struggle with synkinesis had been ignored. He was told he was simply funny looking, not well adjusted, distractible, perhaps just not good at school; his initial onset and lack of treatment impacted his concentration in a competitive school environment. It was assumed he wouldn't amount to much, and that was OK with his family and friends—but not with him. The story he sent me was about meeting his spouse in college. They both enjoyed racquet sports, shared a deep religious commitment, enjoyed the outdoors. He got his degree, married, went on to earn a graduate degree, has a successful career, is a respected member of his religious community, and finally found doctors willing to take him seriously. But he wanted to talk to someone else who *had* synkinesis—who actually had it. He found me.

So many people have expressed the terrible fear that they were alone in this. That they were the only one. That this was a special punishment visited on them for vanity, for a cruel remark, for having bullied a peer in childhood, for something they couldn't conceive, for a host of sins, imagined, committed, and lived. That they (we) were supposed to have recovered, and,

SOMEONE I WOULD RATHER BE

in failing to do so, that they (we) had somehow revealed their inner portrait of Dorian Gray,[3] their status as a villain, marked and branded. But we also know that's not true. That it's not fair what our culture, our histories, our world tell us about ourselves now. It's a lot to live, and to simply be in a space with others living it, where you don't have to explain, is glorious. Any embodied otherness needs this kinship. Support groups, both online and in person, as well as support events have been impactful and crucial to the rebuilding of a sense of self.

Reframing the Self

Oh, yeah, big time. It changed me in a different way meaning that I value myself more now than I did before. I learned how to love myself again. I learned to find more things about myself to like. I learned how to appreciate what other people did for me; it just changed the way I see everything. I value other people more. I'm kinder. (Maria M.)

I'm definitely stronger. Sitting there, having to talk to new people with a funny face, or dealing with new parents, going out and doing everyday activities. . . . You overcome your fear of going out and having things look messed up, so I think that that's helped me a lot. I've always been confident, but I think it definitely gives you more confidence when you feel like you could do more because you have to. Because you are doing more. And you are doing it! You can either choose to sit inside and stay in your little bubble if you need to, or you could choose to go beyond that and say, "Eff it. I'm going to rock this. Got to do what I got to do." And I found out, I can still rock it. (Mandy D.)

Maria M. and Mandy D., who were both previously introduced, shared with me the growth they experienced personally through this process. People are resilient, in all the ways people are typically resilient after loss. People found ways to reframe who that loss had made them, within a narrative of the self that was consistent with existing identity. (Sort of like an academic writing a book. Anyway, you get the point.) People tended to reframe the self in complicated and sometimes contradictory ways, seeing a self who both gained and lost, who struggled, failed, and succeeded. The perceived proportions varied by person, by moment, by circumstances impacted, by facets of identity, by experience, and so forth. We will return to this in a moment. But this balance of loss and growth typified the re-creation of a narrative of the self after synkinesis.

Despite facing discrimination at work, Jennifer D., a white cisgendered cosmetologist and hair stylist, was able to reframe her talents as a way to give to others, and her experience provides insight:

It just reminds me that there are far worse things that can happen to you, and to your health physically or mentally, and that you come first. It makes me look at people a whole lot different to know that you never know where someone is in their life. You never know how they're feeling deep down inside, even if on the outside they look good. I learned to always try to be a little bit kinder to people . . .

And I guess it's a little bit, I guess the positive thing I'm getting out of it is I want to continue in my career, but I guess I've been in the wrong places, wrong environments, to really give people what I want to give. . . . And it's not just the haircut. I want to change the outlook on hair dressers and stylists, to expand what is beauty, to make more people feel beautiful.

And I actually I feel like the one thing I've been good at was listening to people, and that has helped me in this time. I know that a hairdresser can make someone feel so much better, even regardless of everything that's going on. So that I guess it's something I'm working on to change myself, and my job, for the better. I can make people feel better about themselves, and that's something.

In her mid-twenties, Bell's palsy and the developing synkinesis had left Jennifer D., an attractive hair stylist, shaken. Working in the beauty industry, so much of her core identity had been undermined by her postsynkinesis experiences. But, as noted previously, she reconsidered beauty as something unique to individuals rather than an objective standard. Jennifer D. had a role model, someone who modeled disability identity:

I guess the one thing is I have my other cousin who is eighteen years old, she was born premature, and she has some visible differences—and she's had to have a lot of surgeries, things like that. And I've always been close with her, and this past summer I was able to get her ready for her prom, and she didn't have anybody to go with, but she still went.

I guess the fact that I was able to go with her—I went to her house, and my goal was to make sure that she felt as beautiful as she could, and I couldn't grasp the idea of going to a prom by myself, or not being asked because, like I said, my social life was so much different from hers. And I know that she probably sat alone at lunch because people think she looks different—not normal—and the fact that she was so fearless to go to prom. . . . It just honestly was such an eye-opener. She wasn't too nervous; this is something she's been living with her whole life.

And now she's choosing to go away to a college that's five hours away, and her mom is freaking out because she's been so protective of her daughter, of knowing how the society may look at her and treat her just because she looks different, but here she is making that choice for

SOMEONE I WOULD RATHER BE

herself to just live a normal life. And I've gotten so close to her this summer . . .

And it was this moment a light bulb kind of went off, and I was like, "I didn't deal with half the stuff she dealt with, but she chooses to not let that affect her." And so she makes me stronger, to know that things are good, everything's good. No matter how different you think you may look; you kind of still have to put yourself out there and do what you want to do.

"Do what you want to do." After I got Bell's palsy, people were surprised I still took a long-planned trip. It was hard—the stares, questions, and unwanted commiserations. Being called a monster by a child. That will never leave me. But I would still have been the same monster if I hadn't gone, and I would have missed out on so much I enjoyed as well as on the knowledge of my own resilience. But it's so much easier to push through on a vacation, with one's unthreatened career, than it is when more of the ground on which identity rests is unstable, unsafe.

Privilege and Coping

Arriving at coping is a process. The people I was able to find at support groups (in person or online), on social media, at awareness events, and through organizations were all coping to some degree. A few gave me a glimpse into their experience of struggling. A few were still dealing with isolation, depression, pain, and lacked access to resources to make significant changes in their circumstances. Some recounted depression, anxiety, and attempts at suicide; one person recounted almost total isolation.

The U.S. healthcare system, from which the majority of my participants hailed, is a challenge. Even with health insurance, rare diseases are difficult to get correctly diagnosed and treated. Even living in one of the few major cities with significant centers that treat synkinesis, it was difficult to find and access services. That was the case for me even though I have a PhD-requiring job in which I teach statistics, interpreting data, and accessing appropriate resources, even with a spouse who is a physician. Even with a supportive functional family, long-standing friend network, and a loving partner, the emotional drain of seeking help for a rare condition has been overwhelming. Those in regions with medical coverage often still find that newer (and more impactful) treatments aren't covered and still face difficulty in obtaining correct information and treatment. (Though one person living in another country mentioned that the obvious impact on her face resulted in her not needing the usual bribes to access healthcare.)

Appropriate Botox treatment and occupational or physical therapy from experienced practitioners is the exception, not the rule, when it should be the standard of care. Synkinesis doesn't kill you, but it creates a host of challenges. There are a variety of effective treatments that can mitigate pain, reduce inappropriate motion, and improve functionality. There are also a plethora of promises from untested, unproven, and sometimes problematic treatment providers. There was no question that family stability, class, and intersecting categories of otherness (race, gender, other disabilities, immigration status, and so forth) were indicative of ability to access higher quality care. Higher quality care facilitates coping.

Overall, the medical models fail to consider the social impact of disability adequately (Mauldin and Brown 2021). In chapter 3, I shared a few examples of medical microaggressions. As is unfortunately typical for nonwhite patients (Schalk 2018), my nonwhite participants were far more likely to describe hostile, negative, unhelpful, or inappropriate interactions with healthcare providers. The ability to persevere in obtaining appropriate care is impacted by the perceptions of and treatment by others, and appropriate care is integral to physical and mental health.

Location was a critical factor in care and recovery: there are very few specialists, and they are generally found in urban areas or near major medical universities. Given the dearth of specialists in synkinesis, many of my interviewees had been faced with the prospect of being the first patient in their community. The lower income rural patients often had few options for access to specialists and treatment, even if their insurance covered the treatment itself. One frustrated low-income rural patient found that insurance would cover the Botox injections essential for pain management, but no one within an accessible distance could perform the injections. Without a car in an area with limited transit options and working from home at a minimum wage job, the trip to an urban center three to four times a year to receive this treatment was impossible.

Pierre Bourdieu's (1984) concept of symbolic violence highlights the way the system does violence to the self through our own enactment and embodiment of systemic inequity. Living as "other" undermines physical and mental well-being and reifies the inequality. The belief that facial disfigurement is indicative of moral failings, is a deserved retribution, or is a punishment of some kind, as has been highlighted throughout this book, reveals one way that disability identity is undermined and privilege reproduced. The ways our vulnerabilities are rendered market opportunities reinforces the systemic inequity of neoliberal late-stage industrial capitalism (Featherstone and Turner 1995). So, basically, more privilege allows more engagement in compensatory strategies, body work, and fashion display. But it's set against a backdrop of assumptions about what signifies a host of positive attributes and identities versus stigmatized attributes and identities.

The experiences of identity within networks of privilege mean doing and being can feel good. There are many meaningful, self-reflective projects of the self (physical, physiological, mental, and social). As Shari Dworkin and I discussed in our previous work (2009), investment in the body, even within hierarchical systems, can be and often is pleasurable and identity affirming. People find ways to communicate self, style, and identity while managing facial difference; in some cases, facial difference allowed a previously unexplored part of the self to be developed. Two examples come from cisgendered young women: Val L., a Latina who acquired her facial difference in her teens, and Vi V., originally from Southeast Asia, who acquired hers while pregnant. Val developed a unique and fun fashion sense to express a whimsical personality whereas Vi made use of makeup to completely obscure an otherwise noticeable asymmetry.

Val shared how she learned to express her personality with wild fashion: "So I kind of just forced myself in a way to go out of my comfort zone because I knew my confidence was already shot, so I can—[I] just wore really outlandish things with fashion instead. . . . And then I settled down, and now I have my own style. Neon high-tops, fun accessories. . . . And I get compliments on that all the time. It took some time, but I have it now." Val shared how much she enjoyed finding just the right accessory, and how it led her to explore the local area more as she found thrift stores, boutiques, and crafters who matched her tastes.

Practical and analytic Vi was proud of her children, her success as a healthcare provider, and her caring daughter and sister. But she also enjoyed being able to "not let it show" at special events. Vi used makeup for such special events, though they might have been something personal such as an anniversary dinner for two or a family wedding; however, she found it too time consuming and costly for everyday use.

Most who were willing to speak with me individually or at support events were coping. Well . . . that was the case most of the time. But they were coping enough. If I had to say what the common denominators were of those who coped and those who were not finding ways to do so, it was having support. They had someone, somewhere, standing by them, caring about them, who saw them as like themselves in other ways. That person or people didn't have to be perfect, but they had to provide unconditional acceptance.

The other factor was having meaningful responsibilities for those who one values, which provides a barrier between oneself and the damage of judgment that being on the wrong side of privilege inflicts. In chapter 3 I noted the importance of having a support network of those whom we see as like ourselves for bolstering our identity. The people who had such groups to act as a buffer between the ideological impositions of systems and their vulnerable self were more insulated. But it also takes a certain amount of privilege to have any control over your daily experiences. It is imperative that we understand not coping, to some degree, as the inability to enact an environment in which one can cope.

Coping Is an Ongoing Process That Requires Ongoing Support

"I don't have a social life anymore, for the past six months since it happened. I couldn't drive at first. . . . Then they weren't sure what was going on, so they put me on medications that made me gain weight, so I felt even worse. Fat and messed-up face. I just don't want to go anywhere." Jen P. ended our interview by acknowledging she wasn't coping but wanted to—she was planning to call a therapist. It was heartbreaking because she was fun, lively, and had a great sense of humor, and I had very much enjoyed the time I spent with her. She also had health insurance that would cover her therapy, a job that allowed for flexible hours, and supportive friends and family. She has the ability to exercise a fair degree of control over her life while being physically, emotionally, and psychologically safe in her home and work environments.

The ability to cope is a privilege. Almost all participants described a process of struggle through which they adapted and began to cope. Things like mental health setbacks, drug and alcohol use, relationship struggles, eating disorders emerging or reappearing, and suicidal ideation were recounted. But the ability to be safe through a process was something that many also shared.

One of my participants had the privilege of a process. Mary D., a white, cisgendered professional, so aptly described a period of being a "sad sobby mess." She said that she sought temporary help from her doctor: "I called my doctor and went and talked to him. He put me on a really low dose of Zoloft because it was awful. I just said to my husband, 'You can just divorce me, and you can go get married to somebody else. You go through that whole "my face is never going to be the same again" feeling sorry for yourself. Just let me visit my daughter. Just let her come visit me.' You kind of go through that sad, sobby mess. But then you start to get better, and feel like you can go out again." Coping is a process. And those who felt secure in their relationships, financial situation, and support network were able to rebuild a sense of self and identity.

So What Helps Put Yourself Back Together?

"You go on; you cope. Everybody does. But it's heartbreaking. And you lose a piece of yourself. . . . It takes time to rebuild." Lori M., who has a graduate degree and a fulfilling career, described the process of grieving her old self. Synkinesis creates a host of challenges—physical, emotional, and psychological—to the self. So what specifically has gotten people with synkinesis back on track? What are the things that have given people . . .

Here, I must pause because what I was going to write seems trite. Strength? Support? Whatever. As I've said previously, most of those things weren't one shot deals—they were built with a lifetime of support, safety, positive reinforcement, and an array of privileges. Really, what I can best talk about here is what has made it easier.

Appropriate Medical Treatment

As I researched this book, it remained frustratingly obvious that there is no clear standard of care for synkinesis or its preconditions. The role of electrical stimulation (e-stim) in alleviating or potentially negatively impacting the condition remains unclear. The risk factors are poorly understood or seldom publicized. Double-blind clinical studies on the treatments have been rare. In support groups, online forums, and across the internet, people continue to share what has "worked" for them, with little substantiation. Given that most people heal regardless, their anecdotal evidence is problematic at best. Finding people who have had experience with the treatments is difficult, and funding such care can be even more so. More research and well-disseminated and funded care are essential.

Surgery and Medical Interventions

"I want to keep doing Botox. I want to have the surgery, but the Botox is $1,500, and I am happy with it. Surgery is even more. I don't think I can afford the surgery. But I want it . . . I want to feel good again. I want to feel sexy and attractive again. I want to feel good again. I want my life back." Jen P., who was introduced previously, has employer-provided medical insurance but still pays out of pocket for effective Botox treatments. Surgery remains financially out of reach for her, despite being a professional with no children. Similarly, Angie C., a cisgendered, Latina, graduate-educated professional, remains frustrated in finding medical care from providers who are at least as well informed as she is:

> I forget the word they used, but they said nothing is covered unless it's physiological function or something to that effect. . . . Yeah, I have a lot of pain, and it's hard to eat and talk . . . I can't talk for long. I don't eat in public anymore. It's a lot of pain. So not sure why that's not covered . . . I wish I could at least get Botox for pain. . . . I don't think it's not lack of support. I think it's just lack of knowledge. They just don't know. Usually when I go to the doctor, I know more than they do. They don't know how to help me. They don't know how to advocate.

Being taken seriously and referred to appropriate treatment is essential. I spent years consulting with people who didn't really understand synkinesis, didn't understand the pain and functional challenges, and therefore didn't provide the right advice, treatment, or even empathy. That experience was more common than not. Unnecessary and painful procedures (I had a spinal tap I didn't need, and a post-tap headache that sidelined me for two weeks),

148   METAMORPHOSIS

dismissive responses to requests, and inappropriate advice bordering on malpractice were common experiences.[4] One participant recounted painful, expensive, and unnecessary electroshock therapies from a specialist. Worse, most of us end up paying out of pocket for these treatments that may not be effective.

We can do better. People reported finding Botox, surgery, and specialized occupational therapy as impactful, and many mentioned mental healthcare as necessary. Although the physical care was difficult, mental health care was rarely recommended, despite the ubiquity of negative mental health impacts on those living with acquired facial difference and synkinesis.

Therapy

People tended to report positive experiences when they could access mental health support. Therapy, support groups, accountability groups, other medical professionals providing emotional support and care were generally reported as being impactful. It turns out therapy works. People who acquire facial difference have higher rates of anxiety, depression, and isolation, although in the long term most people cope, and their anxiety and depression return to the nonclinical range (Daker-White et al. 2014; VanSwearingenet al. 1998). This indicates immediate intervention could be very impactful.

Many sought therapy and support groups, and they made ongoing attempts to find the right therapist, therapy, or group. Being a healthcare professional herself, Kelly H. knew not to give up when the first group she tried wasn't right for her: "The first group I tried was more about hearing loss, so that wasn't right for me. I do have single-sided deafness now, but I was there about my face. So I found [the group where I met her]. This is better for me." Several of my participants had founded or initiated support groups in their own region or online after they had initially sought support and found it lacking. "There needs to be a space for people to express and share, and that's what makes people connect. There needs to be up as much as down. We need to share the down and 'here's what worked for me.' It's good to listen; this is devastating. People are devastated. But they need to hear that we can get back, and there's not a lot of information on that out there." Brad A., who introduced in previous chapters, founded a satellite group locally after attending groups over two hours away. He expressed how impactful support groups and personal therapy had been for improving his outlook on his condition and his life. Despite his permanent facial difference, therapy after his synkinesis began resulted in improved mental health; he found himself achieving other life goals, such as managing his weight.

Similarly, Abby B., who was previously introduced, found online support groups gave her an outlet when there were no local options: "There's nothing around here I can go to, so I go online. I'm in a few of them on Facebook. I'm very open about what this, what Bell's did to me. It feels really good to also be supportive, because if I can save one person from getting stuck like I did for a while, I've done my job. There's pictures of me at difference stages of this stuff. I'm really vocal. I talk about healing. A little bit on Twitter, too. The one I find most helpful is [name of online group]. I get help; I give help."

But, like therapy, finding the right match for what you need at the time you need it is crucial. Support groups for people in different phases of their process and with different impactions are crucial. The wrong fit comes mostly from either wanting something different at that moment or from being more, or less, healed than others in the group. For example, those with long-term impacts often found their support groups to be either too focused on recent grief or on healing, rather than on long-term mental health. Angie C., who was previously introduced, was fairly impacted but ready to move on. Her grieving process was winding down, and Angie just wanted to focus on enjoying life. But there have been challenges, both physical and social. Having moved past her venting, Angie was looking for suggestions, solutions, and sometimes commiseration; instead, she found many groups were focused on recent diagnoses, and they tended to feel bogged down in immiseration: "I joined one group on Facebook for a while. It just got really depressing. New people just kept joining, and it was like getting it over and over. It was all just a lot of saying what a nightmare it is and whining. . . . No solutions. . . . No help in moving on. Just venting over and over." Angie instead joined a group for long-term survivors, which she found better matched her needs and place in the healing process.

Brad A, who was cited earlier as founding his own local group, eventually created a podcast to share his experiences. He knew that coping was a hard, difficult process, but he really needed to hear more from people who had gotten through it, moved on, and were OK. He wasn't finding those spaces. He had gone through his own self-pathologizing period and emerged with a burgeoning sense of disability identity. He wanted support in reframing, rebuilding, and in advocacy.

I joined this forum, and it was supposed to be a support forum, but I ended up more depressed. I mean it was nice to have people be like, "Hey, welcome, blah blah blah . . ." But there was nothing, there was no good story like, "I fully recovered, and it's great." Or "I didn't recover, and it's still great." . . . There was none of that. It was just, "I can't stand it, I'm so miserable." . . . "It's been years . . . nothing helps, still miserable." Lots of really unhappy, depressed people on that forum. I certainly don't blame them because I was one of them, but going there to try to lift my spirits and it just ended up sinking me deeper into a depression. . . . But then you told me about [in-person group], and it was a whole different experience. It was about advocacy.

Brad A. also did a series of podcasts focused on survival, on living with facial difference. That was one of the really amazing things: people stepped up to fill the niches they saw vacant in the areas they needed. People became empowered advocates, and they shared their experiences in starting charities, organizing support events, creating and managing online support communities, applying for grants, and speaking with the media.

Consistent with Rosalyn Darling's (2019) observations on affirmative activism and identity, some, like Brad A., who despite having internalized the larger cultural views toward facial difference (stigma of acquired disabilities), develop a sense of disability identity after becoming involved in a support network (encounters with activists). It's a clear recognition that they(we) aren't the problem—it's the systemic view and treatment of those viewed as "different" or "other" (Darling 2019; Schalk 2018; Siebers 2008, 2013). Finding ways to update a for-profit healthcare system mired in traditional models into one that actively considers identity, self, and lived experience seems impossible. But people living with synkinesis have been advocating for better physical and medical care; over time, it has had an impact.

Two examples stand out. First, a group developed scales for use in understanding facial difference and specifically paralysis in children and youth. The working group included medical personnel, researchers with facial difference, researchers with the appropriate specialties, advocates, and people with different types of facial paralysis. Measurement tools designed to be used in an international context were made widely available. The participants had little to gain, yet we showed up for the bimonthly global online meetings. (In my own case, I was awake for the call by 5:00 A.M. on a Saturday. Others stayed up late for it.) We reviewed documents, shared insights, and successfully produced a useful tool that included patient centered measures.

The second example was a doctor who heard the concerns raised by patients during an in-person support group that this physician regularly attended. This physician realized that the focal point for vision appears to be impacted by synkinesis; after consulting with colleagues, the doctor began to study this issue and look for ways to mitigate it in the meantime, such as adjusting glasses or contacts.

Friends and Family

"My daughter. If it weren't for her, I think I would have crawled into a hole and never come out. But because of her, I knew I had to keep going. And I am so glad I had the strength to do that because I have two beautiful granddaughters now. They don't care about my face. They just love me, and I just love them for who they are." Erica B., a Black, middle-aged, cisgendered woman with an associate's degree, noted the importance of unconditional acceptance in recovery. The support and acceptance of family and friends is impactful in helping people recover, repair, rebuild, and rearticulate their identity.

People are different. What makes one individual feel better might not be meaningful to another or might even feel hurtful. Earlier I mentioned that many of my interviewees had found they had relationships that weren't good for them and discovered the ability to exit through this process. Others found their relationships strengthened and renewed. It was about being seen, known, valued, and cared for. One person shared stories of quiet walks with a friend. Another spoke of her friends forcing her to go out to the clubs she loved. One had a friend who also attended the support events and changed her behavior unasked, based on what she had heard. One had a group friends who had always mercilessly teased each other—who finally teased him about his face as well. One shared the outrageous pictures that had been taken with sisters making faces so hers didn't stand out.

Darling (2019) discusses the challenge people with disabilities face in their relationships as others often fail to meaningfully engage. The valued relationships are those that acknowledge the person's experience without applying a label or stigma, or pathologizing the individual.

Pets

Before we move on, I just had to give a shout out to our animal companions because pets came up during my interviews a lot. Basically, pets treat us the same—for them, our identity doesn't change. Whether it was "dogs don't care if you can smile," or enjoying the clucking of chickens or petting the cat, pets were noted as sources of support. Pets were seen as pivotal in two key ways. First, pets were emotional support as companions, courage providers, and buffers for the larger social world. My participants highlighted a host of ways their pets provided emotional support, making them feel "normal," "useful," or "loved."

Second, after synkinesis, pets make it easier to enter new and strange situations. Pets are wonderful icebreakers; someone with a pet seems more approachable. Previously introduced Jen P. found that, without her smile, her endearing yorkies could serve as a friendly introduction: "I have two yorkies. They come with me to work, and most places I go. It's hard to meet new people now, so that helps. It's just easier with them with me. . . . They are adorable, and they break the ice, make it easier to start a conversation and seem friendly."

Being able to afford, care for, and maintain an animal companion requires a certain amount of privilege. The cost of emotional support animals—or just pets for emotional support—was a frequent lament among those who desired, wanted, and needed a pet but lacked means to care for one. An interesting thing that emerged during this and larger discussions was the opening that pets gave one to create and control the narrative of the self.

Controlling the Narrative

Finding ways to rearticulate the self or create a positive narrative of the self in a world in which one has stigma was a key challenge that my participants struggled to find ways to overcome. As highlighted by Darling's (2019) work, the narrative of disability becomes central to how others see one, and it impedes relations. Otherness is having an imposed narrative that one is always having to manage. Part of the process of rebuilding the self was finding ways to reclaim narrative.

As Darling (2019) highlights, for those with an acquired mild disability or the ability to pass, an identity of typicality or rejection of disability identity emerges. As discussed in the previous chapter, some of my participants rejected the idea that synkinesis was a disability or that they were seen as disabled. Some could and did choose to "pass" much of the time, and they did not see themselves as disabled. But many cannot, did not want to, or believed they weren't able to (even if they were). Instead, finding ways to control, reclaim, or present the narrative were highlighted as critical to rebuilding the self. Amanda G., a young, outgoing professional, was previously introduced. She found telling her story with humor while reclaiming a potentially harmful piece of imagery was an important part of healing:

> Actually, one thing. My fiancé at the time, he suggested that I make a humorous post on the website Reddit, basically photoshopping my face [and] saying, this is how Bell's palsy feels, and this is what it looks like, and I compared myself to Two-Face from the Batman movies and photoshopped myself to look like that.
>
> It was funny, and it garnered so much response from the Reddit community. I think over 20,000 people commented and liked or disliked the photo in a twenty-four-hour span. I was inundated with tons of people questioning, what is Bell's palsy? What are you doing to treat it? Just curious at the condition.
>
> It actually really helped me talk about it and get over my own insecurity about myself, because if I could laugh at myself and these people could laugh with me and be so kind and understanding, it wasn't that big of a deal. It was a great and cathartic experience for me.

Another educator describes always explaining to students on the first day so they won't misinterpret her lack of affect. Similarly, I usually work my facial paralysis into lectures, discussions, or examples. Acknowledging that one may be misread and explaining about it feels so much better than just seeing reactions and responses or feeling helpless and misunderstood. Gerald W., an educator with a graduate degree, explained, "I just stood up in front of the class, and I said, 'This is Bell's palsy.' I explained for about five minutes what's going on, that I'm going through a tough time, and if you don't understand me, I'm not going to take it personally, I understand. If you have any recommendations, if you know anybody, if you want to talk about it, I'll be more than happy to talk about it because I didn't want it to be something that students went, Hey, what the heck is that? What's wrong with you?"

People put themselves back together. But it's really a great deal more. If microaggressions are the individual-level expression of systemic inequity, the battle over the narrative is pushback. The tension between identity and systemic inequity in neoliberal market systems reveals itself in that one of the primary areas of display discussed—imagery and social media.

Coping with the Ubiquity of Images in a Social Media World

It's complicated: rebuilding identity, embracing disability, engaging in a highly visual culture, and participating in a pleasurable beauty culture that also pathologizes are confusing. Recall the experience I shared of Cathy W., someone who is embracing disability identity and her smile, and is using her free time to do outreach and advocacy. She mentioned wanting just one hour without facial difference so she could take a ton of social media pictures and post them. This was someone who also mentioned the frustration of a photographer who couldn't understand that she wanted pictures "that look like her." It's not that she isn't coping, but she was responding to a cultural phenomenon; even with filters, even with angles, and makeup, the spontaneous (yet obviously posed) images of social media are not easily achieved.

The primacy of the visual and the social pressure toward aesthetic visuals— the aesthetization of everyday life (Talley 2014)—is well documented and linked to colonialist commercialized capital market interests (Featherstone and Turner 1995). The ubiquity of social media has rendered imagery as central to communication. Photos and social media came up so often: the wish to have a photo that conveys joy, love, lightness, fun. Simply, it hurt and never stops hurting. For me, I am always a little sad even while I am happy for you. I love all your photos with your kids, or your parents, or your friends, on your anniversary, on your trip, with your beloved pet. You are rendered beautiful by the joy you exude, and I always smile. Then I feel the pull. I know that when I try to mirror back that unrestrained joie de vie I will both feel and look awkward. The people I interviewed felt like they were always missing out on an increasingly integral part of socializing—taking and sharing pictures that accurately and spontaneously convey human experience and emotion.

Many expressed that social events were more challenging because of how central photos and now social media are. Abby B., who has a large family with many special events, shared both her anxieties and how she is pushing past them:

My middle child is getting married next summer. I am saving up for laser treatments. I'm the mother of the groom, so I am going to be in a lot of pictures. . . . I don't want to be in pictures with this face. I know I shouldn't feel that way, but I do . . . I am so happy for them. But with this face, it's going to be very difficult, getting all those pictures done. And the day of, being worried about it all the time. But I have to do it, so I'll just do the best I can. Try to be there for them, and not worry about how I look and the pictures.

Similarly, Angie C., who was introduced previously, acknowledged the difficulty of attending events, especially with people she knows love to share images on social media: "They take so many pictures. For those events, I don't really attend, or if I go, I only go for a little while, just to show, you know, hey, I'm here, and then I leave. No pictures! I mean I've had to take some pictures . . . I hate them . . . I don't put any on Facebook or Instagram. I just don't want my image out there like that."

Mary D., a white, cisgendered, community college–educated stay-at-home mother, shared her frustration at being singled out during a photo, and the pain it triggered:

We were on a girls' trip back from Mother's Day, and we're down in Palm Beach. There were four of us, and my girlfriends were like, "Let's take a picture." I don't love photos, but okay. And when you're with your good girlfriends, you're like, "Whatever." You know, you have to try and make it work; I just hope they take ten, whoever's taking the picture.

I handed my phone over to a waitress, and the four of us girls got around the firepit. We had the ocean in the background; it was so beautiful. And she starts taking a picture, and she goes, "You're not smiling. Can you smile?" And I just had a flood of emotions. They just overwhelmed me. I wished I could. And it hurt so much. And I go, "Nope! I'm done, thanks." And one of the other girls, she's like, "Let's just take a couple more." And I looked at her and go, "I'm done."

And that's what happens sometimes, you go from the nice, sweet person that we normally are to like this raging, angry b-tch. Can I have my old smile back? You have no idea what I'm going through. Should I go tell the manager that you need to be fired? Because there's people out there with problems, and the last thing you should do is tell somebody to smile.

You have this flood of crazy thoughts that go through your head, and then you're like, "You can't tell the manager that, she doesn't know." And you take a deep breath and calm down, but all that over a picture for social media.

Mary shared that unexpected grief temporarily overwhelmed her when faced with a fairly common social situation.

SOMEONE I WOULD RATHER BE

Control over the image, the presentation, the context, and how one should feel about it mattered more to people than "looking good." What frustrated, infuriated, annoyed, and undermined people was that the agency in telling their story was being taken away. Matt E., who was previously introduced, remembered his reaction to his mother when she wanted to airbrush his senior class photos:

> My mother wanted me in my senior photos to have it airbrushed. They wanted a picture of their boy the way they wanted him to look like, not the way I looked. That was the only time in my life I ever was forced to get a photograph taken. It wasn't the photograph itself. It was the fact that they wanted it airbrushed and doctored to hide my disfigurement. They got what they wanted—I bit the bullet, [and] they got what they wanted. But when my mother died I took the photograph and I threw it away. It was nothing to me when I had it done. It meant nothing to me when I was in the senior album when I graduated from high school. It meant nothing to me thirty years later when I threw it in the trash.

That incident highlights the deep tension. It's not about wanting to "look" normal but about wanting to be as we are. That image wasn't him. It was a lie.

Recall Cathy W. made a similar point in chapter 3 when she described being told not to look like herself in her honeymoon photos. She said, "I wasn't bothered by the question. I thought he was just trying to do his job. But to tell me not to smile . . . I know how I look when I smile. It's OK. This is me. This is me happy."

We don't like synkinesis, and we don't like living with it, but we also want to like ourselves. The microaggressions and internalizations described in previous chapters are the existing culture and structure reified. Because if you aren't normal, then you aren't fully human, and not being fully human leaves one vulnerable. I like the scar in my eyebrow. It probably highlights the problems I have with my eye, but who cares? For whatever reason, that scar from my third surgery makes me smile. It's rachet. It's right down the line of the knife in my head, the point of pain. It's my survival scar. It's my point of interest. I hate when people notice my eye looks different, but I still love my scar. It's complicated. But maybe I can love myself, my survival and my strength, and still hate that I had to build those capacities to cope.

Let's Do a Silly One

People are resilient. Friends can "get it." Though some would have been horrified by this, many of those I interviewed mentioned incidents like what my students would call "let's do a silly one."

A young, handsome, cisgendered, Latino professional, Will M. shared that his friends doing the "Bell's palsy picture" really helped him.

What really helped me, like I said earlier, was just making light a bit. Me and my friends would take photos, and we decided, "Let's do the Bell's palsy picture in it." Some people didn't get it, like my old boss at that time; she was telling me, "Don't do that. Don't let people make fun of you." But I was explaining to her, "It actually feels like I'm not sticking out in the picture or something."

So we would take group photos and call them my Bell's palsy support group. So we would take pictures. All of us . . . always them—well, me normal, and them making the Bell's palsy face—and I guess. . . . Yeah, this is a way for me to get through those first three months, was just making light of it. I had a lot of friends that just—would come over for dinner and just check up on me.

My original boss at that time, every time she'd come in, she would just say, "Hey honey, smile for me. Let me see what you look like today." And just [those] kind of things are really helpful, just knowing that someone was constantly thinking about you and wondering how you're doing, wanting to know the progress, if I'm progressing.

Lively Maddie G., a cisgendered college-educated marketing professional, shared a similar story. It was easy to see how Maddie, who was bursting with energy, had entered her field initially through event planning. Once she had loved photos and social media; now, she told me, she hates all that—except with her sister. "My sister does this thing with me. When we take photos together, she purposely makes a silly face, and I scrunch my face up even more. Then we call it 'sisters face,' and it's something that we do now because she knows that three-quarters of the pictures I take with her I'm not going to be happy with anyway, so let's just make them funny."

As I write this, I glance up at the photos I have taped to a bookshelf above my desk. I smile at the photobooth square from a trip with two of my best friends about six months after my diagnosis. We are sticking our tongues out sideways and making crooked faces. And that's exactly it: it's three people making silly faces, so I don't stick out. We all look like we are being silly and having fun because we were all being silly and having fun.

Gaining Perspectives

As Matt E. alluded to in the opening vignette, there was something gained: a perspective on the facile nature of appearance and the need to start to question assumptions about categories, identities, systemic orderings, and the systems that order. I remember reading Foucault's *The Order of Things*, struggling through it and still not fully understanding the text. But the value and danger of categories—what they mean, how they make meaning, what they engender, and

SOMEONE I WOULD RATHER BE

the power inherent in wielding them—is worth considering. To become a person who can get past assumptions, stares, cultural denigrations and who can advocate to change those views, that is something gained.

But there's something deeper: knowledge of what it means to be other and an awakening to there being lots of ways to be other. It doesn't have to be that way. Foucault describes the microphysics of power by which our bodies are rendered docile. Synkinesis disrupts our docility and makes it impossible to be a docile body, to be a norm. There is a terrible cost to that, but there is also an amazing freedom. We step outside the categories into an abyss of nonmeaning; we reject the histories of what it should mean, and we have to rebuild a new self with a new process, generated a reframing of self, others, and the social world.

7

Walking Away

The Challenge of Change

One upside to facial paralysis . . . I grew up in a pretty segregated society. My brother and my family were, were Barry Goldwater conservative Republicans. OK. Racist. And I'm the only one that's still in the family that's not that way. I just can't do that. It would just be against everything I stand for. I can understand what it is to be is treated differently or not waited on in a restaurant because that's happened to me, to be overlooked or discounted just because of how you appear to others.

So I know what it's like to a certain extent to be seen as different. I can't say I know how it feels to be Black or Latino, but I do know what it's like to be treated not equal. I can't say that I know what it's like being a woman, but I know what it's like to be not taken seriously and to not be truly valued or not paid fairly. I'm more open and more tolerant of people who are different, and that's made me a better person. By far a better person.

Matt E., a cisgendered white man, developed a disability identity growing up with visible facial difference. As he faced physical assault, bullying, and harassment at work, he saw his experiences as challenging to his core systemic beliefs, which allowed him to grow in meaningful ways.

Our lives are a project of the self, and our relationship with the self is surprisingly complicated. Synkinesis fundamentally disrupts the external display and communication of self, as well as the internal communication with and experience of self. This self is communicated, understood, and experienced within a culture that overlays meaning on identities and reifies through experience. The idea of a self, shaped by and shaping circumstance, is captured in the complicated term *subjectivity*. What is it to be a subject? It is to be human, counted, valued, and to have voice. What is it to experience self, and how do people at different subject locations experience, express, and reify self and self-identity in ways that overlap and differentiate? What does it mean to be a subject within a system that renders us all objects? What happens when it's disrupted, externally and internally?

158

Chapter 1 introduced the project: What is synkinesis? How did I study it? What does it mean to study something one has/is/lives? Chapter 2 was the painful one—that is, for you. The rest of the book reveals others' pain, my pain, shared pain, but the second chapter was the one that most have told me causes pain. This theory chapter is where I tried to explain why I, as a member of my field and a product of my educational environment, study, expand, divulge, express, and move toward an understanding in the way that I do. As I write this, Pierre Bourdieu and Loïc Wacquant's *Invitation to a Reflexive Sociology* (1992), the first book my advisor in graduate school, Mike Messner, suggested I read, is obvious— my work is a project of reflexive sociology.

The theory chapter is not an attempt to prove my place, to destroy/reproduce/renegotiate tradition, or even to build knowledge. Rather it is meant to reveal, explore, and examine the role of structure in shaping thought, in shaping identity, and in shaping subjectivity as well as defining objects. Not just what we think about but every aspect of the process of thought is systemically infused. I know that most people were no doubt sorely tempted to skip that chapter, but if you didn't, thank you! Social theory is beautiful, but also painful. It is like a harsh landscape: stark, brutal, and enveloping, with undeniable revelations, quashed hubris, and never-ending trepidation, where whatever comes next will be even more disturbing but also enticing. It's thinking about what's discomforting. It's eternally wrongfooting oneself, and accepting that one now remains perpetually off-balance. It's about knowing that you forever will not know, but seeking anyway. It's accepting there are always trade-offs, and choosing to face that harsh reality.

When I began studying sociology, what resonated most deeply for me was the potential for praxis, action underscored by theory. Action that can be directed toward a better lived experience; though we can debate the meanings of better and the colonist hierarchical mindset that attempts to rank experience, we can still attempt it. We can work for the inevitable failure of systems, with the eternal optimism of agency. Agency may need that optimism to have any impetus to make a small space more livable for at least some span of time. So maybe "better" is the wrong word. It's the old system reimposing values when we say "better." As Margaret Atwood aptly observed, "Better never means better for everyone. . . . It always means worse, for some." I would argue that some can handle a bit more worse with greater ease. But *more livable* is a different goal than *better*. It centers embodied experiences.

The need to have embodied, experiencing people in the narratives that debate these things is glaring, and a wider range of voices sharing in the discussion is necessary/imperative. Chapter 2 traces a journey through sociology of embodiment, which highlights the struggle to decolonize our thinking with tools that are inadequate, designed to undermine our efforts, and largely supplied by and developed under the direction of the colonizers. We ourselves become the colonizers, even as we struggle against this. How do I decolonize when I am a product, an instrument, and a tool of colonization, regardless of what I want to be? Chapter 2 comprises that struggle.

I remain indebted to so many who situated identity and consciousness within social relations. Karl Marx, W.E.B. Du Bois, Georg Simmel, Emile Durkheim, and Max Weber created a space in which structure and agency were a relationship—complicated, eternal, processual. Critical theorists and cultural studies scholars like Stuart Hall force a struggle with ideology and material culture, revealing subtle relations of power. I looked to Michel Foucault and Pierre Bourdieu for challenging embodied subject experiences and for questioning the subjectivity emergent from practices normalized, imposed, embraced, and rejected by bodies within systems that impose meaning. Through practices that are institutionalized, personalized, and normalized, people come to embody social relations at unique historical conjunctural moments. Bourdieu highlights the reproduction of hierarchy and class privilege within our daily lives, habits, practices, tastes, and bodies. Foucault reminds us of the role of institutions, meanings, and processes of knowledge. Both problematize the ways that our sense of self, our pleasures, and our desires are infused with hierarchical social relations.

Judith Butler, Donna Haraway, and Sylvia Wynter undermine certitudes and boundaries, forcing us into the spaces between. I must interrogate my questions. Patricia Hill Collins, Cedric Robinson, C.L.R. James, Audre Lorde, and bell hooks bridge structure and embodied experience, and they provide new tools to build new houses or maybe communal halls. Critical race theory, postcolonial, queer, and disability theory, and intersectional feminism expand our understanding of inequity, equity, and the challenges inherent in creating equity in systems predicated on exploitation. We struggle on, but these are my tools.

Chapter 3 highlights the internalization of systems and strategies of protection and resistance. There are so many ways bodies are made aware of and experience their status. One of the reasons synkinesis is so disruptive is it involves an abrupt status change, in many cases, without much ostensible difference in initial sense of self or abilities. One suddenly becomes the other in a new way—a way not ingrained, embodied, or socialized. And this makes one painfully aware of how otherness operates on this specific axis of identity. The systemic costs, the inherent assumptions, and the devaluations are so often internalized, with long-term consequences. Chapter 3 highlights the imposition of otherness onto us.

Using critical race theory, disability studies, and intersectional feminism, how structure infuses social interactions and lived experience with identity markers that reinforce systems, privilege, and hierarchy at the expense of people is the focus. How identity is inherently legitimating or discrediting as well as how this is communicated, felt, lived, believed, and denied is an experience that shapes how we see ourselves, our limits, and our possibilities. How one internalizes stigma and is invested in a body project in relation to self, stigma, and society has meaningful consequences. Systems protect themselves. We rarely question hierarchy; instead we spend our resources trying to fix ourselves.

Chapter 4 focuses on the face. All our parts matter, and to lose any of them creates disruption to one's sense of self in important ways. This chapter centers on the face. Faces are discussed as central to the experience of self, emotion, identity, and communication. Western culture imbues faces, facial expression, and facial difference with deep meaning. Morality, beauty, and privilege are conflated, so facial difference carries a heavy cost. Individuals experience real costs to not "fixing" or "normalizing" or "hiding" their "difference." Chapter 4 highlights the negative assumptions and the ways the market offers solutions while individualizing and monetizing. Hence, privilege is a key factor in access to treatment. Western individualized market-based "solutions" focus on appearance rather than experience, function, or communication. Solutions that serve the needs of the market rather than people are heartbreakingly apparent as struggles to access pain management, mental health support, and more comprehensive care are the norm. Although popular culture loves the myth of extraordinary individuals who overcome challenges, that narrative is largely at odds with the lived experience of the ordinary individuals who are faced with a market system that expects them to pay to manage their bodily failures.

Chapter 5 highlights the embodied experience of synkinesis. Synkinesis includes the physical manifestations of a disability that challenges one's access to self. The tragedy of synkinesis is the loss of the internal experience of self, the disruptions to the best experiences of human life, and the inability to effectively communicate. That will always be a loss and a challenge. That will always be a pain endured. But people have internalized the experience in very different ways, which emerges in a discussion of disability identity. How disability and disability identity are understood and expressed by those with synkinesis is central: some have embraced a disability identity, and others have distanced themselves from it. For some, embracing a disability identity challenged their thinking and changed some of their fundamental assumptions, which is the focus of chapter 6.

People are resilient, and we find ways to re-create self and identity. Chapter 6 explores regaining a sense of subjectivity, and explicitly that of coming to question otherness, othering, and the system in which we construct subjectivity. Beyond functional coping (and let me be clear, functional coping is significantly better than the alternatives), I had to stop and think about disability, about rights, about to whom we extend humanity, citizenship, fellowship, and general privileges—about a lot. I had to ask myself, what kind of a world do I want, and why am I not doing more to live in that world? As Audre Lorde ([1984] 2007) observed, "For the master's tools will never dismantle the master's house. They may allow us temporarily to beat him at his own game, but they will never enable us to bring about genuine change." But could that house be abandoned? More people seem to want to walk away.

The World Is Changing

The Western world is at a moment of ideological change. Some fundamental assumptions about narratives, subjects, objects, knowledge, and their production are in flux. Dichotomies and hierarchies are being questioned. Categories are being destabilized. Positions are being interrogated, and identities and subjectivities infused with new meanings. As the changes compile, a paradigmatic shift looms.

"All that is solid melts into air, all that is holy is profaned." Marx's words return to me. "And humanity is at last compelled to face with sober senses the real conditions of life. And relations with humankind." Most don't include the next line: "The need of a constantly expanding market for its products chases the bourgeoisie over the entire surface of the globe" (Marx and Engels [1848] 2015). Though critical theories and cultural studies have exposed the vulgarities of Marxism in the overestimation of the role of economics, the ideologies embedded, our deepest assumptions, fears, hopes, prides, joys, and failures, and the expressions in which we experience and express identity, I can't help but return to his observations. In so many ways the interests of the system are embedded.

In what ways do we resist? It's nice to believe in the purity of resistance, but it's always more complicated. Resistance is always in opposition to. The remnants of ideological structures always already infuse what follows. As we rail against older ideologies and structures, we bring them into our new creations. Those creations, that we build so lovingly for the following generations, will be dismantled by them, but will also infuse what they build unless we change things. As Foucault observes in *The Order of Things* (1970), the fundamental epistemological standpoint of Western culture hinges on difference, embedded in hierarchy. It's not just understanding racism, sexism, heterosexism or any other *ism*. It's that they are borne out in a system that understands things through a lens of hierarchical binary difference. Specific Western histories overlay morality onto these differences: good and evil, pure and tainted, always already in our minds when considering categories for those around us. But more often, we are dissatisfied with ourselves and the ideological foundations of the world around us.

There are also moments of paradigmatic change, when foundational ideologies rupture. Foucault suggests it is epistemic shifts that represent changes in ways of thinking. His archeology of knowledge highlights an understanding of knowledge as something produced within a system, an object of study, integral to the production of culturally meaningful subjects, complicit and invested in (re)production. The tenuous relationship between those with legitimated knowledge and systems of power is central to his theorizing. The irony of his own work as systematizing that self-knowledge and the eventual acceptance of this inevitable contradiction does not discredit the idea. It better captures the lived experience of the embodied subject within a system that reproduces.

Bourdieu (1984) highlights how, through practice, we come to embody our social positions. We don't merely look the part; we think the part, we act the part, we become the part. Those experiences that shape our habitus contain powerful expectations. Often, this hinges on binary identities assigned and earned. We are all "dummy variables" in our otherness, "other" or "not other" on each category. But each strand of otherness gives us a unique subject location. The cost of otherness adding up. We are expected to conform to the confluence of expected identities. Nonconformity with perceived location is often met with correctives. But there are communities of others, and we find them: the *like us*-es, on more or fewer axes of identity. We "code switch" across different fields, our bodies adjusting as we move between our roles, obligations, and expectations. Our unthought expressions of social position, our bodies' systemic manifestations, and our minds, infused with superstructure. We are always benefiting from and subject to the symbolic violence of our culture. When we fight against this, so often it's codified in another body, acting out the results of living in an inequitable system. But is resistance composed of shifting what makes an "other"? Or is it a rearticulation?

What does it mean to challenge otherness, difference, and hierarchy as dominant paradigms? What is being delegitimated? What foundational truths, assumptions, and embodied reactions are being dereified? Our social locations are what Patricia Hill Collins (1990) terms the matrix of domination, the embodied intersections of our perceived identities across a host of historically manifest dichotomies, with otherness adding up, weighing down, but signifying systemic power. The embodied nature of thought and experience and subjectivity(ies) in Foucault, Bourdieu, critical race theory, intersectional feminism, queer theory, disability studies, and others questions not just epistemic certitude but also ontological underpinnings. Difference, inequity, and hierarchy are embodied, lived realities generated by a system reliant on them. They create bodies that reinforce, symbolize, and reinfuse ideologies, beliefs, and lived experiences that conform. But critical theories are demanding a reckoning. We are being asked to learn to live and, therefore, think differently. The goal is not an abstract revolutionary future but a host of immediate practices, which together can change lived realities. The goal is to create a system that foregrounds ongoing lived experience rather than profit.

Disputing images, representation, and cultural consciousness is a start, but it's not enough. Moving beyond representation is challenging (Schalk and Kim 2020). Even for those committed, it means never-ending brutal and painful confrontations with our own complicity. In what ways are we making real, reifying, and creating the categories that give the dark and brilliant meanings to our bodies and souls, and those of others? The traumas, the hurts, the beliefs, and what we are told, what we come to know about bodies like ours, and what we know about bodies we have the gratitude to not be. The toxicity of our relief eats away at our humanity. Our bodies learn to react and adapt so that the sick feeling of fear or the undermined confidence of an identity with questioned ability is deeply engrained. But's it's over now, right? Didn't [insert person, film, etc.] win an [Oscar, Emmy, Nobel Prize]? Wasn't there that great movie about that exceptional person? Ableism? Racism? Sexism? Heterosexist? Cisism? Aren't the markets now offering inclusion? My group finally is winning awards, getting a series, being recognized. Dolls, toys, roles, imagery . . . can't we just add representation and stir?

It seems so seductive. The first barriers broken. Celebrating entrances, recognition, acceptance, and tolerance. The lived pain of being disabled, BIPOC, female, or any other "other" in our current system is a visceral reality, and it's wonderful to have joy, celebration, and pride. But within the ideological parameters of late-stage capitalism, the project of the self can never be innocuous. The other is not merely what one should not be, but is what must be. Exploitation requires justification. Colonialism, racism, sexism, and ableism are necessary. They infuse the system with painful justifications for hierarchies of bodies. A system of hierarchy requires that we are always already considering our place. Are these people like me, a threat to me, or beneath me? Our insecurities are being perpetually assuaged through market-dependent body projects. The looming threat of dependency and all the vulnerability it implies are in our lived experience of self. With this comes an impetus toward judgment. All that gratitude I feel that I am not is the judgment on someone else's lived reality.[1] Every time I "don't understand," I am judging and creating more others. It is also there in our altruism, our compassion, and our kindness toward those who are "less fortunate," absolving ourselves from the systemic reproduction of their misfortune while simultaneously creating cultures of altruism and deserving (and undeserving) victims.

Synkinesis is a brutal disruption. It opens with a moment of trauma then follows with a visible stigma, fears of dependence, feelings of freakishness, and assumptions of moral failure coupled with the stain of "not healing." It's a cruel confrontation with vulnerability, with otherness, with difference. Some move past it; for others that challenge was not only empowering but epiphanic. It changed how they saw not only themselves, but others and the world in which we live. It changed what they value and how they live. One of the cisgendered white men I interviewed shared that synkinesis had damaged his career, and that he had endured medically prescribed but inappropriate and painful treatments. He didn't want to be who he had been—driven, career-focused, competitive, and not very kind. He liked the person he was now better. He saw himself as more thoughtful, more compassionate, more empathetic, and more willing to help and accept help. His hand covered his inescapable smile as he recounted that he had found love. Investing in his relationship and being a caring and available partner were more important to him now. Despite the challenges he was facing, he was happy. He was satisfied in who he is, how he is living, and what he continues to do to be a member of a wider community. It becomes apparent that we need a new way to think about things, and new methods of study (Schalk and Kim 2020).

"The Ones Who Walk away from Omelas" ([1973] 1975), the short story by Ursula K. Le Guin, haunts me. In the story, the perfect society of Omelas depends upon a single child being kept in degradation, isolation, filth, and confinement, a truth revealed to residents when they come of age. We learn that most citizens choose to ignore the plight of the child who has been sacrificed for the many. But some will walk away from the city; they venture into a world they aren't yet sure of because they cannot reconcile the cost of their security that has been revealed. The road they take leads to somewhere uncertain, but they find it necessary to accede to uncertainty when confronted with the known.

I'm concerned by the idea that *we* need an "other" upon which to build our foundation, whether psychic, economic, social, or physiological. In our current system, there is always an other. Moving the boundaries doesn't change what hierarchical binaries impose on our thinking, on our production of thought, on our tolerances, on our commitments, and on our willingness to engage. I thought I was writing a book about struggling with a rare condition. Really, I was writing a book about struggling with a common condition. Synkinesis forced that. Brutally, painfully, desperately. I can't be sorry about that, but only regret what I hadn't learned sooner.

I continue to be brutally confronted by my ableism and by what fundamentally underlies it. The fear of being unworthy, unsafe, vulnerable, alone, unacknowledged, unaccepted, and unwanted. The resentment of those who reproduce the system and their privilege and their reification of the system. Hating *those* people is so much easier. We could just help everyone see that *they* are the problem. That *they* should be shunned. That *they* are really the bad, dirty, unworthy, and useless ones. Not me! We should other the ableists, other the racists, and other the sexists. We should take away their security, make them afraid, and make them hate themselves.

What have I become?

Changing the narrative of who the villain is isn't the third way so many came to seek. The point wasn't to make someone else the movie monster villain. Creating a world where we aren't so apt to create villains seems a more worthy goal. Maybe that also means we have to let go of our desire to be the hero.

The myth of the "great person" who changes the course of history looms large in our consciousness. Rectifying past misdeeds has largely been choosing new heroes so that we can all aspire and feel pride of kinship. We fail to celebrate the ordinary, without which the exceptional does not exist. We eat the food of the ordinary, wear the clothes of the ordinary, mostly use devices made by the ordinary, and build our communities among the ordinary. Robinson (1983) challenges us to forgo heroes as well as villains. To let go of our fantasies of ourselves and others as the singular exceptionals who drive the course of history. To recognize and celebrate our common humanity and our common struggles. To focus on providing for the least of these, rather than reveling in the possibilities of the most privileged. To recognize the necessity, interdependence, and humanity of all of us. To build a world in which we endeavor to generate humanity rather than reward those who can achieve it against the odds.

It seems an impossible shift.

We have a system that puts profit ahead of people. It heaps rewards on a chosen few while ignoring the immiseration of many. Systems self-perpetuate. We internalize these beliefs. They buoy us up, and they drag us down. Those who have are inherently better than those who have not. Fault and blame, the other sides of pride (of place) and privilege, are the internalization of systemic inequity. There is so much fear: rejection, an inability to care for oneself and others, failure, falling, and not being "good" enough. My son asked me whether he was "good," and I almost said, "Of course you are honey." But I stopped myself. Instead I told him "good" and "bad" those are colonialist notions.

Let's decolonize our minds a little.

Let's think about learning to be part of a community. Is what we are doing working for us and those around us? What can we be doing that would be more fulfilling, more compassionate, and kinder? Can we work toward knowing ourselves and what we need, and making that fit without judging others? It's such a relief to free oneself from needing to constantly judge, from always seeking salvation in the project of the self, a salvation promised from accumulation. For some, in order to be inherently "good," someone else must be revealed as "bad," with Calvinist traps laid out against a life designed to prove privilege and oppression are deserved, the security provided by moral certitude. To let go of that certitude is to step into the abyss willingly and joyfully, not without fear but accepting fear, and finding joy in how it binds us together.

The Threat of Being Other

The other is in all of our consciousnesses as an external and an internal threat. We fear what the other will do to us, and what will be done to us if we are the other. The threat of what the other will do to us dominates our public discourse. But rarely do we look at the threat of becoming other. The threat of being other hangs over all of us. What does it mean to be the other, and what will I do/pay/ risk to avoid it? Who has the privilege to do that? What does not being or appearing as the other provide or promise?

The first word that explodes, enormous and expanding, is *safety*. Safety on a deep level is the knowledge I am generally safe at any given moment—not just physically, but also psychically, emotionally. I am going to feel that my physical being and sense of self—who I am—will be valued, protected, and nourished. Being the other risks damage. The risks are enumerated as people find themselves subjected to physical and verbal abuse; the matrix of categories into which one is assigned compounds the threats. Differential care, access to resources, freedom from the assault of psychological indignities, microaggressions, discrediting, are all problematic; they are even more so if one is already identified as other.

Microaggressions, the effort it requires to access appropriate care, the research necessary to understand the options, all take a tremendous toll on the psychological health of individuals. Whether I am hiding or covering or disciplining my otherness, or celebrating, embracing, and normalizing it, I am still acting within a system. Embracing is better and feels like a step in the right direction, but it is still mired in toxicity. For so long we hid the piece of us that could be the other. Most of us are "passing," hiding, segregating, covering, or fixing whatever other the market is opening up, threatening us with, forcing us to work against, or promising us relief from. Taking it out, valorizing it, and embracing it feels better. Hugging that wounded frightened piece of ourself close feels more like me.

Now what? It's still other.

It's still difference. It's still perpetuating a system designed around that position. Maybe it's a place I can never fully abandon because it is structured into my thinking, my being. But there's a place I can imagine. Someplace I feel at the edges of my consciousness, in the waking dream state of almost. That is the place I hope for; and through that hope, someday it will be there. In that place the past looms less large, and the way we do things here and now won't really be understood. The past will just be guessed at, wondered about, studied, but will fade into the realm of the unfathomable.

This thing in ourselves that is ourselves, made out of our experiences with the world, is us but also the larger world made material. The internal/external of this dynamic of a self-understanding from within an individual body, programed by a social world, each with a unique operating system patchworked over time, cannot be separated from the systems in which it is living. We are in perpetual dialogue with ourselves, nuanced by the meanings culture(s) afford(s). But dialogue sanitizes the experience. It's embodied. It may not be words we feel. So many pains are our bodies carrying the trauma of the self in a hierarchical system. But our bodies also carry pleasures, expected flavors, savors. We know the smells and sounds of our safe places, and our bodies relax. We tense at the triggers of past trauma. A system indifferently inflicts, without care for the person, and leaves some advantaged in the way their body anticipates. I feel good about who I am, or I don't; I feel pride or mortification, or anger, or frustration, or fear, or pleasure. Maybe they are mixed up together in complicated ways because synkinesis messes with this process in a deeply profound way—wrong tastes, changes in how smell impacts, wrong feel. These things and more will always haunt me. But they also have opened me, taught me, and forced me to confront so many assumptions. It's made me kinder, more open, and more willing to walk into the abyss.

The conjunctural moment of late-stage capitalism privileges the market as savior. Certainly, the market has offered some impactful solutions, and ongoing research promises more. But even basic Botox injections for pain reduction and improved communication are out of reach for more people than those for whom it was easily accessible. People found effective, meaningful treatments, but those most satisfied with their care paid out of pocket, had GoFundMe accounts, or fought for insurance coverage, sometimes for years. The healthcare industry has left most of us defeated, worn out, and humiliated at a moment when we most needed compassion, care, understanding, and assistance. My hard-won union-backed health insurance with one of the "best" companies in the business got me Botox only after several *years* of repeated requests. But I also paid out of pocket for some of my most impactful treatments—the two surgeries and the neuromuscular retraining. That was most of us: it's a system in which the needs of individuals aren't paramount.

The market also offers panaceas. There are lots of other symbols of body work, class status, and success with which I can adorn and validate myself. It offers lots of pleasures I can use to erase, hide, and minimize my pains. Many participants in my study extolled treatments that they, themselves, had been dubious of as medical treatments. But they noted the treatments helped them to relax, or the treatments were provided by people who made them feel safe, valued, and heard or provided them with a safe space to express their fears and concerns. That's not bad, but it's also reserving and limiting access. It leaves many unsure of the best way to allocate limited resources. It drains resources. But it is neoliberal late-stage capitalism, and that is exactly how it's supposed to work. The profits of healthcare companies supersede the needs of individuals. Caveat emptor. Do your research. It's always your responsibility or your fault. Those who can afford it get help, and those who can't carry the stigma.

The Kids Are Alright

We are at a moment of crisis; a conjunctural moment could move us toward policy and practices that improve the lived experience and process of many. Although critiques of Gen Z and Millennials abound, there's a great deal to be appreciated in their practice, process, and priorities. The most distressing stories of exclusion, bullying, and isolation came more often from my older participants. A pattern emerged among the younger participants of being more open, finding more support, and working through the experience with therapy.

Terri A., who eighteen years old, in college, and stressed, is new to Bell's palsy. But unlike many of the older participants in my study, she's already sharing photos and finding support rather than critiques and exclusion. She talked about realizing that she needed social emotional support immediately and finding it: "I mean, I have a lot of really supportive friends. I have posted some pictures of it, and everybody that I work with, all my friends know what happened. . . . I use the hashtag #BellsPalsy, and the hashtag #BellsPalsyFace. Everybody . . . like, I've gotten all really, really nice comments, like, 'Oh, you're so beautiful! Stay strong! You'll get through this!' Like, they're all really, really nice about it." Self-reflection on reactions came far more easily to the younger participants. Working through, processing, seeking assistance, seeking support, and offering support were all more a part of the younger person's social repertoire, part of the expected presentation of self. The stigma that haunted so many was much less a stain and much more a thing to be worked through.

Standards and quality of care are changing as a result. People who had acquired facial difference less recently almost never reported being advised to seek a range of physical and mental health treatments; they were usually given the initial medications and sent home to heal. The people with more recent diagnoses were far more likely to be encouraged to seek a range of treatments, which explicitly included mental health counseling or support groups. People like Maria M., who was previously introduced, were initially referred to therapy and a support group. She reported that it made a difficult transition more manageable and helped her feel not so "alone." Knowing that others were struggling with the physical challenges was key, and having a laugh or sharing useful treatment suggestions mattered.

As we peeled back the layers of pain, shame, and fear that come with a loss of ability and change in status, and as I worked on myself, there was also something else that needed to be vanquished. It's in wondering about hierarchical categorical imperatives, the damage they do, and the systems perpetuated.

170 METAMORPHOSIS

The Day before the Revolution

To return to Le Guin, she also wrote a short story as a preface to her masterwork, *The Dispossessed* (1974). *The Dispossessed* explores a more equitable world based on the teachings of the character Odo, an anarchist philosopher. Though it is not a "perfect" world, it seems to offer less shame, less hate, and less deprivation. But Odo never lived to see this world: "The Day before the Revolution" is her death. The imaginings of what could be better are something incapable in the bodies that reify the existing system, even if those are the bodies that bring it down.

What we are trying to create is a new world in which to become. As I and so many others struggle to rebuild, reshape, and refashion ourselves, the old tools seem inadequate—more destructive than creative. We push forward nevertheless: refashioning, rebuilding, and reconstructing not only ourselves, but the world around us. As I look around, I see lots of other people working toward that same thing: a world in which we can be and become in ways that allow us to create more whole, more safe, and more secure bodies. For my own life, I've always said there's always a point where you just have to shut your eyes and jump. No matter how much preparation was performed, that leap of faith is always a terrifying step into the unknown.

This book is me, letting go . . .

JUMP!

APPENDIX A

SUMMARIZING FACIAL DIFFERENCE

Facial difference can be *acquired* or *congenital* (present at birth).

Let's start with *congenital*. Congenital facial difference means it is present from birth. Facial difference at birth is usually either genetic or developmental. Genetic difference–based facial difference refers to facial difference as the result of a difference in one's genetic code relative to what is expected. Facial difference could be one aspect of a wider range of genetic differences, or it could be the primary difference. In many cases, it is unclear whether congenital facial difference is genetic or developmental.

Moebius syndrome, the underdevelopment of the sixth and/or seventh cranial nerve, is one of the more common causes of congenital facial difference. People with Moebius syndrome do not have synkinesis but do have paralysis. There may be other issues as well with Moebius syndrome, such as affected vision. It is unclear what causes Moebius syndrome, but there is some evidence it is inherited (see the NORD site for more information at https://rarediseases .org/rare-diseases/moebius-syndrome/).

The people in my study sample who were born with single-sided facial paralysis generally did not know if the cause was genetic or developmental. In congenital unilateral lower lip palsy (CULLP), a condition more people may be familiar with, the lower lip is not responsive on one side. As for single-sided congenital paralysis, the condition was rare, and most did not report synkinesis— although it could not be ruled out completely as some did report symptoms consistent with synkinesis.

Acquired facial difference is damage to the seventh cranial nerve as the result of illness or injury. If the nerve is damaged beyond repair or any healing, single-sided paralysis occurs. If one is experiencing full paralysis, synkinesis is not occurring. The most common cause of single-sided facial paralysis is Bell's palsy.

171

Other causes include Ramsay Hunt syndrome, tumors (and their removal, especially acoustic neuroma), neurological disorders, and trauma.

If the nerves do not heal, an individual experiences paralysis. The muscles will be slack, and no movement will occur. By contrast, synkinesis involves nerves healing too much—the nerve regrows in too many places. Synkinesis, which is considered a movement disorder, can result in cramps, inappropriate muscle movement, and miswiring of body functions such as saliva and tears (i.e., one salivates when the eye is irritated or tears up when trying to eat). Synkinesis can look like paralysis and can even feel a bit like paralysis, but it is actually the opposite: rather than things not moving at all because the wire isn't connected, the wire is telling too many places to move. It may mimic paralysis requires very different forms of treatment.

Although the same range of treatments can assist people with paralysis and those with synkinesis, they are applied and practiced very differently for the two conditions. Surgery can be impactful. For individuals with full paralysis, surgeries such as the Gracilis muscle transfer can give people some fullness, tone, and the ability to achieve a smile. For those with synkinesis, surgeries such as selective neurolysis can reduce the pain and tightness and restore movement.

Occupational therapy with someone who has the proper experience and training can be useful for either set of conditions; however, very different treatments are applied. For synkinesis, learning to "turn off" movement was as important to me as figuring out where to turn it on. It requires deep thought about things that are usually innate. Botox injections also can be incredibly useful for reducing any additional discomfort that surgery can't address as well as for assisting with occupational therapy and restoring symmetry to appearance. Finally, cosmetic enhancement to restore symmetry and to improve communication is incredibly helpful.

The bottom line is that we really don't know enough about these conditions. But hopefully, as more people begin to communicate about them, their advocacy will lead to improvements in our knowledge and care.

APPENDIX B

OVERVIEW OF METHODS

Interviews

The interviews I conducted were semistructured, meaning some questions were asked of everyone, but each person's unique story also allowed for a range of questions and probes tailored to their experience (Corbin and Strauss 2015). The shortest interview was just over forty minutes, and the longest was over two hours.

Everyone was asked a series of basic demographic questions (gender, age, ethnicity, education, profession, age at onset of facial difference, relationship status). Everyone was also asked to tell their story in their own words. Questions about medical treatments, hopes or plans for future treatment, perceptions of self, social experiences, special events, disability identity, social disability, and social media were asked of everyone.

As an "insider" researcher, I always self-disclosed my personal experience and my potential professional benefits at the start of each interview. The participants were given the opportunity to provide informed consent, and I obtained permission to record the interviews. All interviews were conducted in English. Participants were offered more secure options for interviews, but everyone preferred the technology with which they were already familiar (FaceTime, Skype, Zoom, telephone, or in person); no one opted to use the more-secure online platforms.

I spent almost two years conducting the interviews, though the majority were conducted during the first year. The second year I looked for more of the type of participant who was less likely to volunteer—such as individuals who identified as male or BIPOC (black, Indigenous and people of color). I transcribed the first few interviews, then a transcription service was used for the others. I also corrected the consistent (and often highly humorous) errors the service made (it's Botox to the face, not buttocks—*Botox*).

Participant Observation

I attended in-person support groups and events as well as online events, which became more prevalent during the COVID-19 pandemic. If I could be unobtrusive sometimes during but always after support events and at other important moments, I would take notes, especially of potential interview questions, themes, or potential areas of analysis (Lofland et al. 2006). I also joined and participated in multiple online support platforms. Although I use what I see there to validate or supplement ideas, I do not use examples or observations from online platforms. Some of the platforms are closed groups, so there is an expectation of privacy, even though I disclose my research to the administrators and participants.

As a participant observer, one must also contend with how one's presence impacts the data. Given my research, I became a regular speaker as well as an attendee and an advocate. I participated in other studies and contributed to other research projects. I shared what I had learned with the respondents, and I invited the participants to attend the support groups after their interviews. So yes, I was definitely impacting the environment. But isn't that the point? I am not doing this research to document ableism and exclusion—I am doing it to end it.

Participant Input

The regular attendees at the initial support group where I recruited participants became the people with whom I could share analyses and ideas, and ask for feedback, verification, or refutation. Some key participants were apprised of my progress and provided enhanced insights.

Coding

I practiced an open coding procedure (Corbin and Strauss 2015; R. S. Weiss 1994), but I also listened to interviews more than I ever have in past projects. I just listened. I played the recordings over and over again as I worked out, walked around my neighborhood, and cleaned my house. I also listened to Brian Apprille's Unique Smiles Podcast (https://uniquesmiles.podbean.com)— each episode, several times.

I considered using a software program, but simply using "find" on each transcript proved more effective for me. I began by reading the transcripts and identifying broad categories of analysis, and potential themes and subthemes. For each theme, I categorized the responses and collected quotes. Under each theme and subtheme I wrote memos, integrating the quotes, observations, and theoretical insights. Key memos focused on topics such as microaggressions, attitudes toward being perceived as disabled, feelings of anxiety, sexuality, and

OVERVIEW OF METHODS 175

many other topics, some of which became critical to this work and others I hope to develop in later pieces.

In addition to standard memos, I also spent considerable time writing about my own feelings about the process, what I was seeing and hearing, and how it impacted my experience of identity. A piece on this process is being developed separately for publication.

Analysis

I used a grounded theory approach to analysis (Holton and Walsh 2016). The analysis developed out of the memos and codes and trying to make sense of these set against my own experience. I ultimately wrote a very different book than I had expected to write. While I initially thought medical experiences would be central, internalization and social disability emerged as key.

For a period of time, thinking through the many voices and my own experience set against social theories of the body consumed my mental space. I essentially wallowed in voices and experiences until a clear pathway to this manuscript began to emerge from what seemed like endless memos and drafts. I even revisited my doctoral dissertation to explore what I had done then and what I was doing now; I was pleasantly surprised by the consistency and development of my thinking.

APPENDIX C

SUMMARY OF PARTICIPANTS WITH FACIAL DIFFERENCES

Pseudonym	Gender	Race	Age	Age of Event	Level of Education	Occupation	Cause
Dierdre M.	Female	Mixed	50	40	Associate's degree	Small business	Bell's palsy
Janice M.	Female	White	56	48	College degree	Company administrator/ childcare provider	Tumor
Enna T.	Female	White	56	0	Graduate or professional degree	Engineer	Congenital
Samantha G.	Female	White	65	0	Graduate or professional degree	Education	Congenital
Cathy W.	Female	White	25	4	Some college	Healthcare administration	Trauma
Linda Madison K.	Female	White	53	0	Graduate or professional degree	Accountant, activist	Congenital
Toni R.	Female	White	49	44	Some college	Engineer	Bell's palsy
Valerie K.	Female	Asian American	40	30	Graduate or professional degree	Librarian	Bell's palsy
Maddi D.	Female	White	37	35	Associate's degree	Event planner	Bell's palsy
Carolyn A.	Female	African American/ Black	45	35	Graduate or professional degree	Education	Bell's palsy

(continued)

Pseudonym	Gender	Race	Age	Age of Event	Level of Education	Occupation	Cause
Georgia A.	Female	White	59	45	Graduate or professional degree	Mental health care	Acquired, cause unknown
Marissa S.	Female	White	45	40	Four-year college degree	Marketing	Bell's palsy
Katie O'Connor	Female	White	42	42	Associate's degree	Health care	Bell's palsy
Nancy Sara L.	Female	White	46	34	Graduate or professional degree	Education	Bell's palsy
Julie G.	Female	White	61	41	Some college	Sales	Bell's palsy
Harriet B.	Female	White	54	36	Four-year degree	Finance management	Acoustic neuroma
Tonya D.	Female	Other	49	45	Four-year degree	Artist	Other tumor
Lori E.	Female	Mixed	51	0	Four-year degree	Information technology	Congenital, cause unclear
Viv V.	Female	Asian American	32	30	Associate's degree	Health care	Bell's palsy
Larissa H.	Female	White	31	28	Four-year degree	Service/sales	Bell's palsy
Hilda S.	Female	White	57	30	Four-year degree	Mural artist	Bell's palsy
Ruth-Ellen	Female	White	62	32	Graduate or professional degree	Marketing	Acoustic neuroma
Rachel B.	Female	White	55	49	Four-year degree	Sales	Other tumor

Janelle W.	Female	African American/ Black	50	41	Associate's degree	Service/sales	Bell's palsy
Brenda M.	Female	White	43	34	College degree	Education	Bell's palsy
Annette Q.	Female	White	31	24	High school diploma/ GED	Logistics	Bell's palsy
Teresa W.	Female	White	26	23	Four-year degree	Education	Acoustic neuroma
Katherine M.	Female	White	34	33	Associate's degree	Stay-at-home mom	Bell's palsy
Marisa B.	Female	White	37	33	Associate's degree	Event planner	Bell's palsy
Dani S.	Female	White	34	11	Associate's degree	Service/sales	Bell's palsy
Amanda G.	Female	White	28	19	Four-year degree	Office management	Bell's palsy
Georgina W.	Female	White	53	48	Graduate or professional degree	Marketing consultant	Bell's palsy
Jamie M.	Female	White	75	69	Associate's degree	Health care	Bell's palsy
Madeline D.	Female	White	38	37	Four-year degree	Health care	Bell's palsy
Anita S.	Female	Other	38	28	Graduate or professional degree	Military, education	Other tumor
Dolores F.	Female	White	67	62	Four-year degree	Health care	Bell's palsy
Anastasia Z.	Female	White	22	20	Four-year degree	Graduate student	Acoustic neuroma

(continued)

Pseudonym	Gender	Race	Age	Age of Event	Level of Education	Occupation	Cause
Elaine S.	Female	White	28	12	Four-year degree	Education	Bell's palsy
Patricia B.	Female	White	31	21	Four-year degree	Project manager	Bell's palsy
Janine S.	Female	White	57	25	Four-year degree	Entertainment	Bell's palsy
Guillermo M.	Male	Latino/a	28	27	A.A.-two-year, technical degree	Personal banker	Bell's palsy
Jason A.	Male	White	50	42	Graduate or professional degree	Marketing	Ramsay Hunt syndrome
Patti D.	Female	White	58	42	Four-year degree	Retired, laboratory work	Bell's palsy
Caitlin Marie	Female	Other	38	31	Graduate or professional degree	Health care	Other tumor
Vero R.	Female	Latino/a	26	14	Current student	Current student	Acoustic neuroma
Jen P.	Female	White	42	41	Some college	Entertainment	Bell's palsy
Sara K.	Female	White	36	1	Associate's degree	Health care	Trauma
Kelly H.	Female	White	50	35	Some college	Secretary	Acoustic neuroma
Samantha H.	Female	White	55	53	Graduate or professional degree	Program manager	Bell's palsy
Zoe S.	Female	White	22	11	Current student	Current student	Congenital, cause unknown

Sam M.	Male	White	51	34	Associate's degree	Scheduler	Bell's palsy
Erika B.	Female	African American/ Black	46	42	Some college	Disability	Bell's palsy
Doris L.	Female	White	62	57	Some college	Accounts receivable	Bell's palsy
Elaine E.	Female	White	50	47	Four-year degree	Mental health care	Bell's palsy
Melinda C.	Female	White	24	21	High school diploma/ GED	Childcare	Bell's palsy
Denise S.	Female	Other	50	30	Graduate or professional degree	Marketing director	Bell's palsy
George S.	Male	White	54	21	Associate's degree	Teacher	Bell's palsy
Abby B.	Female	White	49	46	Associate's degree	Health care	Bell's palsy
Penelope H.	Female	White	46	45	Associate's degree	Disabled	Bell's palsy
Christine W.	Female	White	70	68	Graduate or professional degree	Lawyer, retired	Bell's palsy
Laura C.	Female	African American/ Black	38	34	Four-year degree	Public relations	Bell's palsy
Carey R.	Female	White	27	18	Graduate or professional degree	First-grade teacher	Acoustic neuroma

(continued)

Pseudonym	Gender	Race	Age	Age of Event	Level of Education	Occupation	Cause
Rita B.	Female	White	50	46	Graduate or professional degree	Attorney	Acoustic neuroma
Janette G.	Female	White	41	32	Four-year degree	Sales	Bell's palsy
Hilaria L.	Female	Latino/a	49	48	High school diploma/GED	Corrections officer	Bell's palsy
Sandra C.	Female	White	42	35	Four-year degree	Education	Acoustic neuroma
Araceli B.	Female	Latino/a	30	27	Four-year degree	Multiple service jobs	Bell's palsy
Emma S.	Female	White	29	7	Graduate or professional degree	High school teacher	Other
Christine S.	Female	Mixed	27	26	Four-year degree	Behavior interventionist for kids with autism	Bell's palsy
Danielle S.	Female	White	49	0	Four-year degree	Video production, inspirational speaker	Other tumor
Bettina S.	Female	African American/Black	62	61	Four-year degree	Management	Bell's palsy

Jerald W.	Male	White	47	46	Graduate or professional degree	Graduate student in STEM field	Bell's palsy
Matt E.	Male	White	66	1	Four-year degree	Technology industry, author	Other
Deborah S.	Female	White	48	46	Graduate or professional degree	Educator	Acoustic neuroma
Brian A.	Male	White	36	29	High school diploma/GED	Entertainment	Bell's palsy
Paul L.	Male	White	53	24	Graduate or professional degree	Consultant, accountant	Acoustic neuroma
Mandy V.	Female	White	62	56	Graduate or professional degree	Software engineer	Bell's palsy
Emily Sheila H.	Female	White	48	30	Four-year Degree	Artist, graphic and fine	Bell's palsy
Maryann C.	Female	White	61	37	High school diploma/GED	Stay-at-home parent	Trauma
Toni R.	Female	African American/Black	52	41	Graduate or professional degree	Manager, human resources	Other tumor
Caroline S.	Female	African American/Black	40	26	Graduate or professional degree	Educator, banking	Bell's palsy

(continued)

Pseudonym	Gender	Race	Age	Age of Event	Level of Education	Occupation	Cause
Kristina C.	Female	African American/ Black	40	18	Graduate or professional degree	Counselor	Bell's palsy
Mike H.	Male	Other	38	37	Graduate or professional degree	Professor	Bell's palsy
Tanya A.	Female	White	18	18	Some college	Student, customer service	Bell's palsy
Karen S.	Female	White	51	47	Graduate or professional degree	Nursing	Other tumor
Selina D.	Female	White	64	13	Graduate or professional degree	Mental health care	Other tumor
Kristina L.	Female	White	27	18	Four-year degree	Graduate student, health care	Bell's palsy
Angie C.	Female	Latino/a	56	48	Graduate or professional degree	Administrative assistant	Bell's palsy
Dina S.	Female	White	21	19	Some college	Student, food service worker	Bell's palsy
Maribel M.	Female	Latino/a	31	26	Some college	Medical assistant	Bell's palsy
Jennifer D.	Female	White	25	24	Associate's degree	Hair dresser, coding	Bell's palsy
Melissa F.	Female	White	27	26	Current student	In-school service job	Bell's palsy

Edna B.	Female	White	69	54	Four-year degree	Telemarketing sales	Bell's palsy
Elizabeth G.	Female	White	70	52	Graduate or professional degree	Fund raiser, retired	Bell's palsy
Laura M.	Female	White	52	50	Four-year degree	Marketing/ advertising	Bell's palsy
Amy D.	Female	Latino/a	34	1	Graduate or professional degree	Gerontologist	Other tumor
Maria M.	Female	Latino/a	55	54	Associate's degree	Insurance agent	Acoustic neuroma
Lois Z.	Female	White	61	55	Graduate or professional degree	Mental health counselor	Ramsay Hunt syndrome
Matti L.	Female	Latino/a	54	48	Associate's degree	Business certificate works for school district	Bell's palsy
Miranda G.	Female	White	42	8	High school diploma/ GED	Information technology	Trauma
Carrie R.	Female	White	22	22	High school diploma/ GED	In-home care provider	Ramsay Hunt syndrome
Teri B.	Female	White	59	13	Graduate or professional degree	Professor	Bell's palsy

(continued)

Pseudonym	Gender	Race	Age	Age of Event	Level of Education	Occupation	Cause
Erica R.	Female	White				Small business owner	Ramsay Hunt syndrome
Gerald F.	Male	White	54	49	Graduate or professional degree	Former lawyer, now personal trainer	Ramsay Hunt syndrome
Kevin S.	Male	White	51	49	Some college	Manager	Other
Melinda H.	Female	White	52	43	Four-year degree	Management entertainment	Bell's palsy
Jessica T.	Female	White	65	61	Associate's degree	Flight attendant	Bell's palsy
Lou C.	Male	Asian American	55	11	Graduate or professional degree	Education	Acquired, cause unknown
Al L.	Male	Latino/a	30	13	Some college	Medical billing	Other
Melissa Ann	Female	White	66	59	Graduate or professional degree		Bell's palsy
Corrine C.	Female	White	61	53	Four-year degree	Certified mediator, consultant	Bell's palsy
Marcy Louise L.	Female	White	41	36	Four-year degree	Healthcare administration	Other tumor
Bob H.	Male	White	57	56	Four-year degree	Information technology (laid off)	Bell's palsy

ACKNOWLEDGMENTS

I would like to express my profound gratitude to the participants in my project and the wider community of those with facial differences who welcomed a new member with compassion and support. To the many who have taken their time to speak with me in person, online, or by email, I am deeply appreciative of your willingness to disclose complicated and sometimes painful stories. The courage, compassion, and care I continue to witness is inspiring. Thank you.

Special thanks to Dr. Babak Azzizadeh, founder of the Facial Paralysis Institute and a pioneer in developing treatments for synkinesis. In addition to performing two surgeries that improved my ability to concentrate and significantly reduced my ongoing pain, Babak has been an ardent supporter of my work. I appreciate the time he has taken to assist in so many different aspects of this project. To Jackie Diels, my occupational therapist, your ongoing research, activism, and care have been critical to my thinking and my healing. Thank you for your advocacy and caring outreach.

I am also deeply grateful to Lisa McKinley, the director of the Facial Paralysis and Bell's Palsy Foundation, for her support and assistance. Lisa has done so much to create a community of support and activism in the United States. Lisa is the type of person who always underestimates the enormity of her impact—Lisa, you are amazing. Thank you.

So many people have invited me to their support groups and events—thank you to everyone. I would like to highlight Barbara Pasternacki's invaluable assistance as well as her thoughtful advocacy, which has initiated lines of medical inquiry. She has assisted many newcomers, and she probably doesn't realize what a wonderful role model and inspiration she is. Thank you, Barbara!

My deepest appreciation also goes to Elizabeth Robinson, the founder of the online support group Bell's Palsy and Facial Support Network Australia New Zealand World, who also provided the amazing cover art. Your openness and caring is appreciated by so many. Thank you as well to Kathleen Bogart and Amanda Hemmesch for your thoughts and inspiration. I also want to give a shout out to Brian Aprille for his comedy and podcast. We all appreciate your openness and advocacy. I give special thanks to the folks at Ascend Physical Therapy and Balance Center and to Casey Chaney for creating spaces and practices that heal.

ACKNOWLEDGMENTS

To my loving spouse, Navid Arefi Ardakani, who happily surrendered his place in the dedication to this book in favor our son, I offer my deepest appreciation. Writing an academic book is intensely time and mind consuming—thank you for your patience and tolerance. I truly appreciate you pointing out to me that I should mention Franz Kafka's book of the same title: the duplication is intentional. (I offer a posthumous thank you to Rose Gilbert, English teacher at Palisades High School and inspiration for Star Wars character Maz.) What if we all feel a little Gregorish (thanks to my kid for the term) at times, but that in our transformation we become something better for our imperfections.

Ziya Robert Wachs Ardakani, thank you for challenging and pushing my thinking. I know it irritates you to no end when I won't tell you if someone is "good" or "bad"; but without your challenges I wouldn't have realized that these aren't words for people. You will never let us take the easy way out. Thank you for that accountability—I am a better person because of it. And along those lines, thank you as well to Doris Urrutia, J. L. Woodson, Isabel Hernandez, and Alexis "Lexi" Madara, who aided with childcare and our home chaos so I could work.

Thank you to my wonderful parents, Helen and Martin Wachs. Unfortunately, during the process of finishing this book my father passed away. Even more galling, he published his own book posthumously before I managed to finish my draft. But, unlike many of my colleagues who lament that their parents have no understanding of their worldview or what they do, I am very much a product of my environment. My parents have lived praxis, and they always encouraged me to do the same, joining me at marches for the climate, against children in cages, and for undocumented students. Thank you to my brother, Steve Wachs, my awesome sister-in-law, Shirley Tse Wachs, and my niece, Leia, who have supported me throughout the health crises and the book-writing process. In my extended family, I shout out to my mother-in-law, Nahid Friberg, her spouse, Lennart, my brother-in-law, Saeed, my sister-in-law, Jennifer, and my nephews, Parker and Arsalan. I always have appreciated their kind words of encouragement throughout this process.

To the many people who have read my drafts or sections or attended my presentations, thank you. I give extra special thanks to Steph D. Jones, whose early readings greatly improved the theorizing. I give copious amounts of appreciation to Travers for their thoughtful input and ongoing support and friendship. Thank you also to Anthony C. Ocampo, Melissa Barragan, Kathryn Daniels, Anjana Narayan, and the Sociology Department at Cal Poly Pomona for their "Third Thursday" readings and comments on one chapter, which I then applied to the entire manuscript to its betterment. I give special thanks to my colleague Mary Danico, for her support and guidance through the process. I would like to voice my appreciation for Juliana Fuqua, who had lots of random conversations when we were supposed to be working on our other research, and also to Caitlin Vitoskly Clarke for all the encouragement along the way.

ACKNOWLEDGMENTS

A shout out goes to Erika DeJonghe for being the first person to say "Bell's palsy" to me, and to Niki Morris for correctly diagnosing over the phone and sending me to the ER, and all the extra medical advice has been appreciated. Thank you to Cheryl Cooky and Shari Dworkin, my long-time co-authors, friends, and inspirations, without whose initial encouragement I might not have done this. And, as always, thanks to Mike Messner for being a wonderful mentor, advisor, and role model. His fingerprints are all over my work, much to its betterment, and he remains a role model as he dedicates his retirement to activism; I, too, now have a cohesive exit strategy.

Without Brooke Jones and Harmony Nguyen I would still be taking out spaces between sentences and just generally struggling with formatting issues; thank you for your willingness to assist and your ongoing work as research assistants. Thanks also to David Dimas for his assistance with the reference section. And thank you to the many wonderful Cal Poly Pomona students who have reminded and continue to remind me of the importance of being: when I showed up to teach with my paralysis at its worst, I was met with compassion, kindness, and support. CPP students are the best! We say that a lot at my job because they really are. Thank you also to my colleagues and our administration at CPP: I genuinely like and respect my colleagues, and I can honestly say that my department, my college, and my university have been a wonderful place to do this work. Cal Poly Pomona is a lovely place to call my academic home.

Thank you to my animal companions. To our dogs for their loyal companionship throughout: Bobo (best dog ever, always missed), Briggs (going strong at 19+ years of age), Ziggy (Baron von Ziggelstein, gone too soon), and Zorro (Don Diego de la Vega, still forced on long hikes despite his desire to just get fat). The cats provided not only recognition that we are all mortal servants of our more beautiful overlords, but also lots of confused and now tail-less lizards for me to enjoy along with the occasional rat. Generally, these treats are brought live and released under my desk, bed, or in my closet—for that ongoing entertainment, thank you Hermione and Minerva. To Henry and Elizabeth (our parakeets), thank you for endangering your lives by entertaining the cats so that I could actually get something done.

NOTES

CHAPTER 1   WHEN LIFE GIVES YOU LEMONS

1. I admire artisans who are able to do this well. If I were one of them, I would be writing feminist speculative fiction à la Margaret Atwood or Ursula Le Guin. I am not one of them. Relegated to the world of academia, this is about as creative as I am capable of being.
2. Weber uses the term *verstehen*, empathetic understanding, to refer to a methodological framework for analysis that takes into account the perspective or viewpoint of the person acting.

CHAPTER 2   THEORIZING CHANGE

1. Governmentality demonstrates the link between the edicts of government and the subjectivity of members of the larger population (Wachs and Chase 2013; Lemke 2011).

CHAPTER 3   MICROAGGRESSIONS, INTERNALIZATIONS, AND CONTESTED IDEOLOGICAL TERRAIN

1. This is not to discount the psychological and perhaps physiological impact of many of the therapies engaged by people with Bell's palsy. It seems that specialized occupational or physical therapy, Botox (to eliminate unwanted movement and restore symmetry), and some surgeries (i.e., selective neurolysis) will improve function, appearance, and communication and can mitigate pain and discomfort. There are many things that may work for lots of valid reasons; for example, a roller did do some of what I did in occupational therapy. There are some therapies that are dubious, but the experience may be relaxing for the patient. And there are lots of people who believe lots of things that lack verification. And there are people who take advantage of others' vulnerabilities.
2. Being unable to blink is a serious problem. It means one cannot spontaneously close one eye. This puts vision at perpetual risk and requires management and care. Eyelid weights (permanent or stick on) can be used for sleep or for assisted blinking.

CHAPTER 4   IT'S MY FACE–WHY THAT MATTERS

1. Existing studies have compared cisgendered men and women. Studies on nonbinary and transgender individuals is an area requiring redress.
2. Poverty is visible and stigmatized as unattractive and revealing of moral degeneracy. Lack of access to dental care, lack of access to nutrient-dense diets, overwork, and

191

NOTES

other aspects of poverty generate bodies labeled as unattractive of "ugly." Social ideologies mislabel the effects of poverty as the signifiers of the cause.

CHAPTER 5   DISRUPTED SELVES

1. Sorry, there's no noncolloquial way to really capture that.
2. Gender/sex provides a prime example. Although biology has insisted on "two sexes" for mammals for a long time, it relies on classifying many as "abnormal" for functional, hormonal, chromosomal, or chosen "deviations." Hence, biology is not merely describing what's in the natural world but making judgments that have larger implications relating to power and privilege.
3. People with social anxiety are concerned about being judged, about being embarrassed, about others being aware of their discomfort, about causing offense, or about having attention drawn to them (Robinson 2010).
4. Acknowledgment to Brit Friedman for her *Blazing Saddles* reference when I requested a synonym for myriad.
5. Certainly, Max Weber's assertion that predictability, control by nonhuman technologies, calculability, and efficiency are the hallmarks of modern rational evaluation ([1905] 2003), as updated by George Ritzer's McDonaldization (1993), exemplify this type of thought.
6. In the United States, 21.3 percent of those aged fifteen and older had a disability or impairment according to the 2010 U.S. census. Impairment describes the loss of ability or capacity, while disability is the repercussions of the impairment (Howson 2013).
7. I am using three to refer to any number greater than two.
8. For example, several people asked if Greta Thunberg, the climate activist, had facial difference; her autism would also fall into this category.

CHAPTER 6   SOMEONE I WOULD RATHER BE

1. The way I see staff visibly relax when I give off my California "no worries" vibe is astonishing. They are expecting what our current cultural parlance refers to as a Karen, a dissatisfied, entitled, privileged, and difficult person.
2. I don't know why I wrote this, but I heard the author Patrick Rothfuss later describe a stone similarly on one of his podcasts, so I am just leaving it as it is.
3. *The Picture of Dorian Gray* is a novel by Oscar Wilde. First published in 1890, the novel depicts the moral degeneration of a young man, which is rendered visible in his portrait while his physical self remains unblemished.
4. E-stim machines were often given to people who were developing synkinesis, and it is something that remains controversial. It is not clear whether it is helpful, or it contributes to synkinesis, or it does little.

CHAPTER 7   WALKING AWAY

1. Basically, that's why I roll my eyes at cursory requests for "gratitude" statements. It's lovely we are all aware of our relative privilege, but is it really OK to just be grateful without working to extend that option to everyone?

REFERENCES

Adler, Peter, and Patricia A. Adler. 1991. *Backboards and Blackboards: College Athletics and Role Engulfment*. New York: Columbia University Press.

American Society of Plastic Surgeons. 2018. "2018 Plastic Surgery Statistics." https://www.plasticsurgery.org/news/plastic-surgery-statistics?sub=2018+Plastic+Surgery+Statistics.

Anderson, L. 2006. "Analytic Autoethnography." *Journal of Contemporary Ethnography* 35 (4): 373–395.

Anzani, Annalisa, Simona Sacchi, and Antonio Prunas. 2021. "Microaggressions towards Lesbian and Transgender Women: Biased Information Gathering When Working Alongside Gender and Sexual Minorities." *Journal of Clinical Psychology* 77 (9): 2027–2040. https://doi.org/10.1002/jclp.23140.

Arayasirikul, Sean, and Erin C. Wilson. 2019. "Spilling the T on Trans-Misogyny and Microaggressions: An Intersectional Oppression and Social Process among Trans Women." *Journal of homosexuality* 66 (10): 1415–1438. https://doi.org/10.1080/00918369.2018.1542203.

Bailey, Moya, and Izetta A. Mobley. 2019. "Work in the Intersections: A Black Feminist Disability Framework." *Gender and Society* 33 (1): 19–40. https://doi.org/10.1177/0891243218801523.

Baker, L. Dana. 2011. *The Politics of Neurodiversity: Why Public Policy Matters*. Boulder, CO: Lynne Rienner.

Barnwell, M. Alison, and David J. Kavanagh. 1997. "Prediction of Psychological Adjustment to Multiple Sclerosis." *Social Science and Medicine* 45 (3): 411–418. https://doi.org/10.1016/S0277-9536(96)00356-5.

Bates, Laura. 2016. *Everyday Sexism: The Project That Inspired a Worldwide Movement*. New York: St. Martin's Griffin.

Bauman, Zygmunt. 1992. *Mortality, Immortality, and Other Life Strategies*. Stanford, CA: Stanford University Press.

Bearman, Steve, and Marielle Amrhein. 2013. "Girls, Women, and Internalized Sexism." In *Internalized Oppression: The Psychology of Marginalized Groups*, edited by E.J.R. David, 191–226. New York: Springer.

Becker, D. Vaughn, Rebecca Neel, and Uriah S. Anderson. 2010. "Illusory Conjunctions of Angry Facial Expressions follow Intergroup Biases." *Psychological Science* 21 (7): 938–940. https://doi.org/10.1177/0956797610373374.

Begum, Nasa. 1992. "Disabled Women and the Feminist Agenda." *Feminist Review* 40 (1): 70–84. https://doi.org/10.1057/fr.1992.6.

Berger, J. Ronald. 2013. *Introducing Disability Studies*. Boulder, CO: Lynne Rienner.

Blairy, Sylvie, Pedro Herrera, and Ursula Hess. 1999. "Mimicry and the Judgment of Emotional Facial Expressions." *Journal of Nonverbal Behavior* 23 (1): 5–41. https://doi.org/10.1023/A:1021370825283.

Bochner, Arthur, and Carolyn Ellis. 2016. *Evocative Autoethnography: Writing Lives and Telling Stories*. New York: Routledge.

Bogart, Kathleen R. 2014. "The Role of Disability Self-Concept in Adaptation to Congenital or Acquired Disability. *Rehabilitation Psychology* 59 (1): 107–115. https://doi.org/10.1037/a0035800.

———. 2015. "'People Are All about Appearances': A Focus Group of Teenagers with Moebius Syndrome." *Journal of Health Psychology* 20 (12): 1579–1588. https://doi.org/10.1177/1359105313517277.

———. 2021. "Masks in the Time of COVID-19 as an Inadvertent Simulation of Facial Paralysis." *Disability and Society* 36 (5): 840–843.

Bogart, Kathleen R., and Amanda R. Hemmesch. 2016. "Benefits of Support Conferences for Parents of and People with Moebius Syndrome." *Stigma and Health* 1 (2): 109–121. https://doi.org/10.1037/sah0000018.

Bogart, Kathleen R., and David Matsumoto. 2010. "Living with Moebius Syndrome: Adjustment, Social Competence, and Satisfaction with Life." *Cleft Palate-Craniofacial Journal* 47 (2): 134–142. https://doi.org/10.1597/08-257_1.

Bogart, K. R., N. Rosa, and M. L. Slepian. 2019. "Born That Way or Became That Way: Stigma toward Congenital versus Acquired Disability." *Group Processes and Intergroup Relations* 22 (4): 594–612. https://doi.org/10.1177/1368430218757897.

Bogart, Kathleen R., Adena Rottenstein, Emily M. Lund, and Lauren Bouchard. 2017. "Who Self-Identifies as Disabled? An Examination of Impairment and Contextual Predictors." *Rehabilitation Psychology* 62 (4): 553–562. https://doi.org/10.1037/rep0000132.

Bogart, Kathleen R., and Linda Tickle-Degnen. 2015. "Looking beyond the Face: A Training to Improve Perceivers' Impressions of People with Facial Paralysis." *Patient Education and Counseling* 98 (2): 251–256. https://doi.org/10.1016/j.pec.2014.09.010.

Bogart, Kathleen R., Linda Tickle-Degnen, and Nalini Ambady. 2014. "Communicating without the Face: Holistic Perception of Emotions of People with Facial Paralysis." *Basic and Applied Social Psychology* 36 (4): 309–320. https://doi.org/10.1080/01973533.2014.917973.

Bogart, Kathleen R., Linda Tickle-Degnen, and Matthew S. Joffe. 2012. "Social Interaction Experiences of Adults with Moebius Syndrome: A Focus Group." *Journal of Health Psychology* 17 (8): 1212–1222. https://doi.org/10.1177/1359105311432491.

Bogdan, Robert. 1990. *Freak Show: Presenting Human Oddities for Amusement and Profit*. Chicago: University of Chicago Press.

Bonilla-Silva, Eduardo. 2003. *Racism without Racists: Color-Blind Racism and the Persistence of Racial Inequality in the United States*. Lanham, MD: Rowman & Littlefield.

———. 2018. *Racism without Racists: Color-Blind Racism and the Persistence of Racial Inequality in America*. 5th ed. Lanham, MD: Rowman & Littlefield.

Bourdieu, Pierre. 1984. *Distinction: A Social Critique of the Judgment of Taste*. Boston: Harvard University Press.

———. 2001. *Masculine Domination*. Cambridge: Polity Press.

Bourdieu, Pierre., and J. C. Passeron. 1977. *Reproduction in Education, Society and Culture*. Translated by Richard Nice. Sage Studies in Social and Educational Change 5. London: Sage.

Bourdieu, Pierre, and Loïc Wacquant. 1992. *An Invitation to a Reflexive Sociology*. Chicago: University of Chicago Press.

Braun Virginia, and Victoria Clarke. 2008. "Using Thematic Analysis in Psychology." *Qualitative Research in Psychology* 3 (2): 77–101. https://doi.org/10.1191/1478088706qp063oa.

Brewster, Thackeray. 2003. "State of the Union for People with Disabilities." Presentation at the annual conference of the National Organization on Disability (www.nod.org).

REFERENCES

Brooks, Nancy A., and Ronald R. Matson. 1982. "Social-Psychological Adjustment to Multiple Sclerosis: A Longitudinal Study." *Social Science and Medicine* 16 (24): 2129–2135. https://doi.org/10.1016/0277-9536(82)90262-3.

Brown, Robyn L., and Mairead E. Moloney. 2019. "Intersectionality, Work, and Well-Being: The Effects of Gender & Disability." *Gender and Society* 33 (1): 94–122. https://doi.org/10.1177/0891243218800636.

Brown, Tony N., Sherrill L. Sellers, and John P. Gomez. 2002. "The Relationship between Internalization and Self-Esteem among Black Adults." *Sociological Focus.* 35 (1): 55–71. https://www.jstor.org/stable/20832150.

Browne, Susan, Debra Connors, and Nanci Stern. 1985. *With the Power of Each Breath.* Pittsburgh: Cleis Press.

Burnett, Kathryn A., and Mary Holmes. 2001. "Bodies, Battlefields and Biographies: Scars and the Construction of the Body as Heritage." In *Exploring the Body*, edited by Kathryn Backett-Milburn and Sarah Cunningham-Burley, 21–36. London: Palgrave Macmillan.

Butler, Judith. 1990. *Gender Trouble: Feminism and the Subversion of Identity.* New York: Routledge.

———. 1993. *Bodies That Matter: On the Discursive Limits of "Sex."* New York: Routledge.

———. 1996. "Performativity's Social Magic." In *The Social and Political Body*, edited by T. R. Schatzki and W. Natter, 29–47. New York: Guilford.

Bylund, N., D. Jensson, S. Enghag, T. Berg, E. Marsk, M. Hultcrantz, N. Hadziosmanovic, A. Rodriguez-Lorenzo, and L. Jonsson. 2017. "Synkinesis in Bell's Palsy in a Randomised Controlled Trial." *Clinical Otolaryngology* 42 (3): 673–680. https://doi.org/10.1111/coa.12799.

Campbell, Fiona. 2009. *Contours of Ableism: The Production of Disability and Ableness.* New York: Palgrave Macmillan.

Cavico, Frank J., Stephen C. Muffler, and Bahaudin G. Mujtaba. 2012. "Appearance Discrimination in Employment." *Equality, Diversity and Inclusion* 32 (1): 83–119.

Charmaz, Kathy. 1983. "Loss of Self: A Fundamental Form of Suffering in the Chronically Ill." *Sociology of Health and Illness.* 5 (2): 168–197.

Clare, Eli. 2017. *Brilliant Imperfection: Grappling with Cure.* Durham, NC: Duke University Press.

Clarke, David B., Marcus A. Doel, and Kate M. L. Housiaux. 2003. *The Consumption Reader.* New York: Routledge.

Cole, C. L. 1993. "Resisting the Canon: Feminist Cultural Studies, 'Sport' and Technologies of the Body." *Journal of Sport and Social Issues* 17 (2): 77–97. https://doi.org/10.1177/019372359301700202.

Collins, Patricia Hill. 1990. *Black Feminist Thought: Knowledge, Consciousness, and the Politics of Empowerment.* Boston: Unwin Hyman.

Colwell, John, Sadi Schröder, and David Sladen. 2000. "The Ability to Detect Unseen Staring: A Literature Review and Empirical Tests." *British Journal of Psychology* 91 (1): 71–85. https://doi.org/10.1348/000712600161682.

Connell, R. W. 1987. *Gender and Power.* Cambridge: Polity Press.

Conover, Kristin J., Tania Israel, and Karen Nylund-Gibson. 2017. "Development and Validation of the Ableist Microaggressions Scale." *Counseling Psychologist* 45 (4): 570–599. https://doi.org/10.1177/0011000017715317.

Cooley, Charles Horton. (1902) 2010. "The Looking-Glass Self." In *Social Theory: The Multicultural Readings*, edited by Charles Lemert, 188–189. Philadelphia: Westview.

Corbin, Juliet, and Anselm Strauss. 2015. *Basics of Qualitative Research: Techniques and Procedures for Developing Grounded Theory.* Thousand Oaks, CA: Sage.

REFERENCES

Coulson, S. 2017. "Perceived Face Value: The Cost of Facial Nerve Paralysis." Paper presented at the 13th Facial Nerve Symposium, Hollywood, CA, August 3–6, 2017.

Coulson, Susan, Nicholas J. O'Dwyer, Roger Adams, and Glen R. Croxson. 2004. "Expression of Emotion and Quality of Life after Facial Nerve Paralysis." *Otology and Neurotology* 25 (6): 1014–1019.

Couser, G. Thomas. 2009. *Signifying Bodies: Disability in Contemporary Life Writing. Corporealities.* Ann Arbor: University of Michigan Press.

Craig, A. R., K. Hancock, and E. Chang. 1994. "The Influence of Spinal Cord Injury on Coping Styles and Self-perceptions Two Years after the Injury." *Australian and New Zealand Journal of Psychiatry* 28: 307–312. https://doi.org/10.1080/00048679409075644.

Cregan, Kate. 2006. *The Sociology of the Body.* Thousand Oaks, CA: Sage.

Crenshaw, Kimberle. 1989. "Demarginalizing the Intersection of Race and Sex: A Black Feminist Critique of Antidiscrimination Doctrine, Feminist Theory and Antiracist Policies." *University of Chicago Legal Forum* 1989 (1): 139–167.

———. 1991. "Mapping the Margins: Intersectionality, Identity, and Violence against Women of Color." *Stanford Law Review* 43 (6): 1241–1300.

Croteau, David, and William Hoynes. 2019. *Media/Society: Technology, Industries, Content, and Users.* 6th ed. Thousand Oaks, CA: Sage.

Daker-White, Gavin, Helen Kingston, Katherine Payne, Julia Greenfield, John Ealing, and Caroline Sanders. 2012. "'You Don't Get Told Anything, They Don't Do Anything and Nothing Changes.' Medicine as a Resource and Constraint in Progressive Ataxia." *Health Expectations* 18 (2): 177–187. https://doi.org/10.1111/hex.12016.

Darling, Rosalyn B. 2000. "Stigma of Disability." In *Encyclopedia of Criminology and Deviant Behavior,* edited by C. D. Bryant, 482–485. Philadelphia: Brunner-Routledge.

———. 2019. *Disability and Identity: Negotiating Self in a Changing Society.* Boulder, CO: Lynne Rienner.

Davis, Fred. 1961. "Deviance Disavowal: The Management of Strained Interaction by the Visibly Handicapped." *Social Problems* 9 (2): 120–132. https://doi.org/10.2307/799007.

Davis, Joshua D., Piotr Winkielman, and Seana Coulson. 2015. "Facial Action and Emotional Language: ERP Evidence that Blocking Facial Feedback Selectively Impairs Sentence Comprehension." *Journal of Cognitive Neuroscience* 27 (11): 2269–2280. https://doi.org/10.1162/jocn_a_00858.

Davis, Lennard J. 1995. *Enforcing Normalcy: Disability, Deafness, and the Body.* London: Verso.

Deegan Mary Jo, and Nancy A. Brooks, ed. 1985. *Women and Disability: The Double Handicap.* New Brunswick, NJ: Transaction.

Dell Orto, Arthur E., and Paul W. Power. 2007. *The Psychological and Social Impact of Illness and Disability.* 5th ed. New York: Springer.

Denzin, N. K. 2014. *Interpretive Autoethnography.* Thousand Oaks, CA: Sage Publications.

Dill, Bonnie Thornton, and Maxine Baca Zinn. 1996. "Theorizing Difference from Multiracial Feminism." *Feminist Studies* 22 (2): 321–331. https://doi.org/10.2307/3178416.

Du Bois, W. E. B. 1897. "Strivings of the Negro People." *The Atlantic,* August 1897. https://www.theatlantic.com/magazine/archive/1897/08/strivings-of-the-negro-people/305446/.

———. 1903. *The Souls of Black Folk.* Chicago: A.C. McClurg & Co. https://www.bartleby.com/114/.

———. 2008. *The Souls of Black Folk.* Edited by Brent Hayes Edwards. Oxford: Oxford University Press.

Duncan, Margaret Carlisle. 1994. "The Politics of Women's Body Images and Practices: Foucault, the Panopticon, and Shape Magazine." *Journal of Sport and Social Issues* 18 (1): 48–65. https://doi.org/10.1177/019372394018001004.

REFERENCES

Dworkin, Shari L., and Faye Linda Wachs. 2009. *Body Panic: Gender, Health, and the Selling of Fitness*. New York: New York University Press. https://doi.org/10.18574/nyu /9780814785256.003.0006.

Ekman, Paul. 1986. "Psychosocial Aspects of Facial Paralysis." In *The Facial Nerve*, edited by Mark May, 781–787. New York: Thieme.

Elliott, Gregory C., Herbert L. Ziegler, Barbara M. Altman, and Deborah R. Scott. 1982. "Understanding Stigma: Dimensions of Deviance and Coping." *Deviant Behavior* 3 (3): 275–300. https://doi.org/10.1080/01639625.1982.9967590.

Emberley, Julia V., and Cynthia Wright. 1999. "[The Cultural Politics of Fur]." *Resources for Feminist Research* 27 (1/2): 170–173.

England, Paula. (1992) 2017. *Comparable Worth: Theories and Evidence*. New York: Routledge.

Ettorre, Elizabeth. 2017. *Autoethnography as Feminist Method: Sensitizing the Feminist I*. New York: Routledge.

Fang, Anyu. 2009. "Hiding Homelessness: 'Quality of life' Laws and the Politics of Development in American Cities." *International Journal of Law in Context* 5 (1): 1–24. https://doi .org/10.1017/S1744552309005011.

Featherstone, Mike. 1991a. "The Body in Consumer Culture." In *The Body: Social Process and Cultural Theory*, edited by Mike Featherstone, Mike Hepworth, and Bryan S. Turner, 170–196. London: Sage.

———. 1991b. *Consumer Culture and Postmodernism*. London: Sage.

Featherstone, Mike, and Bryan S. Turner. 1995. "Body & Society: An Introduction." *Body and Society* 1 (1): 1–12. https://doi.org/10.1177/1357034X95001001001.

Fine, M., and A. Asch. 1988. "Disability beyond Stigma: Social Interaction, Discrimination, and Activism." *Journal of Social Issues* 44 (1): 3–21. https://doi.org/10.1111/j.1540-4560.1988. tb02045.x.

Fitzgerald, F. Scott. (1936) 2017. "The Crack-Up." *Esquire*, March 7, 2017. https://www.esquire .com/lifestyle/a4310/the-crack-up/.

Flecha-García, María L. 2010. "Eyebrow Raises in Dialogue and Their Relation to Discourse Structure, Utterance Function and Pitch Accents in English." *Speech Communication* 52 (6): 542–554. https://doi.org/10.1016/j.specom.2009.12.003.

Foucault, Michel. 1970. *The Order of Things: An Archeology of the Human Sciences*. Translated by Alan Sheridan. New York: Vintage.

———. 1972. *The Archaeology of Knowledge*. Translated by Alan Sheridan. New York: Pantheon.

———. 1978. *The History of Sexuality*. New York: Vintage Press.

———. 1979. *Discipline and Punish: The Birth of the Prison*. New York: Vintage Press.

———. 1980. *Power/Knowledge*. Brighton: Harvester.

———. 1982. "The Subject and Power." *Critical Inquiry* 8 (4): 777–795. http://www.jstor.org /stable/1343197.

———. 1999. *Abnormal: Lectures at the Collège de France*. New York: Picador.

Fowler, Bridget. 1997. *Pierre Bourdieu and Cultural Theory: Critical Investigations*. Thousand Oaks, CA: Sage.

Freeman, Lauren, and Heather Stewart. 2018. "Microaggressions in Clinical Medicine." *Kennedy Institute of Ethics Journal* 28 (4): 411–449. https://doi.org/10.1353/ken.2018.0024.

Garland-Thomson, Rosemarie. 1997. *Extraordinary Bodies: Figuring Physical Disability in American Culture and Literature*. New York: Columbia University Press.

———. 2005. "Feminist Disability Studies." *Signs* 30 (2): 1557–1587. https://doi.org/10.1086 /423352.

———. 2009. *Staring: How We Look*. Oxford: Oxford University Press.

Giddens, Anthony. 1991. *Modernity and Self Identity: Self and Society in the Late Modern Age.* Cambridge: Polity Press.

Gifford, Robert. 2011. "The Role of Nonverbal Communication in Interpersonal Relations." In *Handbook of Interpersonal Psychology: Theory, Research, Assessment, and Therapeutic Interventions*, edited by Leonard M. Horowitz, and Stephen Strack, 171–190. Hoboken, NJ: Wiley.

Gill, Carol. 1989. "Sexuality and Disability Research: Suffering from a Case of the Medical Model." *Disability Studies Quarterly* 9 (3): 12–15.

Giulianotti, Richard. 2005. *Sport: A Critical Sociology.* Cambridge: Polity Press.

Goffman, Erving. 1959. *The Presentation of Self in Everyday Life.* New York: Anchor Books.

———. 1963. *Stigma: Notes on the Management of Spoiled Identity.* Englewood Cliffs, NJ: Prentice-Hall.

———. 1967. *Interaction Ritual: Essays on Face-to-Face Interaction.* Chicago: Aldine.

Goodley, Dan. 2014. *Dis/Ability Studies: Theorising Disablism and Ableism.* New York: Routledge.

Gore, Jonathan. 2009. "The Interaction of Sex, Verbal, and Nonverbal Cues in Same-Sex First Encounters." *Journal of Nonverbal Behavior* 33 (4): 279–299. https://doi.org/10.1007/s10919-009-0074-1.

Hahn, Harlan. 1981. "The Social Component of Sexuality and Disability: Some Problems and Proposals." *Sexuality and Disability* 4: 220–233.

———. 1989. "Masculinity and Disability." *Disability Studies Quarterly* 9: 1–3.

Haines, Kari M., C. Reyn Boyer, Casey Giovanazzi, and M. Paz Galupo. 2018. "'Not a Real Family': Microaggressions Directed toward LGBTQ Families." *Journal of Homosexuality* 65 (9): 1138–1151. https://doi.org/10.1080/00918369.2017.1406217.

Hall, Stuart. 1983. "The Problem of Ideology: Marxism without Guarantees." In *Marx: 100 Years On*, edited by Betty Matthews, 57–84. London: Lawrence & Wishart.

Hanhardt, Christina B. 2013. *Safe Space: Gay Neighborhood History and the Politics of Violence.* Durham, NC: Duke University Press.

Haug, Frigga, et al. 1987. *Female Sexualization: A Collective Work of Memory.* Translated by Erica Carter. New York: Verso.

Havas, David A., Arthur M. Glenberg, Karol A. Gutowski, Mark J. Lucarelli, and Richard J. Davidson. 2010. "Cosmetic Use of Botulinum Toxin-A Affects Processing of Emotional Language." *Psychological Science* 21 (7): 895–900. https://doi.org/10.1177/0956797610374742.

Herring, Cedric, and Anthony Hynes. 2017. "Race, Skin Tone, and Wealth Inequality in America." In *Color Struck. Teaching Race and Ethnicity*, edited by Lori Latrice Martin, Hayward Derrick Horton, Cedric Herring, Verna M. Keith, and Melvin Thomas, 1–17. Rotterdam, The Netherlands: Sense.

Hess, U., and P. Bourgeois. 2010."You Smile—I Smile: Emotion Expression in Social Interaction." *Biological Psychology* 84 (3): 514–520. https://doi.org/10.1016/j.biopsycho.2009.11.001.

Holton, Judith A., and Isabelle Walsh. 2016. *Classic Grounded Theory: Applications with Qualitative and Quantitative Data.* Los Angeles: Sage.

hooks, bell. 1981. *Ain't I a Woman?: Black Women and Feminism.* Boston, MA: South End Press.

Hosseini, Khaled. 2003. *The Kite Runner.* New York: Riverhead Books.

Howson, Alexandra. 2013. *The Body in Society.* Cambridge: Polity Press.

Hughes, Michael J. 1998. *The Social Consequence of Facial Disfigurement.* Aldergate, UK: Ashgate.

REFERENCES

Hwang, Hyisung C., and David Matsumoto. 2016. "Facial Expressions." In *APA Handbook of Nonverbal Communication*, edited by David Matsumoto, Hyisung C. Hwang, and Mark G. Frank, 257–288. Washington, DC: American Psychological Association.

Isenberg, Nancy. 2016. *White Trash: The 400-Year Untold History of Class in America*. New York: Penguin/Random House.

Jagger, Alison M., and Susan R. Bordo, eds. 1992. *Gender/Body/Knowledge: Feminist Reconstructions on Being and Knowing*. New Brunswick, NJ: Rutgers University Press.

Johnson, Allan. 2017. *Privilege, Power, and Difference*. 3rd ed. New York: McGraw-Hill Professional.

Jones, Camara Phyllis. 2000. "Levels of Racism: A Theoretic Framework and a Gardener's Tale." *American Journal of Public Health* 90 (8): 1212–1215. https://doi.org/10.2105/ajph.90.8.1212.

Joseph, John H., Allen Foulad, Amir Aaron Hakimi, Babak Azizzadeh, Brian S. Biesman, Faye L. Wachs, and Laura Eaton. 2022. "Age-Related Craniofacial Morphology: Assessing the Effect of Muscle Action on the Bony Orbit in Subjects with Long-Standing Flaccid Unilateral Facial Nerve Paralysis." *Journal of Cosmetic Dermatology* 21 (7): 3163–3165. https://doi.org/10.1111/jocd.15072.

Kattari, Shanna K., Miranda Olzman, and Michele D. Hanna. 2018. "'You Look Fine!': Ableist Experiences by People with Invisible Disabilities." *Affilia* 33 (4): 477–492. https://doi.org/10.1177/0886109918778073.

Kawai, Kosuke, Alison Tse Kawai, Peter Wollan, and Barbara P. Yawn. 2017. "Adverse Impacts of Chronic Pain on Health-Related Quality of Life, Work Productivity, Depression and Anxiety in a Community-Based Study." *Family Practice* 34 (6): 656–661. https://doi.org/10.1093/fampra/cmx034.

Keller, Richard M., and Corinne E. Galgay. 2010. "Microaggressive Experiences of People with Disabilities." In *Microaggressions and Marginality: Manifestation, Dynamics, and Impact*, edited by Derald Wing Sue, 241–267. Hoboken, NJ: John H. Wiley & Sons.

Kelly, Samantha Murphy. 2020. "Plastic Surgery Inspired by Filters and Photo Editing Apps Isn't Going Away." *CNN Business*, February 10, 2020. https://www.cnn.com/2020/02/08/tech/snapchat-dysmorphia-plastic-surgery/index.html.

Kleinman, Sherryl. 2003. "Feminist Fieldworker: Connecting Research, Teaching and Memoir." In *Our Studies, Ourselves: Sociologists' Lives and Work*, edited by Barry Glassner, and Rosanna Hertz, 215–232. New York: Oxford University Press.

Krnjacki, Lauren, Naomi Priest, Zoe Aitken, Eric Emerson, Gwynnyth Llewellyn, Tania King, and Anne Kavanagh. 2018. "Disability-based Discrimination and Health: Findings from an Australian-based Population Study." *Australian and New Zealand Journal of Public Health* 42 (2): 172–174. https://doi.org/10.1111/1753-6405.

Kvigne, Kari, and Marit Kirkevold. 2003. "Living with Bodily Strangeness: Women's Experiences of their Changing and Unpredictable Body Following a Stroke." *Qualitative Health Research* 13 (19): 1291–1310. https://doi.org/10.1177/1049732303257224.

La France, Betty H., David D. Henningsen, Aubrey Oates, and Christina M. Shaw. 2009. "Social-Sexual Interactions? Meta-Analyses of Sex Differences in Perceptions of Flirtatiousness, Seductiveness, and Promiscuousness." *Communication Monographs* 76 (3): 263–285. https://doi.org/10.1080/03637750903074701.

Lakomski, Gabriele. 1984. "On Agency and Structure: Pierre Bourdieu and Jean-Claude Passeron's Theory of Symbolic Violence." *Curriculum Inquiry* 14 (2): 151–163. https://doi.org/10.1080/03626784.1984.11075918.

Langer, Ellen J. Susan Fiske, Shelley E. Taylor, and Benzion Chanowitz. 1976. "Stigma, Staring, and Discomfort: A Novel-Stimulus Hypothesis." *Journal of Experimental Psychology* 12 (5): 451–463. https://doi.org/10.1016/0022-1031(76)90077-9.

Latour, Bruno. 1993. *We Have Never Been Modern.* Translated by Catherine Porter. Boston: Harvard University Press.

Leder, Drew. 1990. *The Absent Body.* Chicago: University of Chicago Press.

Lefton, Mark. 1984. "Chronic Disease and Applied Sociology: An Essay in Personalized Sociology." *Sociological Inquiry* 54: 466–476. https://doi.org/10.1111/j.1475-682X.1984.tb00070.x.

Le Guin, Ursula K. 1974. *The Dispossessed.* New York: HarperCollins.

———. 1975. "The Ones Who Walk away from Omelas." In *The Wind's Four Quarters,* 275–284. New York: Harper & Row. First published in 1973.

Lemke, Thomas. 2011. *Biopolitics: An Advanced Introduction.* Translated by Eric Fredrick Trump. New York: New York University Press.

Levchak, Charisse C. 2018. *Microaggressions and Modern Racism: Endurance and Evolution.* Cham, Switzerland: Palgrave MacMillan.

Lewis, Jioni A., Ruby Mendenhall, Stacy A. Harwood, and Margaret Browne Huntt. 2016. "'Ain't I a Woman?': Perceived Gendered Racial Microaggressions Experienced by Black Women." *Counseling Psychologist* 44 (5): 758–780. https://doi.org/10.1177/0011000016641193.

Linton, Simi. 1998. *Claiming Disability: Knowledge and Identity.* New York: New York University Press.

Loeser, Cassandra, Barbara Pini, and Vicki Crowley. 2018. "Disability and Sexuality: Desires and Pleasures." *Sexualities* 21 (3): 255–270. https://doi.org/10.1177/1363460716688682.

Lofland, John, David A. Snow, Leon Anderson, and Lyn H. Lofland. 2006. *Analyzing Social Settings: A Guide to Qualitative Observation and Analysis.* 4th ed. Belmont, CA: Wadsworth/Thomson Learning.

Lorde, Audre. (1984) 2007. "The Master's Tools Will Never Dismantle the Master's House." In *Sister Outsider: Essays and Speeches,* 110–114. Berkeley, CA: Crossing Press.

Loue, Sana. 2006. *Assessing Race, Ethnicity, and Gender in Health.* New York: Springer.

Lovallo, William R. 2005. *Stress and Health: Biological and Psychological Interactions.* 2nd ed. Thousand Oaks, CA: Sage.

Lui, P. Priscilla, and Lucia Quezada. 2019. "Associations between Microaggression and Adjustment Outcomes: A Meta-Analytic and Narrative Review." *Psychological Bulletin* 145 (1): 45–78. https://doi.org/10.1037/bul0000172.

Markula, Pirkko. 1996. "Firm but Shapely, Fit but Sexy, Strong but Thin: The Postmodern Aerobicizing Female Bodies." *Sociology of Sport Journal* 12 (4): 424–453. https://doi.org/10.1123/SSJ.12.4.424.

Maroto, Michelle, David Pettinicchio, and Andrew C. Patterson. 2019. "Hierarchies of Categorical Disadvantage: Economic Insecurity at the Intersection of Disability, Gender, and Race." *Gender and Society* 33 (1): 64–93. https://doi.org/10.1177/0891243218794648.

Martin, Emily. 2007. *Bipolar Expeditions: Mania and Depression in American Culture.* Princeton, NJ: Princeton University Press.

Martin, Nicola. 2012. Disability Identity—Disability Pride." *Perspectives: Policy and Practice in Higher Education* 16 (1): 14–18. https://doi.org/10.1080/13603108.2011.611832.

Marx, Karl, and Friedrich Engels. (1848) 2015. *The Communist Manifesto.* New York: Penguin.

Mauldin, Laura, and Robyn Lewis Brown. 2021. "Missing Pieces: Engaging Sociology of Disability in Medical Sociology." *Journal of Health and Social Behavior* 62 (4): 477–492. https://doi.org/10.1177/00221465211019358.

McIntosh, Peggy. 1988. "White Privilege and Male Privilege: A Personal Account of Coming to See Correspondence through Work in Women's Studies." Working paper 189. Wellesley, MA: Center for Research on Women.

———. 1997. "White Privilege and Male Privilege: A Personal Account Coming to See Correspondences through Work in Women's Studies." In *Critical White Studies: Looking behind the Mirror*, edited by Richard Delgado and Jean Stefancic, 291–299. Philadelphia: Temple University Press.

Mead, George Herbert. 1934. *Mind, Self, and Society from the Standpoint of a Social Behaviorist.* Edited by Charles W. Morris. Chicago: University of Chicago.

Merleau-Ponty, Maurice. (1962) 2012. *Phenomenology of Perception.* Translated by Donald A. Landes. New York: Routledge.

Messner, Michael A. 1988. "Sports and Male Domination: The Female Athlete as Contested Ideological Terrain." *Sociology of Sport Journal* 5 (3): 197–211. https://doi.org/10.1123/ssj.5.3.197.

———. 2002. *Taking the Field: Women, Men, and Sports.* Minneapolis: University of Minnesota Press.

Meyer I. H. 2007. "Prejudice and Discrimination as Social Stressors." In *The Health of Sexual Minorities*, edited by I. H. Meyer and M. E. Northridge M. E., 242–267. Washington, DC: APA.

Miles, A. L. 2019. "'Strong Black Women': African American Women with Disabilities Intersecting Identities, and Inequality." *Gender and Society* 33 (1): 41–63. https://doi.org/10.1177/0891243218814820.

Monti, Holly, Lori Reeder, and Martha Stinson. 2014. "The Survey of Income and Program Participation: How Long Do Early Career Decisions Follow Women? The Impact of Industry and Firm Size History on the Gender and Motherhood Wage Gaps." U.S. Department of Commerce, Census Bureau, paper no. 264. Presentation at the 19th Annual Meeting of the Society of Labor Economists (SOLE), Arlington, VA, May 3, 2014. https://www.census.gov/content/dam/Census/library/working-papers/2014/demo/SIPP-WP-264.pdf.

Moody, Anahvia Taiyib, and Jioni A. Lewis. 2019. "Gendered Racial Microaggressions and Traumatic Stress Symptoms among Black Women." *Psychology of Women Quarterly* 43 (2): 201–214. https://doi.org/10.1177/0361684319828288.

Nadal, Kevin L. 2013. *That's So Gay!: Microaggressions and the Lesbian, Gay, Bisexual, and Transgender Community, Perspectives on Sexual Orientation and Gender Diversity Series.* Washington, DC: American Psychological Association.

Nadal, Kevin L., and R. J. Mendoza. 2013. "Internalized Oppression and the Lesbian, Gay, Bisexual, and Transgender Community." In *Internalized Oppression: The Psychology of Marginalized Groups*, edited by E.J.R. David, 227–252. New York: Springer.

Nario-Redmond, Michelle R. Jeffrey G. Noel, and Emily Fern. 2013. "Redefining Disability, Re-imagining the Self: Disability Identification Predicts Self-esteem and Strategic Responses to Stigma." *Self and Identity* 12 (5): 468–488. https://doi.org/10.1080/15298868.201.

Nash, R. 1990. "Bourdieu on Education and Social and Cultural Reproduction." *British Journal of Sociology of Education* 11 (4): 431–447. https://doi.org/10.1080/0142569900110405.

Nelson, Audrey, and Claire Damken Brown. 2012. *The Gender Communication Handbook: Conquering Conversational Collisions between Men and Women.* San Francisco: Pfeiffer.

Neville-Jan, Ann. 2003. "Encounters in a World of Pain: An Autoethnography." *American Journal of Occupational Therapy* 57 (1): 88–98. https://doi.org/10.5014/ajot.57.1.88.

NORD (National Organization for Rare Disorders). 2012. Empowering the Rare Disease Community. http://www. rarediseases.org.

Nosek, Margaret A., Rosemary B. Hughes, Nancy Swedlund, Heather B. Taylor, and Paul Swank. 2003. "Self-esteem and Women with Disabilities." *Social Science and Medicine* 56: 1737–1747. https://doi.org/10.1016/S0277-9536(02)00169-7.

Ocampo, Anthony C. 2022. *Brown and Gay in LA: Queer Sons of Immigrants Coming of Age.* New York: New York University Press.

Olkin, Rhoda. 1999. *What Psychotherapists Should Know about Disability.* New York: Guilford.

Omi, Michael, and Howard Winant. 1994. *Racial Formation in the United States: From the 1960s to the 1990s.* New York: Routledge.

O'Neil, Mary Lou. 2002. "Youth Curfews in the United States: The Creation of Public Spheres for Some Young People." *Journal of Youth Studies* 5 (1): 49–67. https://doi.org/10.1080/13676260120111760.

Ozawa de-Silva, Chikako. 2002. "Beyond the Body/Mind? Japanese Contemporary Thinkers on Alternative Sociologies of the Body." *Body and Society* 8 (2): 21–38. https://doi.org/10.1177/1357034X02008002002.

Papadimitriou, Christina. 2001. "From Dis-ability to Difference: Conceptual and Methodological Issues in the Study of Physical Disability." In *Handbook of Phenomenology and Medicine*, edited by S. Kay Toombs, 475–492. Dordrecht, the Netherlands: Kluwer Academic.

Patterson, Miles L. 2014. "Reflections on Historical Trends and Prospects in Contemporary Nonverbal Research." *Journal of Nonverbal Behavior* 38 (2): 171–180. https://doi.org/10.1007/s10919-013-0171-z.

Paustian-Underdahl, Samantha C., and Lisa Slattery Walker. 2015. "Revisiting the Beauty Is Beastly Effect: Examining When and Why Sex and Attractiveness Impact Hiring Judgments." *International Journal of Human Resource Management* 27 (10): 1–25. http://doi.org/10.1080/09585192.2015.1053963.

Peitersen, Erik. 2002. "Bell's Palsy: The Spontaneous Course of 2,500 Peripheral Facial Nerve Palsies of Different Etiologies." *Acta Oto-laryngologica Supplementum* 549: 4–30.

Preston, Stephanie D., and R. Brent Stansfield. 2008. "I Know How You Feel: Task-Irrelevant Facial Expressions Are Spontaneously Processed at a Semantic Level." *Cognitive, Affective and Behavioral Neuroscience* 8 (1): 54–64. https://doi.org/10.3758/cabn.8.1.54.

Price, Margaret. 2015. "The Bodymind Problem and the Possibilities of Pain." *Hypatia* 30 (1): 268–284. https://doi.org/10.1111/hypa.12127.

Prince, Althea. 2010. *The Politics of Black Women's Hair.* London, ON, Canada: Insomniac Press.

Rail, Geneviève, and Jean Harvey. 1995. "Body at Work: Michel Foucault and the Sociology of Sport." *Sociology of Sport Journal* 12 (2): 164–179. https://doi.org/10.1123/ssj.12.2.164.

Reed-Danahay, Deborah. 1997. *Auto/Ethnography: Rewriting the Self and the Social.* Oxford: Berg.

Richards, Rose. 2008. "Writing the Othered Self: Autoethnography and the Problem of Objectification in Writing about Illness and Disability." *Qualitative Health Research* 18 (12): 1717–1728. https://doi.org/10.1177/1049732308325866.

Riehle, Marcel, Jürgen Kempkensteffen, and Tania M. Lincoln. 2017. "Quantifying Facial Expression Synchrony in Face to Face Dyadic Interactions: Temporal Dynamics of Simultaneously Recorded Facial EMG Signals." *Journal of Nonverbal Behavior* 41 (2): 85–102. https://doi.org/10.1007/s10919-016-0246-8.

Rieser, Richard. 2018. "Achieving Disability Equality: The Continuing Struggle." In *Education, Equality, and Human Rights: Issues of Gender, 'Race,' Disability and Social Class*, 4th ed., edited by Mike Cole, 192–229. London: Routledge.

Rifkin, William J., Rami S. Kantar, Safi Ali-Khan, Natalie M. Plana, J. Rodrigo Diaz-Siso, Manos Tsakiris, and Eduardo D. Rodriguez. 2018. "Facial Disfigurement and Identity: A Review of the Literature and Implications for Facial Transplantation." *AMA Journal of Ethics* 20 (4): 309–323. https://doi.org/10.1001/journalofethics.2018.20.4.peer1-1804.

Ritzer, George. 1993. *The McDonaldization of Society: An Investigation into the Changing Character of Contemporary Social Life.* Thousand Oaks, CA: Pine Forge Press.

REFERENCES

Robinson, Cedric. 1983. *Black Marxism: The Making of the Black Radical Tradition*. Chapel Hill, NC: University of North Carolina Press.

Robinson, Theresa M. 2010. *Social Anxiety: Symptoms, Causes, and Techniques*. Hauppauge, NY: Nova Science.

Ruiz-Soler, Marcos, and Francesc S. Beltran, F. 2012. "The Relative Salience of Facial Features When Differentiating Faces Based on an Interference Paradigm." *Journal of Nonverbal Behavior* 36 (3): 191–203. https://doi.org/10.1007/s10919-012-0131-z.

Rutter, Derek R. 1984. *Looking and Seeing: The Role of Visual Communication in Social Interaction*. Chichester, UK: Wiley.

Ruusuvuori, Johanna, and Anssi Peräkylä. 2009. "Facial and Verbal Expressions in Assessing Stories and Topics." *Research on Language and Social Interaction* 42 (4): 377–394. https://doi.org/10.1080/08351810903296499.

Saguy, Abigail C., and Kjerstin Gruys. 2010. "Morality and Health: News Media Constructions of Overweight and Eating Disorders." *Social Problems* 57 (2): 231–250. https://doi.org/10.1525/sp.2010.57.2.231.

Samuels, Ellen Jean. 2003. "My Body, My Closet: Invisible Disability and the Limits of Coming-Out Disclosure." *GLQ: A Journal of Lesbian and Gay Studies* 9 (1): 233–255.

Saunders, Gerda. 2017. *Memory's Last Breath: Fieldnotes on My Dementia*. New York: Hachette.

Schalk, Samantha Dawn. 2018. *Bodyminds Reimagined: Disability, Race, and Gender in Black Women's Speculative Fiction*. Durham, NC: Duke University Press.

Schalk, Sami. 2022. *Black Disability Politics*. Durham, NC: Duke University Press.

Schalk, Sami, and Jina B. Kim. 2020. "Integrating Race, Transforming Feminist Disability Studies." *Signs: Journal of Women in Culture and Society* 46: (1) 31–55 https://doi.org/10.1086/709213.

Schweik, Susan M. 2009. *The Ugly Laws: Disability in Public*. New York: New York University Press.

Seymour, Elaine. 1998. *Talking about Disability: The Education and Work Experience of Graduates and Undergraduates with Disabilities in Science, Mathematics, and Engineering Majors*. Washington, DC: American Association for the Advancement of Science.

Shakespeare, Tom. 1999. "The Sexual Politics of Disabled Masculinity." *Sexuality and Disability* 17 (1): 53–64. https://doi.org/10.1023/A:1021403829826.

Shell, Marc. 2005. *Polio and Its Aftermath: The Paralysis of Culture*. Cambridge, MA: Harvard University Press.

Shilling, Chris. 2003. *The Body and Social Theory*. London: Sage.

———. 2012. *The Body and Social Theory*. 3rd ed. Thousand Oaks, CA: Sage Publications.

———. 2016. *The Body: Very Short Introductions*. Oxford: Oxford University Press.

Shuttleworth, Russell, Nikki Wedgwood, and Nathan J. Wilson. 2012. "The Dilemma of Disabled Masculinity." *Men and Masculinities* 15 (2): 174–194. https://doi.org/10.1177/1097184X12439879.

Siebers, Tobin. 1995. *Disability Theory*. Ann Arbor: University of Michigan Press.

———. 2003. "What Can Disability Studies Learn from the Culture Wars?" *Cultural Critique* 55: 182–216. https://www.jstor.org/stable/1354652.

———. 2006. "Disability Studies and the Future of Identity Politics." In *Identity Politics Reconsidered*, edited by Linda Martin Alcoff, Michael Hames-García, Satya P. Mohanty, and Paula M. L. Moya, 10–30. New York: Palgrave Macmillan. https://doi.org/10.1057/9781403983398_2.

———. 2008. *Disability Theory*. Ann Arbor: University of Michigan Press.

———. 2010. *Disability Aesthetics*. Ann Arbor: University of Michigan Press.

————. 2013. "Disability and the Theory of Complex Embodiment: For Identity Politics in a New Register." In *The Disability Studies Reader*, 4th ed., edited by Lennard J. Davis, 278–297. New York: Routledge.

Simon, Rachel. 2002. *Riding the Bus with My Sister: A True Life Journey*. Boston: Houghton-Mifflin.

Slatery, William H., III, and Babak Azizzadeh, eds. 2014. *The Facial Nerve*. New York: Thieme.

Smart, Julie. 2009. *Disability, Society, and the Individual*. 2nd ed. Austin: Pro-Ed.

Smith, Brett, and Andrew C. Sparkes. 2005. "Men, Sport, Spinal Cord Injury and Narratives of Hope." *Social Science and Medicine* 61: 1095–105. https://doi.org/10.1016/j.socscimed.2005.01.011.

Solórzano, Daniel, Miguel Ceja, and Tara Yosso. 2000. "Critical Race Theory, Racial Microaggresions, and Campus Racial Climate: The Experiences of African American College Students." *Journal of Negro Education* 69 (1–2): 60–73. https://www.jstor.org/stable/2696265.

Souza, Kim. 2021. "The Supply Side: Retailers Battle for Beauty Sales in 2021." *Talk Business and Politics*, October 16, 2021. https://talkbusiness.net/2021/10/the-supply-side-retailers-battle-for-beauty-sales-in-2021/.

Sue, Derald Wing. 2010a. *Microaggressions and Marginality: Manifestation, Dynamics, and Impact*. Hoboken, NJ: Wiley.

————, ed. 2010b. *Microaggressions in Everyday Life: Race, Gender, and Sexual Orientation*. Hoboken, NJ: Wiley.

Svenaeus, Fredrik. 2000. "Hermeneutics of Clinical Practice: The Question of Textuality." *Theoretical Medicine and Bioethics* 21 (2): 171–189. https://doi.org/10.1023/a:1009942926545.

————. 2015. "The Phenomenology of Chronic Pain: Embodiment and Alienation" *Continental Philosophy Review* 48 (2): 107–122. https://doi.org/10.1007/s11007-015-9325-5.

SWNS. 2017. "Vanity Costs American Women Nearly a Quarter of a Million Dollars." *New York Post*, July 6, 2017. https://nypost.com/2017/07/06/vanity-costs-american-women-nearly-a-quarter-of-a-million-dollars/.

Szymanski, Dawn M., and Christy Henrichs-Beck. 2014. "Exploring Sexual Minority Women's Experiences of External and Internalized Heterosexism and Sexism and Their Links to Coping and Distress." *Sex Roles* 70 (1): 28–42. https://doi.org/10.1007/s11199-013-0329-5.

Talley, Heather Laine. 2014. *Saving Face: Disfigurement and the Politics of Appearance*. New York: New York University Press.

Tepper, Mitchell Steven. 1999. "Letting Go of Restrictive Notions of Manhood: Male Sexuality, Disability and Chronic Illness." *Sexuality and Disability* 17: 37–52. https://doi.org/10.1023/A:1021451712988.

————. 2001. "Lived Experiences That Impede or Facilitate Sexual Pleasure and Orgasm in People with Spinal Cord Injury." PhD diss., University of Pennsylvania.

Thorpe, Holly. 2009. "Bourdieu, Feminism and Female Physical Culture: Gender Reflexivity and the Habitus-Field Complex." *Sociology of Sport Journal* 26 (4): 491–516.

Tickle-Degnen, Linda, L. 2006. "Nonverbal Behavior and Its Functions in the Ecosystem of Rapport." In *The SAGE Handbook of Nonverbal Communication*, edited by Valerie Manusov and Miles L. Patterson, 381–401. Thousand Oaks, CA: Sage.

Tiggemann, Marika, and Amy Slater. 2013. "NetGirls: The Internet, Facebook, and Body Image Concern in Adolescent Girls." *International Journal of Eating Disorders* 46 (6): 630–633. https://doi.org/10.1002/eat.22141.

Tillmann, Lisa M. 2009. "Body and Bulimia Revisited: Reflections on 'A Secret Life.'" *Journal of Applied Communication Research* 37 (1): 98–112. https://doi.org/10.1080/00909880802592615.

REFERENCES

Towler, Annette J., and David J. Schneider. 2005. "Distinctions among Stigmatized Groups." *Journal of Applied Social Psychology* 35 (1): 1–14. https://doi.org/10.1111/j.1559-1816.2005.tb02090.x.

Tumin, Dmitry. 2016. "Marriage Trends among Americans with Childhood-Onset Disabilities, 1997–2013." *Disability and Health Journal* 9 (4): 713–718. https://doi.org/10.1016/j.dhjo.2016.05.004.

Turner, Bryan S. 1992. *Regulating Bodies: Essays in Medical Sociology.* London: Routledge.

Turner, Bryan S. 2008. *The Body & Society: Explorations in Social Theory.* Thousand Oaks, CA: Sage Publications.

Van Dalen, M., B. Dierckx, S.G.M.A. Pasmans, E.W.C. Aendekerk, I.M.J. Mathijssen, M. J. Koudstaal, R. Timman, H. Williamson, M.H.J. Hillegers, E.M.W.J. Utens, J.M.E. Okkerse. 2020. "Anxiety and Depression in Adolescents with a Visible Difference: A Systematic Review and Meta-analysis." *Body Image* 33: 38–46. https://doi.org/10.1016/j.bodyim.2020.02.006.

VanSwearingen Jessie M., Jeffrey F. Cohn, Joanne Turnbull, Todd Mrzai, and Peter Johnson. 1998. "Psychological Distress: Linking Impairment with Disability in Facial Neuromotor Disorders." *Otolaryngology—Head and Neck Surgery* 118 (6):790–796. https://doi.org/10.1016/S0194-5998(98)70270-0.

Veblen, Thorstein. (1899) 1994. *The Theory of the Leisure Class.* New York: Penguin.

Vernon, Ayesha. 1999. "The Dialectics of Multiple Identities and the Disabled People's Movement." *Disability and Society* 14 (3): 385–398. https://doi.org/10.1080/09687599926217.

Wachs, Faye L. 2005. "The Boundaries of Difference: Negotiating Gender in Recreational Sport." *Sociological Inquiry* 75 (4): 527–547. https://doi.org/10.1111/j.1475-682X.2005.00135.x.

Wachs, Faye L., and Laura F. Chase. 2013. "Explaining the Failure of an Obesity Intervention: Combining Bourdieu's Symbolic Violence and the Foucault's Microphysics of Power to Reconsider State Interventions." *Sociology of Sport Journal* 30 (2): 111–131.

Wacquant, Loïc J. D. 1995a. "Pugs at Work: Bodily Capital and Bodily Labour among Professional Boxers." *Body and Society* 1 (1): 65–94. https://doi.org/10.1177/1357034X95001001005.

———. 1995b. "Why Men Desire Muscles." *Body and Society* 1 (1): 163–180. https://doi.org/10.1177/1357034X95001001010.

Walkowitz, Daniel J., and Lisa Maya Knauer. 2009. *Public Space: Memory, Race, and Nation.* Durham, NC: Duke University Press.

Walsh, Anthony, and Patricia Ann Walsh. 1989. "Love, Self-Esteem, and Multiple Sclerosis." *Social Science and Medicine* 29 (7): 793. https://doi.org/10.1016/0277-9536(89)90078-6.

Watermeyer, Brian, and Tristan Görgens. 2013. "Disability and Internalized Oppression." In *Internalized Oppression: The Psychology of Marginalized Groups,* edited by E.J.R. David, 253–280. New York: Springer.

Watson, Nick. 2002. "Well, I Know This Is Going to Sound Very Strange to You, but I Don't See Myself as a Disabled Person: Identity and Disability." *Disability and Society* 17 (5): 509–527. https://doi.org/10.1080/09687590220148496.

Weber, Max. (1905) 2003. *The Protestant Ethic and the Spirit of Capitalism.* Translated by Talcott Parsons. Mineola, NY: Dover.

Weiss, Gregory L., and Lynne E. Lonquist. 2017. *The Sociology of Health, Healing and Illness.* New York: Routledge.

Weiss, R. S. 1994. *Learning from Strangers: The Art and Method of Qualitative Interview Studies.* New York: Free Press.

Weiss, Stephen E. 1994. "Negotiating with 'Romans'—Part 1." *MIT Sloan Management Review,* January 15, 1994. https://sloanreview.mit.edu/article/negotiating-with-romans-part/.

Wendell, Susan. 1996. *The Rejected Body: Feminist Philosophical Reflections on Disability*. New York: Routledge.

West, Candace, and Don H. Zimmerman. 1987. "Doing Gender." *Gender and Society* 1 (2): 125–151. https://doi.org/10.1177/0891243287001002002.

Westbrook, Laurel, and Kriten Schilt. 2014. "Doing Gender, Determining Gender: Transgender People, Gender Panics, and the Maintenance of the Sex/Gender/Sexuality System." *Gender and Society* 28 (1): 32–57. https://doi.org/10.1177/0891243213503203.

Western, Bruce, and Elizabeth M. Pettit. 2005. "Black-White Wage Inequality, Employment Rates, and Incarceration." *American Journal of Sociology* 111 (2): 553–578. https://doi.org/10.1086/432780.

Westland, Gill. 2015. *Verbal and Non-Verbal Communication in Psychotherapy*. New York: W.W. Norton.

Wheatley, Elizabeth E. 2005. "Risk, Reflexivity and an Elusory Body: Transformations in Studying Illness." *Journal of Contemporary Ethnography* 34 (1): 68–100. https://doi.org/10.1177/0891241604271341.

White, Gillian B. 2015. "Black Workers Really Do Need to Be Twice as Good." *The Atlantic*, October 7, 2015. http://www.theatlantic.com/business/archive/2015/10/why-Black-workers-really-do-need-to-be-twice-as-good/409276.

Williams, Christine L., Kirsten Dellinger, and Lisa Keister. 2010. *Gender and Sexuality in the Workplace*. Vol. 20. Bingley, UK: Emerald Group.

Williams, David R., and Ruth Williams-Morris. 2000. "Racism and Mental Health: The African American Experience." *Ethnicity and Health* 5 (3–4): 243–268. https://doi.org/10.1080/713667453.

Willingham, Daniel T. 2010. *Why Students Don't Like School: A Cognitive Scientist Answers Questions about How the Mind Works and What It Means for the Classroom*. San Francisco: Jossy-Bass.

Willis, Paul. 1977. *Learning to Labor: How Working Class Kids Get Working Class Jobs*. Farmborough, UK: Saxon House.

Wright, J. 2009. "Biopower, Biopedagogies and the Obesity Epidemic." In *Biopolitics and the "Obesity Epidemic": Governing Bodies*, edited by J. Wright and V. Harwood, 1–14. New York: Routledge.

Wynter, Sylvia. 1999. "Towards the Sociogenic Principle: Fanon, the Puzzle of Conscious Experience, of Identity and What It's Like to be 'Black.'" In *National Identities and Socio-Political Changes in Latin America*, edited by Mercedes Durán-Cogan and Antonio Gómez-Moriana, 30–66. London: Routledge.

Yaron, Gili, Agnes Meershoek, Guy Widdershoven, Michiel van den Brekel, and Jenny Slatman. 2017. "Facing a Disruptive Face: Embodiment in the Everyday Experiences of 'Disfigured' Individuals." *Human Studies* 40 (2): 285–307. https://doi.org/10.1007/s10746-017-9426-8.

Zarifa, David, David Walters, and Brad Seward. 2015. "The Earnings and Employment Outcomes of the 2005 Cohort of Canadian Postsecondary Graduates with Disabilities." *Canadian Review of Sociology* 52 (4): 343–376. https://doi.org/10.1111/cars.12082.

Zitzelsberger, Hilde. 2005. "(In)visibility: Accounts of Embodiment of Women with Physical Disabilities and Differences." *Disability and Society* 4: 389–403. https://doi.org/10.1080/09687590500086492.

INDEX

ableism, 7, 9, 29, 37, 56, 137, 138, 164; boundaries of disability and, 123; confrontation with, 165; microinvalidations and, 60; popular culture and, 95

ableism, internalized, 40, 68, 104, 109, 118, 127; advocacy and, 122; mental health and, 70; passing and, 72; struggles with, 129–130

abnormality, 7, 37

acceptance, 13, 35, 139, 150–151

accommodations, 66, 119, 120

acoustic neuroma, 3, 20, 84, 89, 172; balance/vertigo issues and, 105; deafness and, 110; summary of participants and, 178–183, 185. *See also* tumors and removal of tumors

addiction, 14, 16

ADHD (attention-deficit/hyperactivity disorder), 127

advocacy work, 20, 135–136, 149; control of narrative and, 137; shared community and, 139; storytelling as advocacy, 74

affect, flattening of, 73, 114

agency, 28, 68, 159

aggression, direct, 51–52, 53

alienation, 110–111; from shared social experience, 113–114; from subjective experience, 112–113; from the "I" (producing/displaying self), 111–112; from the Me (displayed/performed self), 111

Americans with Disabilities Act (ADA), 125

anger, 12, 137, 168

anger, appearance of, 55, 77, 83; bias in interpretations of, 86–87; disrupted communication and, 106; as obstacle to employment and socializing, 83

animal companions, 52, 151–152

anxiety, 4, 7, 13, 42, 143; coding procedure memos on, 174; compensatory strategies and, 78; contradictory feedback and, 83; generated by consumer culture, 96; over miscommunication, 107; passing as relief from, 72; in social interactions, 117; social physique, 70–71

appearance, 11, 37, 74, 79; classism and, 97; communication capital and, 99; as form of physical capital, 97; imagination of appearance to others, 25; perception of, 6

ASD (autism spectrum disorder), 127

Asian American female participants, 20, 56–57, 177, 178

Asian American male participants, 186

Atwood, Margaret, 159, 191n1 (chap. 1)

authenticity, 17, 137–138

autism, 127, 192n8

autoethnography, 7, 10; defined, 8; evocative, 10; narrator as subject and object, 15; as a position, 11; reflexive self and, 14

balance, 54, 67, 105. *See also* vertigo

Bauman, Zygmunt, 91

beauty culture and standards, 31, 34, 75, 97, 161

being-as-object, 34, 134, 135

being-as-subject, 34, 75

being-in-the-world, 112

Bell's palsy, 8, 20, 45, 48, 56, 88, 89, 137; causes of, 2; distress at onset of, 109; education about, 152–153; friends' good-natured imitation of, 155–156; as most common cause of synkinesis, 57, 171; onset of, 1–4; pain and, 15, 124; repeat bouts of, 102, 128; spontaneous recovery from, 57, 93; summary of participants and, 177–186; therapies for, 57, 191n1 (chap. 3)

biopower, 30

BIPOC (black, Indigenous and people of color), 24; disability identity and, 45; interview participants, 8–9, 20, 173

Black female participants, 42–43, 115, 150–151, 177, 179, 181–184

Black studies, 42

blame, 34, 93; displacement of, 51; as microinsult, 57, 58; self-blame, 4

blink, inability to, 64, 191n2 (chap. 3)

Bochner, Arthur, 10

body, the: aging process and, 140; bodies at different social locations, 32–33; commodification and, 38, 75; consumer culture and, 136; as contested ideological terrain, 74; docile body, 30; internal feelings generated by expressions, 77; rebel body, 30; as site of being and becoming, 104; sociology of, 9, 13, 23–25, 103

207

INDEX

"bodymind," 25
Body Panic (Dworkin and Wachs), 38, 75
Bogart, Kathleen, 10, 84, 88, 89, 120, 132
Bogdan, Robert, 68
Bonilla-Silva, Eduardo, 65
Botox, 3, 6, 87, 114, 143, 172, 191n1 (chap. 3);
   financial cost of, 94–95, 147; health
   insurance coverage for, 82; as most
   common treatment for pain, 93–94; as
   out-of-reach treatment, 168; social
   emotional processing affected by, 107;
   struggle to afford, 66
Bourdieu, Pierre, 14, 74, 159, 160; on
   embodiment of social positions, 163; on
   forms of capital, 98; habitus concept,
   31–33, 86, 98; on symbolic violence, 33,
   74, 144
bullying, 50, 52, 125, 139
Butler, Judith, 160

Campbell, Fiona, 119
capital: bodily capital, 9; communication
   capital, 99–100; cultural capital, 32;
   invested in the self, 134; physical capital,
   97–99, 132; social capital, 32, 98
capitalism: late-stage, 144, 164, 168; racial,
   93, 121, 136
"careful disattention," 28
change, self and, 18
children, bullying of, 41, 52–53
citizenship, second-class, 51, 61
classism, 95, 97
code switching, 99, 118, 132
coding procedure, 174–176
Collins, Patricia Hill, 44, 160, 163
colonialism, 119, 164, 166
communication, 6, 9, 11, 38; Botox treatments to improve, 66; code switching
   and, 99; communication capital, 99–100;
   communicative events, 104; communicative feedback, 77, 78; communicative
   performance, 131–132; disrupted by
   synkinesis, 22, 36, 64–65, 78, 83, 106–107,
   158; face and, 78–81; frustration from
   inability to communicate, 76–77; gender
   difference and, 87–88, 99; internalization
   and, 69; management and planning of,
   107; misunderstandings, 62; nonverbal
   and facial, 28, 58, 79, 99, 132; shared
   feeling through mimicry, 84–85, 106;
   silence from family members, 62–63;
   ubiquity of social media and, 153. *See also*
   face; smiles/smiling
community, shared experiential, 139–141
compensatory strategies, 28, 78, 79, 88–90,
   144; overcompensation, 90–91
Connell, Raewynn, 34
consent, informed, 12
consumer culture, 31, 34, 38, 96, 136
Cooley, Charles Horton, 25
coping, 116, 117, 134, 146–147, 161; as ongoing
   process, 146, 149; privilege and, 143–145
corporeality, foregrounding of, 25

COVID-19 pandemic: mask-wearing during,
   37, 60, 84, 97; Zoom calls during, 111
cranial nerve, seventh, 2, 171
Crenshaw, Kimberle, 44
crip theory, 120, 123
critical race theory, 13, 22, 24, 33, 160, 163;
   "legitimate knowledge" and, 14; minimalization concept and, 65
CULLP (congenital unilateral lower lip
   palsy), 171
cultural capital, 32
cultural studies, 13, 33, 162

"damaged goods," 49, 72, 135
Darling, Rosalyn, 35, 39, 43, 49, 150, 151; on
   rejection of disability identity, 152; on
   stigma and self-perception, 29
Davis, Fred, 35
deafness, single-sided, 110, 126, 148
decolonization, 159–160, 166
deformity, as congenital condition, 92
dehumanization, 115, 117, 130, 134
dementia, 16
dental problems, 2, 3, 5, 95
depression, 5, 11, 21, 70, 72, 143
desexualization, 51
deviance, 36–37, 93
diagnoses, 10
dialogue, internal, 11
Diels, Jackie, 84
disability: autoethnography of, 16; awareness of, 15; devaluing of bodies viewed as
   disabled, 8; disabling versus disability,
   121–124; evil associated with, 54; hidden,
   51, 72; invisible, 55, 61, 62, 124; limits on
   presentation of self and, 28; loss of
   identity and, 104; microaggressions and,
   51; minimalization of, 63–66; policed in
   public space, 50; professional discrimination and, 46–50; rejection of disability
   status, 120–121; self-esteem and, 29;
   social, 22; stigma and, 34–37; stigmatiza-
   tion of, 119, 120; truth-claims of, 29;
   visible, 18, 56
disability identity, 18, 22, 38, 118, 122, 131, 144,
   149; as challenge to ontological foundations of self, 138; congenital disability
   and, 34; consumer culture normativity
   undermined by, 136; disability identity
   studies, 18, 22; embrace of, 120, 126, 127,
   161; incidence in the United States, 119,
   120; lived experience and, 126; as
   nebulous concept in relation to facial
   difference, 40; range of feelings about,
   129; rejection of, 120, 152, 161; role models
   and, 142–143; self-esteem and, 126; sense
   of self and, 29
disability status, 124–127
disability studies, 33, 37–38, 42, 126, 160,
   163; feminist, 13, 14; social (in)justice
   and, 119
disability theory, 160
Discipline and Punish (Foucault), 1

INDEX

discomfort, 2, 65, 94, 129; of being stared at, 59; inability to perform facial expressions, 111; ongoing, 43; pain described as, 4–5
discrimination, 8, 69, 72, 78, 141
disfigurement, 16, 78, 95, 115, 119; as acquired condition, 92; demarcation with disability, 123; meaning of, 91–96
Dispossessed, The (Le Guin, 1974), 170
double-consciousness, 118, 128
dramaturgy, 27
dualisms: abandonment of, 25; challenged by feminist theory, 33
Du Bois, W.E.B., 128, 160
Durkheim, Emile, 160
Dworkin, Shari, 34, 38, 75, 93, 96, 134, 145

eating disorders, 16
education level, of participants, 20, 177–186
Ellis, Carolyn, 10
embodiment, 6, 7, 22; of evil, 11; identity and, 17; sociology of, 159
emotion: alienation and, 113; conveyed by facial expression and movement, 78, 79; disrupted processing of sensations tied to, 105; flattening of affect, 73, 114–116; inability to share happy moments, 86, 101; socializing and, 153; tightened muscles and negative emotions, 81; uncomfortable experience of, 17
equity, 9, 41, 66, 160
E-stim (electrical stimulation) machines, 192n4 (chap. 6)
Ettorre, Elizabeth, 16
experience, embodied, 17, 29, 33, 106; disruption to experience of self, 101; as simultaneously subject and object, 34
experience of self, 6, 11, 42, 102, 131; communication as, 100; disruption of, 18, 21, 101, 107–110, 158; external judgment and internalization in relation to, 39; gender difference and, 20; injury to, 8; processing of physical experience/sensation, 104–110; radical shift in understanding of, 12; in the social world, 25, 38; tragedy of synkinesis and, 161; trauma and, 104
eyebrows, 78, 79, 108, 131
eye contact, 87, 88
eye watering, 2, 3

face: avoidance of having face on camera, 26, 84; centrality to identity, 22, 76, 78; communication and, 78–81; exhausting task of managing, 83; as form of capital, 33; physical capital and, 97–99; relaxed or at-rest, 83; social cues and, 79; "what's wrong with your face?" 13, 52, 57, 63, 67
facial difference, 3, 12, 94, 160; conflated with ill health, 34; conflated with moral degeneration, 95, 144; disability identity and, 40; evil associated with, 54; mirrored back in unconscious mimicry,

84–85; presumed to signal negative traits, 40; recent diagnoses of young people, 169; response by others to, 42; socially devalued roles and, 27; summarized, 171–172; villains in popular movies with, 99
Facial Palsy UK, 61
facial paralysis, 9, 20, 38, 150; acquired, 3, 10, 26, 47, 171–172; congenital, 10, 88, 120, 171; as disability, 118–120; initial onset of, 4, 109; internal disruption of experience and, 22; mistaken for mental disability, 48–49; professional discrimination and, 46–50; shared experience of, 15
Facial Paralysis Awareness Day, 57
"faint praise," 56
family, 16, 97, 134, 150–151; minimalization and, 65; miscommunication and, 81; pain dismissed by, 15; silence from family members, 62–63
fashion, social self and, 89–90, 144, 145
fat replacement, 87
faux pas, 133, 135, 137
fear, 13, 129, 169
femininity: emphasized, 34; idealized, 32
feminism, 13, 24; black, 13, 41, 45; Latine, 41, 45
feminism, intersectional, 12, 13, 22, 33, 43, 44–45, 160, 163
filtering, challenges with, 105
first impressions, challenge of, 8
fitness, 31, 38, 97
Fitzgerald, F. Scott, 118
food, loss of ability to enjoy, 105, 106
Foucault, Michel, 1, 33, 136, 156, 157, 163; on power and production of knowledge, 119; on role of institutions in defining (ab)normality, 37; on subjectivity, 29–31, 74, 160
freak shows, 16, 68, 92
friends, 97, 150–151; betrayal by, 92; miscommunication and, 81; pain dismissed by, 15; synkinesis minimized by, 64, 65

Galgay, Corinne, 51
Garland-Thomson, Rosemarie, 58, 61, 67, 71, 73
gatekeeping, 18, 100
gaze, disembodied, 24, 58
gender, 30, 43, 44, 65, 74, 140; access to public space and, 50; biology and relations of power, 192n2 (chap. 5); gender difference in communication, 87, 99; gendered norms and self, 32; internalization and, 70; intersection with race, 88; microaggressions and, 51; professional cost of disability and, 46–47; wage gap, 46; women's roles, 87
gender studies, 42
Giddens, Anthony, 28
Goffman, Erving, 27, 28; on "disclosure etiquette," 36; on faux pas, 133; on "identity spoilt," 17, 34, 85; on passing, 85; on role strain, 104; on stigma, 35, 58

INDEX

governmentality, 31, 191n1 (chap. 2)
Gracilis muscle transfer, 172
Gramsci, Antonio, 33
grief, 6, 7, 28, 109; from inability to communicate, 76, 79; loss of smile and, 28; permanent loss and, 116; reminders of, 110
growth, 9, 11, 22, 126, 138

habitus, 31–33, 74, 86, 98
hair, politics of, 45–46
Hall, Stuart, 86, 160
hand gestures, 87
Hanna, Michele, 55, 61
Haraway, Donna, 160
Haug, Frigga, 34, 134
healing process, 2, 139, 149
health: connection between mental and physical health, 138; fitness conflated with, 97; healthcare industry, 168–169; morality linked to, 74; privilege/oppression axes and, 38; U.S. healthcare system, 143
health insurance coverage, 66, 143, 146, 168
Hemmesch, Amanda, 10
herpes viruses, 2
heterosexism, 68, 162
hierarchy, 10, 123, 161, 169; challenge to, 163; difference and, 162; fragility of identity in, 138; hierarchical binaries, 165; reproduced in daily life, 160; symbolic violence and, 33; trauma of self and, 168
hooks, bell, 160
hospital ER (emergency room) experiences, 1–4, 109
Hosseini, Khaled, 117
Hughes, Michael, 73, 91
humor, 36, 55, 79, 133, 146

I and the Me, concept of, 25, 26
identity, 11, 23, 74; affirmative activism and, 150; embodiment and, 17; expression and nonprivileged identity categories, 86–88; "felt identity," 27; "identity spoilt," 17, 34, 36, 42, 85; intersection of identities, 70, 118; performance of, 131; as process, 26; rebuilding of, 153; reforging of, 131; reified identity categories, 103; role expectations and, 104; self-determination of, 39; shift in, 9, 12. *See also* disability identity
ideologies, 51, 86, 160; ideological repair work, 73–74, 91, 115; resistance and, 162; understanding of facial difference and, 93
impression management, 27–28, 133
infantilization, 51
interactionism, 25
internalization, 22, 39, 68–71, 160; passing and, 72; social discrimination and, 97
intersectionality, 42, 44
interviews, 6, 10, 19–22; anxiety about online images of face during, 26; as cathartic process, 16, 19, 21; emotional aspect of, 16–17, 21; online, 26; in-person, 21; rapport over shared pain, 18–19; semi-structured nature of, 21, 173; summary of participants with facial difference, 177–186
Invitation to a Reflexive Sociology (Bourdieu and Wacquant, 1992), 159
isolation, 11, 13, 19, 21, 97; coping process and, 143; social disability and, 128

James, C.L.R., 160
Jewish participants, 69, 85
Joffe, Mathew, 132
joie-de-vivre experiences, alienation from, 112–113, 153
joint pain, 3
Jones, Camara Phyllis, 69

Kattari, Shanna, 55, 61
Keller, Richard, 51
kintsugi (kintsukuroi), as metaphor for embracing damage, 135
Kite Runner, The (Hosseini, 2003), 117
knowledge, 24, 160, 162; about the self, 29; bias and, 14; embodied, 14; Foucault's archeology of, 162–163; inclusion of the visceral in, 14; power relations and, 25, 119; production of, 37

Latine/Latina female participants, 20, 23, 36, 89, 145, 180, 182, 184, 185; on disabled status, 121–123; on discomfort of physical experience, 104–105; disrupted experience of self, 101, 103; on finding appropriate medical care, 147; internalization and, 69; on loneliness, 114; on loss of smile, 80–81; on microaggressions, 57; on mimicry in communication, 84–85; on overcompensation, 90; professional cost of disability and, 48
Latine/Latino male participants, 155–156, 180, 186
Latour, Bruno, 24
laughing, 106, 114, 128; disruption of expression and, 107; as harassment, 52, 135; management of affect and, 113; missed happy moments and, 101, 103, 108
Lefton, Mark, 118
Le Guin, Ursula K., 165, 170, 191n1 (chap. 1)
lived experience, 13, 42, 159, 163, 169; cultural shift toward awareness of, 63; disruption of self and, 11–12; flattening of affect (shutting down), 114–116; habitus and, 74; ideology and, 50; racism and, 65; theory of complex embodiment and, 125
loitering laws, 50
loneliness, 61, 114
looking-glass self, 25
Lorde, Audre, 160, 162

makeup: asymmetry covered by, 92, 145; passing and, 72
marriage, as normative life goal, 18
Marx, Karl, 160, 162
masculinity, idealized, 32

INDEX

Mead, George Herbert, 25, 26, 27, 134
meaning, disrupted ability to share, 107
medical professionals, 10, 14; lack of
    specialists in synkinesis, 144; microin-
    sults from, 57; pain dismissed by, 15
mental health, 16, 18, 19, 31, 70, 120, 123;
    acquired versus congenital disability in
    relation to, 29; appropriate treatment
    and, 144; chronic pain and, 5–6; coping
    process and, 146; disability status and,
    121, 122; Foucault's theories and, 31;
    identity transitions and, 16; internalized
    ableism and, 70; lived experience of
    otherness and, 71; necessity of mental
    health care, 148; participants with
    careers in mental health care, 181, 184,
    185; standards of care and, 169; stress
    and, 43; struggles to access support for,
    161; support groups and, 149
Messner, Michael, 73, 159
microaggressions, 8, 9, 22, 50, 72, 78, 87, 139,
    155; coding procedure memos on, 174;
    defined, 51; expectations infused by, 86;
    experience of self and, 115; genuine
    inquiries distinguished from, 67;
    ideological repair work for systemic
    inequity and, 74; internalized, 68, 71; "the
    look" in first encounters, 58; medical, 144;
    quality of medical care for nonwhite
    patients undermined by, 88; questioning
    of affect and mood, 81; as relations of
    privilege/oppression, 53–54; responses to,
    66–68; safety and freedom from, 167;
    social status and, 11; talked about in
    support groups, 19
microassaults, 51, 54–55
microinsults, 51, 55–59
microinvalidations, 59–63
mind/body dualism, Cartesian, 24, 25
minimalizations, 63–66; internalized, 69;
    responses to, 66–68
mirrors, 1, 15, 26, 76, 77–78, 91
miscommunication, 79, 81–86; anxiety over,
    107; of mood and affect, 80; with the self,
    101, 114
misdiagnosis, 4
mixed-race female participants, 20, 45, 53,
    90, 177, 178, 182
Moebius syndrome, 3, 16, 171
mononucleosis, infectious (Epstein Barr), 2
monster, becoming, 11, 92, 143
morality, 24, 38; consumer culture and, 136;
    facial difference presumed to signal
    immorality, 40, 93; health and, 74–75;
    Victorian culture and, 38, 96, 99;
    Western culture and, 161, 162
mortification, 25, 26, 110, 133, 168
muscle cramps, 15
musculoskeletal problems, 3, 64

narrative, 17, 119; agency in self-fashioning
    of, 28; control of, 137, 152–153; nonverbal
    communication and, 87

nerve pain, 124
neuroatypicality, 127, 138
neurolysis, selective, 172
neuromuscular retraining, 94, 114, 168
normality, 30, 40; masking during COVID-19
    pandemic and, 60; morality, 35; normal
    affect, 38; pressure to achieve, 126;
    removal from category of normal, 99; role
    of institutions in defining, 37
normalization, 39
normativity, 9, 136

objectivity, 13, 17, 33
occupational therapy, 96, 143, 148, 172, 191n1
    (chap. 3)
Olzman, Miranda, 55, 61
"Ones Who Walk away from Omelas, The"
    (Le Guin, [1973] 1975), 165
oppression, 13, 23, 25, 133; embodied
    experience and, 33; expectations and
    assumptions in relation to, 45–46; health
    conflated with "fit" appearance, 38;
    ideological justification of, 166; internal-
    ized, 71; intersectional feminist definition
    of, 44–45; intersectional model of, 42;
    structural systems of, 45
Order of Things, The (Foucault, 1970),
    156, 162
otherness, 12, 46, 49–50, 71, 74, 118, 160;
    alienation and, 113; becoming "other," 34,
    40; disability as experience of, 119; as
    embodied experience, 42; imposed
    narrative and, 152; impression manage-
    ment impeded by, 28; as internalized
    condition, 128; kinship/community and,
    141; shift from "normal" to "othered"
    identity, 16–18; as social disability, 128,
    129; subject locations and, 163; synkinesis
    as confrontation with, 164; threat of
    being other, 167–169; ugliness conflated
    with, 54

pain, 143, 159, 169; autoethnography of, 16;
    Botox treatments to reduce, 66, 93–94,
    147, 168; disabling nature of, 124–125;
    nerve pain, 15; during onset of synkine-
    sis, 2; tolerable and intolerable, 4–5
parotid gland tumors, 3
passing, 28, 35, 36, 39, 71–73, 94, 167;
    compulsory ableness and, 69; as hiding of
    "discrediting attribute," 85
patient advocacy, 12, 13
patriarchy, 73
patronization, 51
people with disabilities, 14, 37, 43, 91
perception, 17, 106; disruptions to, 110;
    somatic, 26–27
performance, 27–28, 68; "authentic," 102;
    communicative, 131–132; relearning of
    social performances, 28; of self, 8, 76, 97,
    137–138; social life as, 61
personhood, 39, 40
pets, 151–152

INDEX

photographs, 56, 77, 91; "Bell's palsy picture," 155–156; family photos hidden from display, 21, 61; photographers' attitudes about smiling, 60, 66–67, 155

Picture of Dorian Gray, The (Wilde, 1890), 141, 192n3 (chap. 6)

politics, as lived reality, 41

postcolonial theory, 160

poststructuralism, 22, 24, 29

power, relations of, 13, 15, 25, 37, 160; biology and, 192n2 (chap. 5); control of narrative and, 86; fields as networks of power, 32; inclusion and, 73; nature and, 104; as ongoing process, 29; subjectivity and, 29–30; symbolic violence and, 69

pregnancy, as risk factor, 2, 56

Price, Margaret, 25

pride, 26, 27, 60, 68, 133, 162, 168; "authentic" performances and, 102; commodified self and, 134; internal dialogues of the self and, 30; of kinship with heroes, 166; me-as-object and, 111, 132, 137; in othered identities, 43, 164; perceived reception and, 104; as "self-feeling," 25; social relations as source of, 29; undercut by disrupted communication, 107

privacy, denial of, 51, 57

privilege, 13, 23, 25, 74, 133; access to healing/treatment and, 15, 161; access to public space and, 50; acquisition of capital and, 32; bodily practices and, 97; coping and, 143–145; embodied experience and, 33; expectations and assumptions in relation to, 45–46; gatekeeping and, 100; gratitude and, 164, 192n1 (chap. 7); health conflated with "fit" appearance, 38; ideological justification of, 166; internalized entitlement, 71; intersectional feminist definition of, 44–45; minimalization and, 66; objectivity as vantage point of, 33; power and, 41; racial, 103; structural systems of, 45; symbolic violence and, 69; white privilege, 7

productivity, traditional measures of, 118, 120, 121, 123

public space, right to, 50, 54, 59

quality of life, 13

queer studies, 42

queer theory, 22, 24, 33, 45, 160, 163

race, 43, 44, 74, 140; access to public space and, 50; earning potential and, 46; internalization and, 70; intersection with gender, 88; material social relations and, 103; microaggressions and, 51; minimalization of, 65

racism, 9, 42, 65, 162, 164, 165

Ramsay Hunt syndrome, 3, 49, 54, 172; balance/vertigo issues and, 105; distress at onset of, 109; summary of participants and, 180, 185, 186

reference groups, 26, 29, 43, 119

rejection, by peers or family, 21, 140

representation, moving beyond, 164

Riding the Bus with My Sister (Simon, 2002), 129–130

Ritzer, George, 192n5

Robinson, Cedric, 160, 166

role strain, 104

safety, 13, 167

salivation. *See* tears/saliva, crosswiring of

Schalk, Sami, 25

schools, 30, 31

Schweik, Susan, 50, 54, 60

science, 17, 25

self: "authentic," 96; as embodied experience, 9, 115; experience and expression of, 6; habitus and, 31–33; looking-glass self, 25; me as object produced, 132–137; performance of, 8, 76, 97, 137–138; as process, 22; rebuilding of, 152, 157; reframing of, 141–143, 149; safety and sense of self, 167; as series of performed experiences, 102; two-part self, 26. *See also* experience of self

self-confrontation, 10

self-disclosure, 63, 64

self-esteem, 61, 97; acquired versus congenital disability, 29; disability status and, 120; impact of being stared at and, 58; rebuilding of body parts and, 65–66, 95

self-estrangement, 110–114

self-expression, 38, 104

self-presentation, 11, 28, 78, 97

self-reflexive scholarship, 14–16

self-representation, 18

self-transition, 6

service professions, physical capital and, 98, 99

sexism, 42, 68, 162, 164, 165

sexuality, 58, 65, 74; (ab)normality and, 24; assumed lack of sexuality, 56; coding procedure memos on, 174; denial of, 104; internalization and, 70; material social relations and, 103; microaggressions and, 51; public space and, 50

sexual orientation, 140

shame, 12, 25, 70, 169; avoidance of, 17; microaggressions and, 54; shaming and countershaming, 54, 66–67

Siebers, Tobin, 126

silence, within families, 62–63

Simmel, Georg, 160

Simon, Rachel, 129

"sincere fictions," 65

smiles/smiling, 7, 63, 133; as form of capital, 83; genuine display of self and, 96; impaired internal feelings and, 77; inability to smile, 64, 169; loss of, 22, 28, 80, 98; loss of self and, 109; microinvalidations and, 60, 62; miscommunication and, 83; power and interpretations of, 86; smiling as conscious effort, 85; surgeries to restore ability to smile, 172; tone/mood of social interaction set by, 80–81

social class, 58, 65, 70, 74, 96; experience shaped by, 117; material social relations and, 103

"social death": defined, 91; social disability contrasted with, 91, 117–118

social disability, 22, 85, 100, 127–128; "social death" contrasted with, 91, 117–118; synkinesis as, 128–129

social locations, 14, 33, 50, 78, 104; Cartesian inability to consider, 24; habitus and, 32, 98; internalized, 104. *See also* oppression; privilege

social media, 12, 63, 96, 153–155

social sciences, 25

social theory, 22

sociopathy, 40

somatic perception, 26–27

staring, 58–59, 67, 126, 139

stereotypes, 40, 51, 68

stigma, 9, 31, 34–37, 85, 118, 121, 164; "courtesy stigma" (by association), 36; disability identity and, 40; internalized, 43, 91, 97; reminders of, 78; self-perception and, 29; socially contingent nature of, 36; social norms and avoidance of, 17; tribal, 35; visible, 28

stress, 43–44, 46, 58, 81, 85

stroke, 1, 28, 122

subjectification, 30

subjectivity, 74, 131, 158, 159, 160, 161

suicidal ideation, 146

suicide attempts, 22, 72, 143

sumptuary laws, 50

support groups, 10, 12, 16, 69, 113–114, 135; advocacy and, 136; anxiety about online images of face during, 26; for different phases of healing, 149; establishment of communion and, 139; founding/initiation of, 148, 149; online, 19, 20, 148; participant observation in, 174; rebuilding of self and, 141; separate groups for newcomers and long-timers, 57–58; sexual issues and, 56; white middle-class women overrepresented in, 74

surgeries, 6, 66, 70, 94, 114, 147–148; cosmetic, 96–97; gender difference and, 87; Gracilis muscle transfer, 172; out-of-pocket payment for, 168; selective neurolysis, 172

surveillance, 30

symbolic interactionism, 29

symmetry and asymmetry, facial, 95, 96, 145, 172

synkinesis, 1, 2, 9, 48, 64, 90, 171; abrupt status change brought by, 160; advocacy movement and, 12; chronic pain and, 4–5; communication disrupted by, 22, 36, 64–65, 78, 83, 106–107, 158; disability in relation to, 7, 37–38, 40, 120–129; disruptive internal experience created by, 104; experience of living with, 13, 40;

experience of self and, 161; gender and, 20; identity shift and, 16, 29, 34; incidence of, 2; lack of specialists in, 144; microaggressions and, 57; miscommunication and, 82; as movement disorder, 2; onset of, 3; physical pain of, 124–125; as result of nerves healing too much, 172; self as object and, 132, 133; as social disability, 128–129; tightened muscles and negative emotions, 81; unnoticed, 71; varying degrees of visibility, 36

Talley, Heather Laine, 38, 92; on centrality of facial appearance in Western culture, 97; on triggers of social death, 91, 117

taste, 32

tears/saliva, crosswiring of, 2, 4

therapy, 21, 36, 70, 138, 143, 148–150, 169; health insurance and, 146; occupational therapy, 96, 148, 172; passing and, 72; physical therapy, 72, 82, 96, 125, 143

Thunberg, Greta, 192n8

Tickle-Degnen, Linda, 132

trauma, 3, 4, 109, 164, 168, 172; addiction and, 14; experience of self and, 104; reminders of, 110; retraumatization, 18; summary of participants and, 177; synkinesis from physical trauma, 110

treatment interventions: appropriate medical treatment, 147; efficacy of treatments, 94, 144; high financial cost of, 94–95; insurance coverage of, 94, 95; level of satisfaction with, 96; patients as active partners in, 13; social privilege and, 20; standard of care, 143–144. *See also* Botox; surgeries

tumors and removal of tumors, 3, 5, 20, 64, 90, 172. *See also* acoustic neuroma

two-part self, 26

"typicality," 39

"ugly laws," 50, 54, 58, 60, 92

verbal cues, 87

verstehen (empathetic understanding), 11, 191n2 (chap. 1)

vertigo, 4, 54, 105. *See also* balance

Victorian culture, 38, 96, 99

video filters, online self-image and, 97

violence, symbolic, 33, 69, 144

visibility, 36, 72, 74

vision problems, 2, 3, 5, 95; inability to blink, 64, 191n2 (chap. 3)

Wacquant, Loïc, 14, 98, 159

Weber, Max, 11, 160, 191n2 (chap. 1), 192n5

white female participants, 23, 34–35, 38, 39, 60–61; on alienation (self-estrangement), 110; on bullying and harassment, 53; on disabled status, 124, 127; disrupted experience of self, 101; on inability to communicate, 76–77; on invalidation,

white female participants (cont.)
61–62; on loss of smile, 80, 81; on lost
ability to have fun, 116; on microassaults,
54; on minimalizations, 64; on miscommunication, 81–82; overrepresented in
the sample, 74; professional cost of
disability and, 47–49; on public
performance, 136; on reframing of self,
141–142; social media image and, 154;
summary of participants, 177–186
white male participants, 40–41, 49, 114–115,
158, 165, 180, 181, 183, 186
Willingham, Daniel, 123
Wynter, Sylvia, 160

ABOUT THE AUTHOR

FAYE LINDA WACHS is professor of sociology at California State Polytechnic University, Pomona. She is the coauthor of the award-winning book *Body Panic: Gender, Health, and the Selling of Fitness* (with Shari L. Dworkin).